God and Creation

God and Creation

St. Thomas Aquinas

Translated and with an Introduction
by William P. Baumgarth and
Richard J. Regan

Scranton: University of Scranton Press
London and Toronto: Associated University Presses

Associated University Presses
440 Forsgate Drive
Cranbury, NJ 08512

Associated University Presses
25 Sicilian Avenue
London WC1A 2QH, England

Associated University Presses
P.O. Box 338, Port Credit
Mississauga, Ontario
Canada L5G 4L8

The paper used in this publication meets the requirements of the American National Standard for Permanence of Paper for Printed Library Materials Z39.48-1984.

Library of Congress Cataloging-in-Publication Data

Thomas, Aquinas, Saint, 1225?–1274.
    [Summa theologica. English. Selections]
    God and creation / Thomas Aquinas; translated and with an
  introduction by William P. Baumgarth and Richard J. Regan.
        p. cm.
    Includes bibliographical references and index.
    ISBN 0-940866-27-7 (alk. paper)
    1. God—Knowableness—Early works to 1800. 2. Faith and reason—
  Christianity—Early works to 1800. 3. Creation—Early works to
  1800. 4. Natural theology—Early works to 1900. I. Baumgarth,
  William P. II. Regan, Richard J. III. Title.
  BT100.T4E5 1994
  231—dc20   92-63002
                                                                   CIP

PRINTED IN THE UNITED STATES OF AMERICA

Contents

6 CONTENTS

Preface

The writings of St. Thomas deserve wide circulation for several reasons. First, they have had such influence on other thinkers. Second, no serious student of Western thought can be considered well-educated without acquaintance with St. Thomas's grand synthesis of faith and reason. Third, we believe that St. Thomas's thought has intrinsic merit and perduring relevance. Even those who do not share St. Thomas's philosophical and theological perspective, should find his writings intellectually stimulating.

This volume is an anthology of St. Thomas's thought about God and creation in the first part of the *Summa theologiae*: proofs of God's existence, his attributes, our knowledge of him by reason, his knowledge and will, his creative act, and its effects. We have included selections from the *Summa* on these topics as St. Thomas deems the topics accessible to human reason, and we have excluded topics related to specifically Christian doctrine, for example, the Trinity, angels. This undoubtedly fragments St. Thomas's perspective and risks misrepresenting his thought. The *Summa* is professedly a summary of theology, not of philosophy, and St. Thomas's perspective is that of a believer seeking to understand his faith. Nonetheless, St. Thomas proposes certain propositions and analyses on the basis of reason, and we think it important for believers and nonbelievers to weigh their merit precisely as rational arguments. Within that context, the anthology is selective, and informed readers can judge for themselves whether the texts selected are sufficiently representative and comprehensive.

Our first purpose, then, is to make available to scholars and the general public in a single, relatively comprehensive volume the thought of St. Thomas on knowledge of God by human reason. Our second purpose is to provide a translation superior to previous translations.

The English Dominican Fathers' translation dates from the first third of this century. That translation is accurate and literal for the most part, but its English rendition of certain key terms is misleading, and its style stilted by contemporary standards. The more recent Blackfriars' translation of a quarter century ago renders key terms more accurately but translates the text very freely and sometimes misleadingly. It is our conviction that only a painstakingly literal translation can capture the nuances of St. Thomas's thought. We aim, therefore, to provide a translation that is more faithful than that of the Blackfriars, and more felicitous than that of the English Dominican Fathers.

To assist the reader, we have provided a glossary of key terms. Hackett Publishing Company has graciously allowed us to incorporate definitions from the glossary we provided in our anthology of St. Thomas's ethical and political writings, *On Law, Morality, and Politics.*

We wish particularly to thank several members of the Classics and Philosophy Departments of Fordham University for their helpful advice: the Reverends Thomas V. Bermingham, S.J., W. Norris Clarke, S.J., Gerald A. McCool, S.J., James A. Sadowsky, S.J., and Andrew C. Varga, S.J. We also wish to thank Professors Patrick Corrigan and Paul Seaton of Assumption College for their suggestions.

Note on the Text and Translation

We have translated the 1952 Marietti recension of the Leonine text of the *Summa*. In citing books of the Bible and numbering the Psalms, we follow the Revised Standard Version. We translate St. Thomas's biblical quotations as he phrases them, not as they may appear in the Vulgate. We cite Plato according to the Stephanus divisions, and we cite Aristotle according to the Bekker divisions. For patristic citations or quotations, we refer the reader to the Migne edition.

Translators should be faithful to the text and express the meaning of the text in felicitous English. The two objectives are often difficult to reconcile. Fidelity to the text has been our highest priority, although we are confident that the reader will find the translation felicitous. The translation of certain key words inevitably involves interpretation. We have, for example, generally translated participial use of the Latin infinitive "*esse*" as "existing" or "existence." Since we interpret that St. Thomas takes "being" in the participial sense to mean "existing," we have chosen to make that interpretation explicit. The translation of other key words varies with the context. We have, for example, translated "*ratio*," the generic Latin word for reason, as "argument," "aspect," "consideration," "nature," "reason," "reasoning," or "respect" as appropriate for different contexts.

WILLIAM P. BAUMGARTH
RICHARD J. REGAN

Introduction

This anthology contains selections from the *Summa theologiae* (Summary of theology) of St. Thomas Aquinas (A.D. 1225–1274) on God and creation. The selections deal with questions about the existence and nature of God, and his creative act and its effects, insofar as these can be known by the light of natural reason. Since these questions deal with God, St. Thomas's answers to them constitute a theology, a study of God. Moreover, since St. Thomas studies God as first cause, this theology is a science in the Aristotelian sense. But a rational or "natural" theology needs to be distinguished from a revealed theology, one that studies questions about God's existence and nature in the light of what God has revealed to human beings about himself. The main sources of such revelation are Scripture (the Bible) and, for the Catholic and Orthodox, Apostolic tradition.

Not everything we learn about God in Scripture and Tradition is, strictly speaking, outside the scope of natural theology. The Bible, for example, affirms God's existence, but so also, according to the natural theologian, does natural reason. The proper objects of revealed theology are mysteries that reason alone does not and cannot discover. The doctrine of the Trinity, the belief that Scripture and Tradition (as set forth in the Nicene Creed, for example) teach about God's existence as three distinct hypostases or persons, is such a mystery. We only know that doctrine because God has chosen to reveal it, not because our mind on its own would be competent to establish such a truth. It bears remembering that, once such a mystery is revealed, the mind can understand its reasonablity, or rather, that nothing in such revealed truth contradicts the truth discovered by human reason alone.

But for reasons of his own, God can reveal certain truths about himself that, in principle, at least the wise could know without special revelation. Such truths command certain things (most of the Ten Commandments, for example) that human reasoning would view as morally obligatory apart from faith. In part, this is so because of the distinction alluded to: what is certain and clear to the philosopher need not be so for the man in the street, and such divinely generated moral commands might be more comprehensible to the nonphilosophical layman than conclusions that require philosophical reflection and reasoning.

The facts that God reveals about his nature that even the wise cannot discover by themselves, are the proper objects of revealed theology. We cannot be said strictly to understand such truths; their intelligibility exceeds our

11

limited reason. About these truths, we are said to have belief, reasonable belief, but not, at least in this life, understanding. Such belief, faith, is, like its
object, a gift of God's initiative. But what we know by reason about God,
we can organize as a science. As such, it is part of a broader science,
metaphysics or first philosophy, which is the science of being. Philosophical
or natural theology is the metaphysics of the highest kind of being: God.

The distinction we have made between natural theology and revealed
theology replaces a much older one. St. Augustine (A.D. 343–430) critically
employed a classification of theologies set forth by the Roman philosopher
Varro (116–27 B.C.).[1] Besides natural theology, Varro recognized poetic
and civil theologies. The theology of the poets anthropomorphizes the gods.
The gods are protrayed as superhumanly powerful beings possessed of base,
all-too-human passions. Among other things, the gods are inclined to be
lustful and cruel. The stories about the gods that Plato (428?–348? B.C.)
criticized in the *Republic*, are illustrative of what poetic theology teaches.[2]
Civil theology comprises the beliefs of cultured, politically involved gentle-
men about the gods. In brief, civil theology stresses the existence of a
hereafter as well as the preoccupation of the divine with justice. A reformed
type of civil theology is one of the goals of the *Republic's* censure of poetry.
Finally, natural theology is the theology of the philosopher, what we have
identified as a branch of metaphysics.

Varro judges each of these theologies to have a proper social role. The
theology of the poets is comic; it makes both human beings and gods laugh-
able. Like tragic catharsis, comedy lets the viewers vicariously indulge in
forbidden pleasures like those sought by the poetic gods. It then channels
potentially harmful appetites into harmless fun. Civil theology emphasizes
the divine concern for the community's laws by focusing upon the rewards
and punishments that await those who have not received just rewards or
punishments in this life. Like poetic theology, civil theology is polytheistic.
Unlike poetic theology, civil theology stresses the nobility of the gods in a
way suitable for the preoccupation of citizens with law and justice. Natural
theology is unequivocally monotheistic. It emphasizes the transcendence of
the divine, not only from the human appetite but even from political concerns. Plato's Good and Aristotle's Unmoved Mover are both examples of
what divinity means to the philosopher.

St. Augustine dismisses poetic theology as emphatically as Socrates did in
the *Republic*. Civil theology and natural theology are conflated. What
emerges is a monotheism whose God both transcends the world and has an
interest in it. In fact, the world itself depends for its beginning and con-
tinued existence on the active will of that God. Unmoved though he may be,
Augustine's God, unlike Aristotle's divinity or Plato's Good, causes things
not only as an object of desire or as a paradigm but also as an efficient
cause. The natural theology of the Augustinian Christian posits a God who

is essentially personal, essentially active in the world, and essentially involved with rewarding and punishing rational, personal creatures.

Why does Christianity seem so interested in natural theology? That interest, after all, is much older than the age of Augustine. Part of the answer becomes clear when we compare Christianity to the other major Western monotheistic faiths. For both Judaism and Islam, the essence of religious devotion consists in the faithful carrying out a comprehensive divine law (for the Jew, the Torah; for the Moslem, the Sharia). Although speculative concerns are not absent, they take second place to comprehending what God as legislator intends us to do in our daily behavior.[3] The primary concern for the two faiths is a practical one: how can we formulate principles of the divine law so that we can apply them to changing circumstances? In short, the Hebrew Scriptures and the Koran give rise to a divine legal system, which is subject to continual commentary and application. The key figures in both religions are those individuals recognized by their communities as skilled interpreters of the divine law: the rabbi in Judaism, the Imam in Islam.

The classic question for philosophers in the Judaic and Islamic communities during the Middle Ages was: does the law prescribe, permit, or prohibit free inquiry into the nature of things, especially legal matters? In other words, does the law prescribe, permit, or prohibit philosophy? Since the divine law regulates behavior but not necessarily belief, the standard response has been that divine law at least permits philosophical inquiry, provided that nothing in the actions of the philosopher violates that law.

St. Thomas, quite to the contrary, begins his *Summa theologiae* with the question: is revealed theology necessary in addition to philosophy? He seems to take for granted the legitimacy of philosophy in the context of revealed religion, the establishment of which was the main object of his Judaic and Islamic counterparts. Why this receptivity to what some Church Fathers, like Tertullian (A.D. 160–220), would have viewed as a pagan inheritance?

One reason for such receptivity becomes clear if we compare a book of the Torah with a gospel or epistle of the Christian Scriptures. Leviticus, for instance, contains detailed prescriptions not only of ceremonial observances but also of judicial processes, dietary rules, and even public health. The New Testament books are silent about most of these themes, and even though those books confirm the moral injunctions of the Commandments, most of the New Testament teachings about behavior are counsels that are not universally binding (e.g., St. Paul's observations on celibacy and marriage). A comprehensive doctrine about politics (e.g., a definition of the best form of government) is not to be found, although Christians are urged to render to Caesar the things that are Caesar's. And what exactly is owed to those who govern us? To answer that question, we need to examine supplementary analyses derived from classical philosophical reflection on political life. Moreover, although the Christian Scriptures indicate such specifically Christian virtues as those of faith, hope, and charity, the nature of natural virtues and their relationship to specifically Christian virtues require elucidation from the ethical teachings of philosophers.

A more fundamental consideration needs to be mentioned. Pious commitment to the Jewish religion is not so much a matter of orthodoxy (correct belief) as it is a matter of orthopraxis (correct behavior). As we have remarked, the Jewish tradition requires a continual application of the principles of the divine law to new circumstances, the development of an authoritative interpretation of that law, the Talmud. Orthodox Judaism is Talmudic Judaism.

Orthodox Christianity, however, requires a continual reflection on the nature and person of Jesus. It requires correct belief about who Jesus really is. Controversies among Christians in the first centuries of the Church's existence involved radically different understandings of Jesus' status. Was he only human, only divine, or both? Christological and Trinitarian debates involve correct belief, not correct behavior. The early Councils concluded that the Scriptures and Tradition ruled out certain speculative propositions about the nature of Christ and the Trinity. Those heretical doctrines were to a large extent set forth in the language of classical Greek philosophy, and the Council Fathers employed the same language when they rejected unacceptable teachings. Christian dialectics, it seems, could not be effectively carried on without concepts elaborated by thinkers like Plato, Aristotle, and Plotinus (A.D. 205–270).

Formal definitions of a subject, or description of its historical origin, are not enough to justify its theoretical value. Does natural theology live up to its potential to explicate how reason on its own establishes God's existence and comes to certain conclusions about his nature? Some religious believers would deny reason's ability to do so. For orthodox Calvinists, for example, the human mind, due to Adam's fall from grace, is as corrupt as the human will. Whatever reliable information we have about God, we derive from revelation, not from reason. For Aquinas, on the contrary, although the appetites of fallen human nature interfere with reason, the human mind is not corrupted by original sin in the same way or to the same degree that the human will is.

Other believers say that religious experience or intuition directly verifies God's existence and nature. St. Thomas, however, doubts that there is a specific faculty for religious experience, or that religious experience differs substantially from our usual sensory and intellectual experience. The "ontological argument" might illustrate one sort of resort to intuition to verify God's existence. This argument holds that once we understand God's nature, we see that he must exist; we cannot have a specific notion of the highest being that does not entail that being's existence. St. Thomas denies that we can judge that a being exists because we know its definition.[4]

Some believers assert that the philosophical borrowings of the Church Fathers and early Councils are foreign to the biblical faith; Hellenism, as it is called, is a mistake. Some of those believers claim that Christians can find in the Scriptures all they need to know. If what we have said about the silence of Christian Scriptures is true, that position is not defensible. Others claim that we only come to experience God by faith, that none of our experience on the natural level could lead us to any knowledge about God's existence or nature. Faith, in short, is necessarily a leap in the dark under divine inspiration.

For St. Thomas, the latter position implies denigration of the power of God and the power of human beings. Could not and did not God give us the power of reason? Is not the power of the creator found in his works? To be sure, what natural theology establishes about God's nature is not identical with what God reveals to believers. The God of faith is much more than the God of the philosophers. But "more" does not mean "inconsistent with." To establish the credentials of God's revelation requires investigation of phenomena like miracles and prophecies, and such phenomena exceed nature. According to St. Thomas, reason can demonstrate that miracles and prophecies are not impossible. Such arguments do not demonstrate that miracles or prophecies occur, but they do demonstrate that miracles and prophecies are possible. One reason for our inclusion of the selections on creation is the light they shed on what St. Thomas holds to be the appropriate boundary between reason and revelation, and the reasonableness of religious belief.

Aside from the objections of various believers, surely the strongest objections to revealed theology are raised by those who claim that reason alone is a reliable source of knowledge about God. In St. Thomas's own time, some philosophers, disciples of Averroes (A.D. 1126–1198), affirmed that God was nothing more than the Unmoved Mover of Aristotle. Though some of these Western Averroists posited a doctrine of double truth (one for philosophy, one for religion), more consistent thinkers, like Marsilius of Padua (A.D. 1275–1342), seem skeptical about revelation. According to the latter thinkers, reason might contradict revelation, and revelation is false if reason does so. These philosophers are thus in paradoxical agreement with fideists about the potential conflict between reason and revelation, although the two schools resolve the conflict in contrary ways. Contrary to the Averroists, St. Thomas attempts to show that the Christian faith is compatible with reason, and that Aristotle can be interpreted in ways that are compatible with Christian belief.

Needless to add, some thinkers flatly deny the possibility of any valid natural theology in that they deny reason's ability to affirm God's existence. Some have even gone so far as to say that human reason proves that God does not exist.

We need now to turn to the heart of St. Thomas's project, his philosophical method. St. Thomas's appropriation of Aristotle makes him very much a revolutionary thinker. In general, before St. Thomas's time, some variety of Neoplatonism dominated Western philosophy and theology. St. Augustine, for example, incorporated many tenets of Neoplatonism into his theology.

Neoplatonism considered knowledge an all-or-nothing affair. Real knowledge is of the unchangeable, the Good and the Ideas. Opposed to real knowledge are ignorance, whose object is nonbeing, and opinion, whose object is the visible world of coming to be and of passing away. Since there cannot be a science about objects that change, there cannot be a science about the objects of sensory experience. The only science, which is wisdom, is of the unchangeable. Through knowledge of the highest intelligible things, which never change, the mind comes to judge sensory objects as symbols of the real beings of the intelligible realm. We should read the book of nature as pointing to the intelligible realm, but nature itself is without any intrinsic reality or theoretical interest. The mind apprehends divine reality and descends from it to the illusory embodiment of that reality in the visible world.[5]

The Aristotelian method St. Thomas adopts has a very different approach. Unlike the Neoplatonists, for whom there is only the one science of the unchangeable, there are for Aristotle many sciences, since we have real knowledge of many really distinct objects. The general science of nature is physics. After understanding physics, the science of nature, we can ascend to metaphysics, the first philosophy. But we must have scientific knowledge of nature before we can ascend to the unchangeable objects that metaphysics studies. Thus nature has an intrinsic structure and significance that leads us beyond itself. We ascend from the sensory to the intelligible, from the changeable to the unchangeable.

In short, St. Thomas appropriates from Aristotle a respect for nature and the evidence of our senses. The excellence of metaphysics does not lead St. Thomas to devalue the world of nature. St. Thomas comes to affirm God's existence and nature by way of no religious experience or mystical intuition of the transcendent; rather, he affirms God's existence and nature by rigorous reflection on phenomena that human beings experience closer to home: motion, causality, contingency, goodness, finality. St. Thomas hopes to convince the reader by reflecting on human sensory and intellectual experience and drawing the proper conclusions about God.

St. Thomas's metaphysics, then, develops from Aristotle's physics, Aristotle's science of nature. But does not that pose a problem for the reliability of Thomistic metaphysics? After all, has not modern science disproved key elements of Aristotle's physics, for example, its teleology and earth-centered cosmology? Our response to this question need not be an unqualified yes. The notion of final causality, for example, seems to have a secure place in at least one modern science, biology. And many modern philosophers will insist on the instrumental nature of science, that science seeks to control physical reality rather than to know it.

We should resist the temptation to throw out the Aristotelian baby with the bathwater. Aristotle's analysis of motion, for example, seems less abstract, closer to common experience, than the maxims of contemporary physics. Non-Thomistic philosophers like Heidegger have pointed out the dogmatic elements, the nonempirical elements, of contemporary science. Although we need not be as skeptical as they, since their skepticism leads to nihilism, we should remain open to the possibility that some principles of Aristotle's philosophy of nature remain reliable, although many specific observations and applications are mistaken.

The *Summa* is primarily addressed to an audience of believers who are beginning to study Christian theology. But we believe that the *Summa*'s philosophical arguments are worthy of study by believers and nonbelievers alike. Where we include arguments germane to revealed theology, those arguments contrast with what St. Thomas thinks human reason on its own can achieve. One selection on creation, for example, deals with the claim that reason can know with certainty that the world is not eternal, as Christian faith professes, and St. Thomas there denies that claim.

The *Summa theologiae* is divided into various sections (questions) dealing with a common theme. Each question in turn is divided into several articles dealing with specific points of inquiry. An article begins with some puzzle; for example: is God a living being? The discussion starts with objections to St. Thomas's position. Each objection may contain one or more reference to some recognized Scriptural, patristic, theological, or philosophical statement. St. Thomas then states his own position, very often in the words of another authoritative text. Next follows the actual argument of St. Thomas in his own words. Finally, St. Thomas answers each of the objections.

Why does the *Summa* have such an elaborate structure? The answer lies in the conventions of medieval academic debate. Each party in those debates first expressed his opponent's position in such a way that the opponent could agree that his position was accurately understood and represented. Only then could the defender of a thesis open the debate by presenting his position.[6] St. Thomas did for the medieval debate what the Platonic dialogue did for classical philosophy: he preserved the spirit of philosophical discussion by means of the written word.

By raising objections to his position, St. Thomas implicitly invites the reader actively to judge the value of the argument, just as Plato's dialogues transpire at least as much between the reader and the platonic text as they do between the characters in the dialogue proper. The reader should be prepared for subtle interpretation; an inquiry in the *Summa* is not a lecture. (Note the difference from the way in which arguments are presented in the more lecture-like format of the *Summa contra Gentiles*.) For instance, St. Thomas very often cites some authority in his introduction to the response, "On the contrary." Sometimes he asserts his position without citing an authority. What does this mean? Perhaps, by implicitly making himself responsible for the position, St. Thomas is pointing to a radical departure from previous thinking, an attempt at an original thesis. This is the sort of phenomenon we have in mind when we suggest the need for an active encounter between the careful reader and the Thomistic text similar to that between the discerning reader and a Platonic dialogue.

St. Thomas's treatment of evil may serve to illustrate the logic of his method of inquiry. We need to know what something is before we inquire about its cause, and so the entire first question on evil (Q. 48) is devoted to the nature of evil. Because we so often speak about evil as if it were some entity, St. Thomas at the outset inquires whether this is so (A. 1). In response, he explains that evil is nothing positive, since evil is the contrary of good, and good is something positive. This, of course, raises the question whether evil is simply an illusion. Taking up this question, St. Thomas affirms that evil is no illusion but consists in things lacking some good (A. 2). But if evil is nothing positive and yet is real in things lacking certain perfections, what exactly is it? St. Thomas replies that evil is the privation, not merely the absence, of a perfection that something ought to have (A. 3). Human beings, for example, ought to have the power of vision, and so blindness is an evil in their regard. St. Thomas asks next whether evil totally destroys good (A. 4). He answers that physical evil does not destroy the goodness of a subject deprived of a due perfection, nor does morally evil behavior eliminate the aptitude of the soul for good. Article Five then distinguishes the evil of punishment for wrongdoing from the evil of wrongdoing itself, and Article Six argues that the latter evil is worse.

With the nature of evil thus determined, Question 49 then takes up the causality of evil. Knowing that there is evil in the world, the mind naturally inquires about the cause of evil, whether the cause is good or evil. In response, St. Thomas argues that evil does have an efficient, that is, active, cause, and that the efficient cause of evil is itself good and produces evil only coincidentally, not intrinsically (A. 1). Since God is the highest good and the first cause of everything, are we not then obliged to admit that he causes evil? St. Thomas replies by distinguishing the causality of physical evil from the causality of moral evil (A. 2). God does cause physical evil coincidentally, that is, God causes the destruction of some things in the course of communicating his goodness to other things for the completion of the universe, but God in no way causes moral evil. Finally, since we may be tempted to think that there needs to be a supreme evil responsible for all evil because there is a supreme good responsible for all good, the question arises whether such a supreme evil exists. St. Thomas answers that there is no supreme evil comparable to the supreme good, since God is the first cause of everything (A. 3).

A revival of interest in religion and the philosophy of religion now seems afoot, both in society in general and in academia in particular. The texts that we have chosen, speak to those religious and philosophical concerns by raising questions and offering answers that may be both perennial and timely. Reason and revelation meet, sometimes in conflict, in the academy and the public forum. St. Thomas was a strong believer in the capacity of philosophy and theology to tolerate and complement each other. That optimism along with our enthusiasm for the project are the animating principles for the selected texts. Speculative curiosity and practical concern make St. Thomas an ideal partner in guiding our judgments and consciences. For the ultimate question for theologians, philosophers, and reflective citizens remains: how should we live our lives?

Notes

1. *The City of God* VI, 5.
2. *Republic* II, 17. 377E.
3. Ralph Lerner and Muhsin Madhi, eds., *Medieval Political Philosophy: A Sourcebook* (New York: Free Press, 1963), p. 6.
4. ST I, Q. 2, A. 1.
5. Cf. Josef Pieper, *Guide to St. Thomas Aquinas* (New York: Pantheon Books, 1962), p. 47.
6. Ibid., p. 79.

Biblical Abbreviations

Cor.	Corinthians
Dt.	Deuteronomy
Eccl.	Ecclesiastes
Eph.	Ephesians
Ex.	Exodus
Ez.	Ezekiel
Gen.	Genesis
Heb.	Hebrews
Hos.	Hosea
Is.	Isaiah
Jas.	James
Jer.	Jeremiah
Jn.	John
Lam.	Lamentations
Lk.	Luke
Mac.	Maccabees
Mal.	Malachi
Mic.	Micah
Mt.	Matthew
Num.	Numbers
Phil.	Philippians
Prov.	Proverbs
Ps.	Psalms
Rev.	Revelation
Rom.	Romans
Sam.	Samuel
Sir.	Sirach
Thess.	Thessalonians
Tim.	Timothy
Tit.	Titus
Wis.	Wisdom

Other Abbreviations

PG   J. P. Migne, *Patrologia Graeca*
PL   J. P. Migne, *Patrologia Latina*
ST   Thomas Aquinas, *Summa theologiae*

Works Cited by St. Thomas

Most titles are in Latin, according to common usage.

Algazel
  Metaphysics
Ambrose
  In Epistolam ad Romanos
  In Epistolam 1am ad Corinthios
  De fide
  De officiis
Anselm
  Contra Gaunilonem
  Proslogium
  De veritate
Aristotle
  De anima
  Categories
  De coelo
  Ethics
  De generatione et corruptione
  De interpretatione
  Metaphysics
  Meteorology
  De plantis
  Physics
  Posterior Analytics
  Prior Analytics
  Topics
Athanasian Creed
Augustine
  Contra adversarium legis et prophetarum
  The City of God
  Confessions
  De correptione et gratia
  De diversis quaestionibus ad Simplicium
  De doctrina Christiana
  De dono perseverantiae
  Enchiridion

Contra Faustum
Super Genesim ad litteram
In Ioannis Evangelium
Contra Iulianum
De libero arbitrio
Contra Maximinum
Octoginta trium quaestionum
De praedestinatione sanctorum
Retractationum
Sermones ad populum
Soliloquiorum
De Trinitate
De utilitate credendi
De vera religione
De videndo Deum
Averroes
  In libros Metaphysicorum
  In libros Physicorum
Avicenna
  Metaphysics
Boethius
  On the Consolation of Philosophy
  De hebdomatibus
  De Trinitate
Chrysostom
  Super Ioannam
Cicero
  De divinatione
  De inventione
  De natura deorum
  De officiis
Damascene
  De fide orthodoxa
Denis the Pseudo-Areopagite
  De coelesti hierarchia
  De divinis nominibus
Glossa ordinaria
Gregory the Great
  Super Cantica Canticorum
  Homiliarum in Ezechielem
  Moralia
Hilary
  De Trinitate

Jerome
  Epistolae
  In Isaiam
Liber de causis
Lombard
  In Epistolam 2am ad Timotheum
  Sentences
Maimonides
  Guide of the Perplexed
Missa dominicae 10ae post Pentecosten
Missa pro viventibus et defunctis
Nemesius
  De natura hominis (erroneously attributed by St. Thomas to Gregory of Nyssa)
Nicene Creed
Origen
  Peri Archon
  In Epistolam ad Romanos
Plato
  Parmenides
  Phaedo
  Phaedrus
  Timaeus

Authors Cited by St. Thomas

Algazel [al-Ghazali] (A.D. 1058–1111)
Almaric of Chartres [Bènes] (d. ca. A.D.1207)
Ambrose, St. (A.D. 340?–397)
Anaxagoras (500?–428? B.C.)
Anselm, St. (A.D. 1033–1109)
Aristotle, "the Philosopher" (384–327 B.C.)
Athanasius, St. (A.D. 293?–373)
Augustine, St. (A.D. 354–430)
Averroes, "the Commentator" (A.D. 1126–1198)
Avicenna (A.D. 980–1037)
Boethius (A.D. 480?–524?)
Chrysostom, St. John (A.D. 354?–407)
Cicero (106–43 B.C.)
Damascene, St. John (A.D. 700?–754?)
David of Dinant (late twelfth–early thirteen century A.D.)
Democritus (460?–370? B.C.)
Denis the Pseudo-Areopagite (early sixth century A.D.)
Empedocles (490?–430 B.C.)
Gregory of Nyssa, St. (A.D. 335?–394?)
Gregory the Great, Pope St. (A.D. 540?–604)
Hilary, St. (A.D. 313?–367)
Isaac ben Solomon Israel (A.D. 845?–940?)
Jerome, St. (A.D. 347?–419/420)
Lombard, Peter (A.D. 1100?–1160)
Maimonides, Moses (A.D. 1135–1204)
Nemesius (late fourth century A.D.)
Origen (A.D. 185?–254?)
Paul, St."the Apostle" (first century A.D.)
Plato (428?–348/347 B.C.)
Pythagoras (580?–500? B.C.)

God and Creation

Part 1
God

ST I
Question 1
On Sacred Instruction, Its Nature, and
Its Extent

[This question is divided into ten articles, the first two of which are included here.]

First Article

Do We Need to Have Another Instruction besides the Philosophical Sciences?

I proceed in this way to the first article: it seems that we do not need to have another instruction besides the philosophical sciences.

Obj. 1. Human beings should not strive for things beyond their power of reason, as the Book of Sirach says: "Seek not after things loftier than yourself."[1] But the philosophical sciences deal sufficiently with things subject to reason. Therefore, it seems superfluous for us to have another instruction besides the philosophical sciences.

Obj. 2. We can be instructed only about being, for we know only the true, and the true is convertible with being. But the philosophical sciences deal with all being and also God, and so we call a certain part of philosophy "theology," or the science of God, as the Philosopher makes clear in the *Metaphysics*.[2] Therefore, we had no need to have another instruction besides the philosophical sciences.

On the contrary, the Second Letter to Timothy says: "All divinely inspired writing is useful for teaching, clarifying, reproving, instructing for justice."[3] But divinely inspired writing does not belong to the philosophical sciences, which we discover by human reason. Therefore, it is useful that there be a divinely inspired science besides the philosophical sciences.

I answer that it was necessary for human salvation that there be certain instruction by divine revelation besides the philosophical sciences, which human reason investigates. First, indeed, because human beings are ordered to God as a certain end that surpasses the grasp of their reason, as the prophet

Isaiah says: "Without you, O God, the eye has not seen the things that you have prepared for those who love you."[4] But human beings, who ought to order their strivings and actions to their end, need first to know that end. And hence it was necessary for the salvation of human beings that divine revelation make known to them certain things that surpass human reason.

Divine revelation needed to instruct human beings even with regard to things that human reason can investigate about God. This is so because few human beings—both after a long time and with an admixture of many errors—would arrive at the truth about God that reason investigates, even though the entire salvation of human beings, which rests in God, depends on knowledge of such truth. Therefore, in order that salvation might come to human beings both more suitably and more surely, divine revelation needed to instruct them about the things of God.

We needed, therefore, to have sacred instruction by revelation besides the philosophical sciences, which reason investigates.

Reply to Obj. 1.   Although human beings should not by reason inquire into things loftier than their power to know, yet they should by faith accept such things when revealed by God. And hence, and in the same place, the text of Sirach adds: "Many things beyond the ken of human beings have been revealed to you."[5] And sacred instruction consists in such things.

Reply to Obj. 2.   Different aspects of knowable objects result in different sciences. For example, the astronomer and the natural scientist demonstrate the same conclusion (for instance, that the earth is round), but the astronomer demonstrates the conclusion by mathematical means, that is, means abstracted from matter, while the natural scientist demonstrates it by means considered with respect to matter. And hence nothing prevents another science also dealing with the same things that the philosophical sciences deal with as knowable by the light of natural reason, as those things are known by the light of divine revelation. And hence the theology that belongs to sacred instruction, differs by genus from the theology that we hold to be part of philosophy.

Second Article

Is Sacred Instruction a Science?

I proceed in this way to the second article: it seems that sacred instruction is not a science.

Obj. 1.   Every science proceeds from self-evident principles. But sacred instruction proceeds from articles of faith, and articles of faith are not self-evident, since some persons do not admit their truth. "For some do not have faith," as the Second Letter to the Thessalonians says.[6] Therefore, sacred instruction is not a science.

Obj. 2. Individual things are not the object of a science. But sacred instruction deals with individual things, such as the deeds of Abraham, Isaac, and Jacob, and the like. Therefore, sacred instruction is not a science.

On the contrary, Augustine says in his *De Trinitate*: "We ascribe to this science only what begets, nourishes, defends, strengthens the most wholesome faith."[7] But such belongs only to the science of sacred instruction. Therefore, sacred instruction is a science.

I answer that sacred instruction is a science. But we should note that there are two kinds of sciences. For certain sciences, such as arithmetic, geometry, and the like, proceed from principles known by the natural light of the intellect. Certain other sciences, however, proceed from principles known by the light of a higher science; for example, optics proceeds from principles known by geometry, and music from principles known by arithmetic. And sacred instruction is a science in the latter way, because it proceeds from principles that the light of a higher science, namely, the science about God and the blessed, makes known. And hence, as music relies on principles transmitted to it by arithmetic, so sacred instruction relies on principles revealed to it by God.

Reply to Obj. 1. The principles of any science are either self-evident or traced back to the knowledge of a higher science. And the principles of sacred instruction are the latter, as I have said.[8]

Reply to Obj. 2. Sacred instruction does not relate individual things because it chiefly deals with such, but they are introduced both as models for our life (as in the moral sciences) and also to make clear the authority of the human beings by whom God's revelation comes to us—and sacred Scripture or instruction is grounded on such authority.

Notes

1. Sir. 3:22.
2. *Metaphysics* V, 1. 1026a18.
3. 2 Tim. 3:16.
4. Is. 64:4.
5. Sir. 3:25.
6. 2 Thess. 3:2.
7. *De Trinitate* XIV, 1, 3. PL 42:1037.
8. In the body of the article.

ST 1
Question 2
On the Existence of God

[This question is divided into three articles, all of which are included here.]

First Article

Is the Existence of God Self-Evident?

I proceed in this way to the first article: it seems that the existence of God is self-evident.

Obj. 1. Things of which we possess knowledge by nature, are said to be self-evident to us, as is manifest in the case of first principles. But, as Damascene says in the beginning of his book, "All are by nature endowed with knowledge of God's existence."[1] Therefore, the existence of God is self-evident.

Obj. 2. Things that we know as soon as we know terms, are said to be self-evident, and the Philosopher in the *Posterior Analytics* attributes this to the first principles of demonstration[2]; when one knows what a whole is, and what a part is, one immediately knows that every whole is greater than one of its parts. But when one understands what the term "God" means, one immediately grasps that God exists, for the term "God" means that than which nothing greater can be signified. What exists in fact as well as in the intellect, however, is greater than what exists in the intellect alone. And so, since God exists in the intellect as soon as we understand the term "God," it also follows that God exists in fact. Therefore, the existence of God is self-evident.[3]

Obj. 3. The existence of truth is self-evident, because one who denies the existence of truth admits its existence: if there is indeed no truth, it is true that truth does not exist; if, on the other hand, something is true, it is necessary that truth exists. But God is truth itself, as John says: "I am the way, the truth, and the life."[4] Therefore, the existence of God is self-evident.

On the contrary, no one can think the opposite of what is self-evident, as the Philosopher makes clear in the *Metaphysics*[5] and the *Posterior Analytics*[6]

38

concerning the first principles of demonstration. But one can think the opposite of the proposition that God exists, as the Psalm says: "The fool has said in his heart, 'God does not exist.'"[7] Therefore, the existence of God is not self-evident.

I answer that something may be self-evident in two ways: in one way, in itself but not to us; in the second way, in itself and to us. For a proposition is self-evident because its predicate is contained in its subject's essence, as in the proposition, "Human beings are animals," for "animal" belongs to the nature of "human being." Therefore, if all know the proposition's predicate and its subject's essence, the proposition will be self-evident to all. This is evident, for example, in the case of the first principles of demonstration, whose terms are general notions that everyone knows: being and nonbeing, whole and part, and the like. If, however, some persons happen not to know the predicate and the subject's essence, the proposition will indeed be self-evident in itself but not to those who do not know the predicate and the subject. And so it happens, as Boethius says in his book *De hebdomatibus*, that only the wise have certain general and self-evident notions, such as "Incorporeal things do not exist in a place."[8]

I say, therefore, that the proposition "God exists," is in itself self-evident, because its predicate is the same as its subject; God is indeed his existence, as we shall make clear later.[9] But because we do not know what God is, the proposition is not self-evident to us but needs to be demonstrated by things more known to us and less known as regards their nature, namely, by effects.

Reply to Obj. 1. We are by nature endowed with knowledge of God's existence in a general way, with a certain confusion, namely, insofar as God is the happiness of human beings, for human beings by nature desire happiness, and they by nature know what they by nature desire. But this is not to know unconditionally that God exists, just as to know that someone is approaching, is not to know Peter, although Peter is the one who is approaching. For many deem riches to be the perfect human good, which is happiness, but certain others deem sensual pleasures the perfect human good, while still others deem something else the perfect human good.

Reply to Obj. 2. Perhaps someone who hears the term "God," does not understand that it means that than which nothing greater can be thought, since some believe that God is a material substance. Even supposing that someone understands that the term "God" means what we assert, namely, that than which nothing greater can be thought, yet it does not thereby follow that such a one would understand that what the term means, exists in the real world, but only that it exists in the intellect's apprehension. Nor can it be proved that God really exists unless one grants that there really exists something than which no greater can be thought, and this is not granted by those who hold that God does not exist.

Reply to Obj. 3.   The existence of truth in general is self-evident, but it is not self-evident to us that a first truth exists.

Second Article

Can We Demonstrate the Existence of God?

I proceed in this way to the second article: it seems that we cannot demonstrate the existence of God.

Obj. 1.   The existence of God is an article of faith. But we cannot demonstrate what belongs to faith, since demonstration causes knowledge, while faith concerns things that are not evident, as the Apostle makes clear in the Letter to the Hebrews.[10] Therefore, we cannot demonstrate the existence of God.

Obj. 2.   The means of a demonstration is something's essence. But we cannot know what God is, but only what he is not, as Damascene says.[11] Therefore, we cannot demonstrate that God exists.

Obj. 3.   If one were to demonstrate the existence of God, this would be only by his effects. But his effects are not proportioned to him, since he himself is infinite, and the effects are finite, while there is no proportion of the finite to the infinite. Therefore, since we cannot demonstrate a cause by an effect that is not proportioned to its cause, it seems that we cannot demonstrate the existence of God.

On the contrary, the Apostle says in the Letter to the Romans: "The invisible things of God are visible when understood through the things that have been made."[12] But this would only be the case if we could demonstrate the existence of God through what he has made, for the first thing that we need to understand about something, is whether or not it exists.

I answer that we demonstrate in two ways. One is by means of a cause, and we call this a "demonstration why" something is so, and it is by means of what is first without qualification. The other is by means of an effect, and we call this a "demonstration that" something is, and this demonstration is by what is first as to us, for we proceed to knowledge of a cause through its effect, because the effect is more manifest to us than its cause is. But we can demonstrate the existence of a particular cause from any of its effects—provided that the cause's effects are nonetheless more known in relation to us—because effects depend on their cause, and so a cause necessarily preexists whenever an effect is posited. Therefore, since God's existence is not self-evident in relation to us, we can demonstrate his existence by means of the effects known to us.

Reply to Obj. 1.   God's existence and other such matters that natural reason can know about God, as the Letter to the Romans says,[13] are not articles of faith but preambles to the articles, for faith in this way presupposes natural knowledge, as grace presupposes nature, and as perfecting presupposes something perfectible. Nothing, however, prevents someone who does not undertake a demonstration, from accepting as an object of faith something that in itself can be demonstrated and known.

Reply to Obj. 2.   When a cause is demonstrated by means of its effect, we need to use the effect instead of the cause's definition to prove that the cause exists, and this happens especially in the case of God. This is so because, in order to prove the existence of something, we need to take as the means of demonstration what the term means, not what the object is, since the question "What is it?" logically follows the question "Does it exist?" We posit names of God, however, from his effects, as I shall show later.[14] Therefore, when we demonstrate the existence of God from effects, we can take as the means of demonstration what the name "God" means.

Reply to Obj. 3.   We cannot have perfect knowledge about a cause by means of effects unproportioned to their cause, but we can nonetheless clearly demonstrate the existence of such a cause by any one of the cause's effects, as I have said.[15] And so we can demonstrate God's existence by means of his effects, although we cannot perfectly know him according to his essence by the effects.

Third Article

Does God Exist?

I proceed in this way to the second article: it seems that God does not exist.

Obj. 1.   If one of two contraries be infinite, the other would be completely destroyed. But we understand by the term "God" something infinite, namely, something good without limit. Therefore, if God were to exist, we would not find anything bad. But we do find bad things in the world. Therefore, God does not exist.

Obj. 2.   More sources do not accomplish what fewer sources can. But, supposing that God does not exist, other sources seem capable of accomplishing everything evident in the world, since we trace things of nature back to nature as their source, and we trace things of free choice back to human reason or will as their source. Therefore, we do not need to posit that God exists.

On the contrary, the Book of Exodus says in the person of God: "I am who am."[16]

I answer that we can prove in five ways that God exists.[17] The FIRST and more evident WAY, moreover, is the one we take from motion,[18] for it is sure and evident to the senses that some things in this world are moved. But everything moved is moved by something else. For an object is only moved insofar as it has potentiality for that to which it is moved, while something produces motion only insofar as it is actual. To move something, certainly, is only to bring it from potentiality to actuality, and only an actual being can bring something to actuality. For example, something actually hot, like fire, causes wood, which is potentially hot, to be actually hot, and thereby moves and changes the wood. The same object, however, cannot at the same time be actual and potential in the same respect but only in different respects; for example, something actually hot cannot at the same time be potentially hot, although it is at the same time potentially cold. Nothing, therefore, can produce and undergo motion, or move itself, in the same respect and in the same way. Everything that is moved, therefore, needs to be moved by something else. Therefore, if the cause of a motion is moved, the cause itself needs to be moved by another, and that other by another. But this regress ought not to be endless, because there would thus be no first cause of motion and so no other cause of motion, since second causes produce motion only because the first cause moves them. A stick, for example, only causes motion because a hand moves it. Therefore, we need to arrive at a first cause of motion, one that is moved by nothing else, and all understand this first cause of motion to be God.

The SECOND WAY is by considering efficient causes. For we find that there is an order of efficient causes in the case of those sensible objects, and yet we do not find, nor can we, that anything is the efficient cause of its very self, because such a thing would thus pre-exist itself, and this is impossible. But we cannot regress endlessly in the matter of efficient causes. This is so because, in all ordered efficient causes, something first causes something intermediate, and something intermediate causes something last, whether the intermediate things be several or only one. But the effect is taken away if its cause is taken away. Therefore, there will be nothing intermediate or last if there be nothing first in the case of efficient causes. But if we should regress endlessly in the case of efficient causes, there will be no first efficient cause, and there will thus be neither a final effect nor intermediate efficient causes, and this is clearly false. Therefore, we need to posit a first efficient cause, and all call this cause God.

We take the THIRD WAY from the possible and the necessary, and the argument proceeds as follows. We certainly find in reality kinds of things that can exist and can not-exist, since we find that certain things come to be and pass away,[19] and so can exist and can not-exist. But it is impossible that all such things always exist, because what can not-exist, at some point of time does not exist. Therefore, if everything can not-exist, there was a time when nothing really existed. But if this is so, nothing would also now exist, because something nonexistent begins to exist only through the agency of something that does exist. Therefore, if nothing existed, nothing could begin to exist, and so nothing would now exist, and this conclusion is obviously false. Therefore, not every being is something that can not-exist, but there needs to be something necessary in reality. But everything necessary either has or does not have the ground of its necessity from another source. There cannot, however, be an endless regress in the case of necessary things that have the ground of their necessity in another source, just as there cannot be an endless regress in the case of efficient causes, as I have shown. We need, therefore, to posit something that is intrinsically necessary, that does not have the ground of its necessity from another source, but which causes other things to be necessary, and all call this intrinsically necessary being God.

We take the FOURTH WAY from the gradations that we find in reality. For we find in reality things that are more good and less good, more true and less true, more excellent and less excellent, and similarly in the case of other such things. But we say "more" and "less" about different things as they in various ways approximate what is most; for example, an object is hotter if it more approximates what is hottest. Therefore, there is something that is most true and most good and most excellent, and so being in the highest degree, for things that are most true, are beings in the highest degree, as the *Metaphysics* says.[20] What we call most in a genus, moreover, causes everything belonging to that genus; for example, fire, which is hottest, causes everything hot, as the same work says.[21] Therefore, there exists something that causes the existing and the goodness and whatever perfection of every being, and we call this cause God.

We take the FIFTH WAY from the governance of things. For we see that certain things that lack knowledge, namely, natural material substances, act for the sake of an end. And this is evident because they always or more frequently act in the same way in order to achieve what is best, and hence it is evident that they reach their goal by striving, not by chance. But things that lack knowledge, do not strive for goals unless a being with knowledge and intelligence directs them, as, for example, an archer aims an arrow. Therefore, there is a being with intelligence who orders all the things of nature to their ends, and we call this being God.

Reply to Obj. 1.   As Augustine says in his *Enchiridion*, "Because God is the highest good, he would in no way allow anything bad to exist in his works were he not so all-powerful and good as to act well even with respect to what is bad."[22] It belongs to the infinite goodness of God, therefore, to permit bad things and to bring forth good things from them.

Reply to Obj. 2.   We also need to trace things produced by nature back to God as their first cause, because nature, by reason of its fixed end, acts at the direction of a higher efficient cause. Likewise, we need to trace even things done by free choice back to a higher cause that is not the reason and will of human beings, since things done by free choice can change and fall short; we indeed need to trace everything that can change and fall short, back to a first source that cannot change and is intrinsically necessary, as I have shown.[23]

Notes

1. *De fide orthodoxa* I, 3. PG 94:793.
2. *Posterior Analytics* I, 3. 72b18–25.
3. Cf. Anselm, *Proslogium* 2–3. PL 158:227–28; *Contra Gaunilonem*. PL 158: 247–60.
4. Jn. 14:6.
5. *Metaphysics* III, 3. 1005b11–12.
6. *Posterior Analytics* I, 10. 89a6–8.
7. Ps. 53:1.
8. Cf. PL 64:1311.
9. Q. 3, A. 4.
10. Heb. 11:1.
11. *De fide orthodoxa* I, 4. PG 94:797.
12. Rom. 1:20.
13. Rom. 1:19.
14. Q. 13, A. 1.
15. In the body of the article.
16. Ex. 3:14.
17. Cf. St. Thomas Aquinas, *Summa contra Gentiles* I, 13, 15, 16, 44; II, 15; III, 44; St. Thomas Aquinas, *De veritate*, Q. 5, A. 2; St. Thomas Aquinas, *De potentia*, Q. 3, A. 5.
18. See Glossary, s.v. "motion."
19. See Glossary, s.v. "generation and corruption."
20. Aristotle, *Metaphysics* Ia, 1. 993b28–31.
21. Ibid.
22. *Enchiridion* 11. PL 40:236.
23. In the body of the article.

ST I
Question 3
On the Simplicity of God

[This question is divided into eight articles, three of which are included here.]

Third Article

Is God Identical with His Essence or Nature?

I proceed in this way to the third article: it seems that God is not identical with his essence or nature.

Obj. 1. Nothing is inside itself. But we say that the essence or nature of God, which is his divinity, is in God. Therefore, it seems that God is not identical with his essence or nature.

Obj. 2. An effect is likened to its cause, since every efficient cause produces something like itself. But in created things, individually existing substances are not identical with their nature; for example, human beings are not identical with their humanity. Therefore, neither is God identical with his divinity.

On the contrary, we say that God is life, and not merely that he is living, as the Gospel of John makes clear: "I am the way, the truth, and the life."[1] As life is related to living beings, however, so divinity is related to God. Therefore, God is his very divinity.

I answer that God is identical with his essence or nature. And to understand this, we need to recognize that the essence or nature and the individually existing substance necessarily differ in things composed of matter and form. This is so because an essence or nature as such includes only what falls within the definition of a species; for example, "humanity" as such includes what falls within the definition of a human being, for human beings are human by such things, and humanity signifies this, namely, the things by which human beings are human. But individual matter, with all the accidents individuating it, does not fall within the definition of the species, for this particular flesh and these particular bones, or whiteness or blackness, or any such thing, does not fall within the definition of being human. And so this

45

particular flesh and these particular bones and the accidents designating this particular matter are not included in humanity. And yet they are included in what human beings are, and so what human beings are, possesses in itself something that humanity does not. And consequently, human being and humanity are not totally identical, but we signify humanity as the formal part of a human being, because the sources determining species are related as form with respect to the individuating matter.

Therefore, in things not composed of matter and form, in which there is no individuation by individual matter, that is, by particular matter, but forms themselves are intrinsically individuated, the very forms necessarily are subsistent, individually existing substances. And hence, individual substance and nature do not differ in them. And so, since God is not composed of matter and form, as I have shown,[2] he is necessarily his divinity, his life, and anything else that we predicate of him in this way.

Reply to Obj. 1. We can speak of uncomposed beings only by way of composite beings, from which we get our knowledge. And so, we use concrete terms to signify God's subsistence when we speak about him, because only composite beings subsist in our world, and we use abstract terms to signify his simplicity. Therefore, we need to trace what we say is the divinity or life or any such thing in God, back to the difference in our intellect's conception and not to any real difference.

Reply to Obj. 2. God's effects do not imitate him perfectly but inasmuch as they can. And it belongs to the deficiency of imitation that only many things can represent what is simple and one. And so there happens to be composition in God's effects, and consequently individually existing substance and nature are not identical in them.

Fourth Article

Are Essence and Existing Identical in God?

I proceed in this way to the fourth article: it seems that essence and existing are not identical in God.

Obj. 1. If this should be so, then nothing is added to God's existing. But the existing to which nothing is added, is existing in general, the existing that is predicated of everything. As a consequence, therefore, God would be existence in general, the existing that we can predicate of everything. But this conclusion is false, as the Book of Wisdom says: "They put the incommunicable Name on pieces of wood and stone."[3] Therefore, God's existing is not his essence.

Obj. 2. We can know that God exists, as I have said before.[4] But we cannot know what he is. Therefore, God's existing is not identical with what he is, that is, with his essence or nature.

On the contrary, Hilary says in his *De Trinitate*: "Existing is not an accident" in God "but is subsistent truth."[5] What subsists in God, therefore, is his existing.

I answer that God is not only his essence, as I have shown,[6] but also his existing. This can be shown in many ways. First, indeed, because whatever exists in something in addition to the thing's essence, needs to be caused in it by the sources of the thing's essence, as are the proper accidents[7] that result from the species (e.g., as the ability to laugh results from being human and is caused by the essential sources of the human species), or by something external (e.g., as heat in water is caused by fire). If, therefore, the very existence of a thing is other than its essence, the existence of that thing is necessarily caused either by an external cause or by the sources of the thing's essence. But such a thing's existence cannot be caused only by the sources of the thing's essence, because nothing suffices to cause its own existence if it has a caused existence. Therefore, something whose existence is other than its essence, needs to have its existence caused by another. But we cannot say this about God, because we say that he is the first efficient cause. Therefore, existence in God cannot be one thing, and his essence something else.

Second, God's existing is identical with his essence because existence is the actuality of every form or nature, for we signify goodness or humanity as actual only as we signify it as existing. Therefore, we necessarily relate existence itself to an essence other than existence itself as actuality to potentiality. Therefore, since there is nothing potential in God, as I have shown,[8] it follows that essence in him is nothing other than his existence. His essence, therefore, is his existing.

Third, God's existing is identical with his essence because, as what possesses fire but is not fire, catches fire by sharing fire, so what has existence but is not existence, is being by participation. But God is his essence, as I have shown.[9] Should God not be his existing, therefore, he will be a being by participation and not by his essence. Therefore, he will not be the first being, and this is absurd to say. Therefore, God is his existing and not only his essence.

Reply to Obj. 1. We can understand "something to which nothing is added" in two ways. In one way, as it belongs to a thing's nature that nothing be added to it, as it belongs to the nature of irrational animals that the latter lack the power of reason. In the second way, we understand something to which nothing is added because it does not belong to the thing's nature that there be an addition to it; for example, animal in general does not include the power of reason, because it does not belong to the nature of animal in general to possess the power of reason, although neither does it belong to the nature of animal in general to lack the power of reason. Existing with nothing added in the first way, therefore, is the divine existing; existing with nothing added in the second way is existing in general.

Reply to Obj. 2. We can speak about "is" in two ways. In one way, "is" means the act of existing; in the other way, "is" signifies composing the proposition that the rational soul effects when it joins a predicate to a subject. If we understand "is" in the first way, therefore, we cannot know God's existence, just as we cannot know his essence, but we can know God's existence only in the second way. For we know that the proposition that we form when we say that God exists, is true. And we know this from his effects, as I have said before.[10]

Eighth Article

Does God Enter into the Composition of Other Things?

I proceed in this way to the eighth article: it seems that God enters into the composition of other things.

Obj. 1. Denis says in his *De coelesti hierarchia:* "The existing of everything is the deity, which surpasses existing."[11] But the existing of everything enters into the composition of each thing. Therefore, God enters into the composition of other things.

Obj. 2. God is a form, for Augustine says in his *De verbis Domini* that "the Word of God," which is God, "is a certain unproduced form."[12] But a form is part of a composite. Therefore, God is part of a composite.

Obj. 3. Whatever things exist and in no way differ, are identical. But God and prime matter exist and in no way differ. Therefore, they are completely identical. But prime matter enters into the composition of things. Therefore, so does God.

Proof of the minor: whatever things differ, differ by some differences and so are necessarily composite; but God and prime matter are altogether simple; therefore, God and prime matter in no way differ.

On the contrary, Denis says in his *De divinis nominibus* that "no touching belongs to him," namely, God, "nor any sort of commingled union with respect to parts."[13] Besides, the *Liber de causis* says that "the first cause governs all things rather than commingles with them."[14]

I answer that there have been three errors in this matter. For example, certain thinkers held that God was the soul of the world, as Augustine makes clear in *The City of God,*[15] and the opinion of certain other thinkers that God is the soul of the first heavens, is also reductively the same. And others said that God is the formal source of all things, and this was reputedly the opinion of the followers of Almaric of Chartres. And the third error was that of David of Dinant, who most absurdly held that God is prime matter. For all of these opinions contain an obvious error: God can in no way enter into the composition of anything, whether as a formal or a material source.

First, indeed, they contain error because God is the first efficient cause, as we have said before.[16] And efficient causes and the forms of the things they make, happen to be only specifically, not numerically, identical; for example, human beings beget human beings. And matter and efficient causes happen to be neither numerically nor specifically identical, because matter is potential, and efficient causes are actual.

Second, the aforementioned opinions contain error because efficient activity belongs to God primarily and intrinsically, since he is the first efficient cause. But composites rather than parts entering into the composition of anything are efficient causes primarily and intrinsically. For example, human beings' hands do not cause, but human beings do by means of their hands, and fire heats by means of heat. And hence God cannot be part of any composite.

Third, the aforementioned opinions contain error because no part of a composite can be absolutely first in beings, not even matter and form, which are the primary parts of composites. For matter is potential, and potentiality is without qualification secondary to actuality, as is clear from what I have said before.[17] Moreover, a form that is part of a composite, is a shared form, and as what shares something, is secondary to what is essentially such, so also is the very thing shared. For example, the fire in things on fire is secondary to what is essentially fire. And I have shown that God is the first being absolutely.[18]

Reply to Obj. 1. We say that the deity is the existing of everything by efficient and exemplary causality and not by essence.

Reply to Obj. 2. The Word is an exemplary form and not a form that is part of a composite.

Reply to Obj. 3. Simple things do not differ by any other differences, for such belongs to composites. Human beings and horses, for example, differ by the distinguishing characteristics of rationality and lack thereof, but these distinguishing characteristics indeed do not further differ from one another by other differences. And hence, to be precise, we say in the strict sense that simple things are different, not that they differ. For according to the Philosopher in the *Metaphysics*, we without qualification say that things are different, but everything that differs, differs by something.[19] And hence, to be precise, prime matter and God do not differ, but they are different by their very selves. And hence it does not follow that they are identical.

Notes

1. Jn. 14:6.
2. Q. 3, A. 2.
3. Wis. 14:21.
4. Q. 2, A. 2.
5. *De Trinitate* 7. PL 10:208.

6. Q. 3, A. 3.
7. See Glossary, s.v. "accident."
8. Q. 3, A. 1.
9. Q. 3, A. 3.
10. Q. 2, A. 2.
11. *De coelesti hierarchia* 4. PG 3:177.
12. *Sermo ad populum* 117, 2. PL 38:662.
13. *De divinis nominibus* 2. PG 3:644.
14. *Liber de causis*, prop. 20.
15. *The City of God* VII, 6. PL 41:199.
16. Q. 2, A. 3.
17. Q. 3, A. 1.
18. Q. 2, A. 3.
19. *Metaphysics* IX, 3. 1054b23–27.

ST I
Question 4
On the Perfection of God

[This question is divided into three articles, all of which are included here.]

First Article

Is God Perfect?

I proceed in this way to the first article: it seems that it is inappropriate for God to be perfect.

Obj. 1. We call something perfect fully made, as it were. But it is inappropriate for God to have been made. Therefore, neither is it appropriate for him to be perfect.

Obj. 2. God is the first source of things. But the sources of things seem to be imperfect, for seeds are the source of animals and plants. Therefore, God is imperfect.

Obj. 3. I have shown before that God's essence is existing itself.[1] But existing itself seems to be most imperfect, because it is most general and takes in the additional notes of everything. Therefore, God is imperfect.

On the contrary, the Gospel of Matthew says: "Be perfect just as your heavenly father is perfect.[2]

I answer that, as the Philosopher relates in the *Metaphysics*,[3] certain ancient philosophers, namely, the Pythagoreans and Speusippus, did not attribute what is best and most perfect to the first source. The reason for this is because the ancient philosophers considered only the material source, and the first material source is the most imperfect. Indeed, since matter as such is potential, the first material source is necessarily the most potential and so the most imperfect.

But we hold God to be the first source in the class of efficient causes, not as something material, and such a first source is necessarily the most perfect. Indeed, just as matter as such is potential, so an efficient cause as such is actual. And hence the first efficient source needs to be the most actual and consequently the most perfect. For we accordingly say that something is per-

51

fect insofar as it is actual, since we say that what lacks nothing as to the mode of its perfection, is perfect.

Reply to Obj. 1. Therefore, as Gregory says, "we resound" the lofty honors of God "by stuttering" as we can, "for we cannot properly call perfect what has not been produced."[4] But because we then say in the case of things produced that something is perfect when brought from potentiality to actuality, we apply the term "perfect" to signify everything that has actual existence, whether or not it possesses existence by being produced.

Reply to Obj. 2. Material sources, which we find to be imperfect, cannot be unconditionally first; rather, something else perfect precedes it. For, granted that seeds are the source of the living beings that they generate, they nonetheless have antecedent to themselves the animals or plants from which the seeds come. For something actual necessarily precedes something potential, since only actual beings bring potential beings into actuality.

Reply to Obj. 3. Existence itself is the most perfect of all things, for it is related to everything as actuality. For nothing has actuality except inasmuch as it exists, and hence existence itself is the actuality of all things and of their forms. And so existence is not related to all things as something receiving to something received, but rather as something received to something receiving. For, when I speak of the existence of a human being or a horse or something else, I consider existence itself as something formal and received, not as something to which existence belongs.

Second Article

Does God Possess the Perfections of All Things?

I proceed in this way to the second article: it seems that God does not possess the perfections of all things.

Obj. 1. God is simple, as I have shown.[5] But the perfections of things are many and diverse. Therefore, God does not contain every perfection of things.

Obj. 2. Contrary attributes cannot exist in the same thing. But things have contrary perfections, for specific differences bring about species, and the differences by which a genus is divided, and species constituted, are contrary. Therefore, since contrary attributes cannot exist in the same thing at the same time, it seems that God does not possess every perfection of things.

Obj. 3. Being alive is more perfect than being, and being rational is more perfect than being alive. Therefore, being alive is more perfect than existing, and being rational is more perfect than being alive. But the essence of God is existence itself. Therefore, God does not possess in himself the perfection of life and rationality and other such perfections.

On the contrary, Denis says in his *De divinis nominibus* that God "possesses beforehand all existing things in one."[6]

I answer that the perfections of all things exist in God. And hence we also say that he is perfect without exception, because he lacks no excellence that we find to exist in any kind of thing, as the Commentator on the *Metaphysics* says.[7] And we can consider this from two perspectives.

First, indeed, because any perfection in an effect needs to be found in its efficient cause, either in the same respect if the cause is univocal,[8] as human beings beget human beings, or in a more outstanding way if the cause is equivocal, as there is in the sun a likeness of the things that the power of the sun produces. For an effect evidently pre-exists in the power of its efficient cause; to pre-exist in the power of an efficient cause, however, is to pre-exist in a more perfect way, not in a less perfect way. Granted that to pre-exist in the power of a material cause is to pre-exist in a less perfect way—because matter as such is imperfect—an efficient cause as such is nonetheless perfect. Therefore, since God is the first efficient cause of things, the perfections of all things necessarily pre-exist in him in a more outstanding way. And Denis touches on this explanation in his *De divinis nominibus* when he says of God that "he is indeed not this thing and not that thing, but he is all things as their cause."[9]

Second, we can consider that the perfections of everything exist in God because of what I have previously shown,[10] that God is intrinsically subsistent existence itself. And so he necessarily contains in himself the whole perfection of existing. For if a hot object does not possess the entire perfection of heat, this is evidently so because heat is not shared in full measure. But heat could not lack any part of heat's power if heat were intrinsically subsistent. And so, since God is subsistent existence itself, he can lack no part of the perfection of existing. But the perfections of everything belong to the perfection of existing, for things are perfect insofar as they possess existence in some way. And hence it follows that God does not lack the perfection of anything. And Denis also touches on this consideration in his *De divinis nominibus*, saying that God "is not something existing in a particular way, but he antecedently contains existence in himself in a uniform way, as a whole without qualification or limitation," and he then adds that God "is himself existence for things that subsist."[11]

Reply to Obj. 1.   As the sun, "itself remaining undivided and by shedding its light uniformly, antecedently includes in itself in a uniform way the substances of sensible objects and their many different qualities, so much more do all things necessarily pre-exist in their cause according to a unity of nature," as Denis says in his *De divinis nominibus*.[12] And so things in themselves different and contrary pre-exist in God as one, without detriment to his simplicity.

Reply to Obj. 2.   The foregoing reply makes the solution to the second objection evident.

Reply to Obj. 3.   Although existence itself is more perfect than life, and life itself is more perfect than rationality itself—if we consider these things as they are distinguished conceptually—yet a living being is more perfect than something that merely exists, and a rational being is a being and a living being, as the same Denis says in the same chapter.[13] Granted, therefore, that being in itself does not include being alive and being rational, because beings that share existence, need not share it in every way of existing, yet God's very existing includes in itself life and reason, because he who is subsistent existing itself, cannot lack any perfection of existing.

Third Article

Can a Creature Be like God?

I proceed in this way to the third article: it seems that no creature can be like God.

Obj. 1.   The Psalm says: "There is not the like of you among the gods, O Lord."[14] But of all creatures, those called "gods" by participation are more excellent. Much less, therefore, can other creatures be called like God.

Obj. 2.   Likeness is a certain comparison. There is, however, no comparison between things of different genera; therefore, neither do these things have any likeness, for we do not say that sweetness is like whiteness. But no creature belongs to the same genus as God, since God is not in a genus, as I have shown before.[15] Therefore, no creature is like God.

Obj. 3.   We call things that agree in form, similar. But nothing is one with God in form, for only God's essence is existence itself. Therefore, no creature can be like God.

Obj. 4.   There is mutual likeness in like things, for what is like, is like something like. If any creature is like God, therefore, God will also be like some creature. And this is contrary to what the Book of Isaiah says: "To whom have you made God like?"[16]

On the contrary, the Book of Genesis says: "Let us make human beings according to our image and likeness"[17]; and the First Letter of John says: "When he has appeared, we shall be like him."[18]

I answer that there are as many kinds of likeness as there are many ways of sharing in a form, since we note likeness by things' agreeing or sharing in a form. For we say that kinds of things sharing in the same form in the same respect and in the same measure are similar, and we say not only that these are similar, but that they are equal in their likeness; for example, we say that two objects equally white are similar in their whiteness. And this is the most perfect likeness.

We say in a second way that things that share in a form in the same respect, but by more or less rather than in the same measure, are similar; as, for example, we say that an object less white is similar to one that is more white. And this is an imperfect likeness.

We say in a third way that things sharing in the same form but in different respects are similar, as is evident in the case of nonunivocal efficient causes. For, since every efficient cause as such produces an effect like itself, although each acts according to its own form, a likeness of the efficient cause's form is necessarily in the effect. If the efficient cause belongs to the same species as the effect, therefore, there will be a likeness in form between the cause and the effect in the same specific respect; for example, human beings beget human beings. But if the efficient cause does not belong to the same species as the effect, there will be a likeness between the cause and the effect but not one in the same specific respect; for example, effects produced by the sun's power indeed approach some likeness to the sun, although such that they receive the sun's form by a generic rather than a specific likeness.

If there is an efficient cause that does not belong to a genus, therefore, its effects approach still more remotely a likeness to the form of the efficient cause, although not such that they share a likeness of the efficient cause's form in the same specific or generic respect. Rather, they share likeness by some kind of analogy, as existing itself is common to all things. And the things that God makes, insofar as they are beings, are likened to him as the first and universal source of all existing.

Reply to Obj. 1.   When sacred Scripture declares that something is not like God, this "is not contrary to its being likened to him," as Denis says in his *De divinis nominibus.*[19] "For the same things are like and unlike God; they are indeed like him insofar as they imitate him, as he who is not perfectly imitable, happens to be imitated, but they are unlike God insofar as they are less than their cause." This dissimilarity is not only to a greater or lesser degree, as, for example, a less white object falls short of one that is more white, but because there is no conformity either specifically or generically.

Reply to Obj. 2.   God is not related to creatures as things of different genera are related to one another, but he is related to creatures as something outside every genus and the source of all genera.

Reply to Obj. 3.   We do not say that there is a likeness of creatures to God because God and creatures share a form in the same generic or specific respect, but we say that there is a likeness only by analogy, namely, as God is a being by his essence, and other things are beings by participation.

Reply to Obj. 4.   Although we may in some way concede that creatures are like God, yet we can in no way grant that God is like creatures, because, as Denis says in his *De divinis nominibus,* "A mutual likeness is admitted in things belonging to one and the same order but not in causes and effects."[20] For example, we say that a portrait is like a human being, but not vice versa. And we likewise can in some way say that creatures are like God, but not that God is like creatures.

Notes

1. Q. 3, A. 4.
2. Mt. 5:48.
3. *Metaphysics* XI, 7. 1072b30–32.
4. *Moralia* V, 36. PL 75:715.
5. Q. 3, A. 7.
6. *De divinis nominibus* 5. PG 3:825.
7. Averroes, *In libros Metaphysicorum* V (IV in the Bekker notation), comm. 21.
8. On univocal and equivocal causes, see Glossary, s.v. "cause."
9. *De divinis nominibus* 5. PG 3:824.
10. Q. 3, A. 4.
11. *De divinis nominibus* 5. PG 3:817.
12. *De divinis nominibus* 5. PG 3:824.
13. Ibid.
14. Ps. 86:8.
15. Q.3, A. 5.
16. Is. 40:18.
17. Gen. 1:26.
18. 1 Jn. 3:2.
19. *De divinis nominibus* 9. PG 3:916.
20. *De divinis nominibus* 9. PG 3:913.

ST I
Question 5
On Good in General

[This question is divided into six articles, five of which are included here.]

First Article

Does Good Really Differ from Being?

I proceed in this way to the first article: it seems that good does not really differ from being.

Obj. 1. Boethius says in his book *De hebdomatibus*: "I see in the world that it is one characteristic for things to be good, and another for them to exist."[1] Therefore, good and being really differ.

Obj. 2. Nothing gives form to itself. But we say that something is good when it receives the form of being, as I explain in my commentary on the *Liber de causis*.[2] Therefore, good really differs from being.

Obj. 3. Good admits of more and less. But existing does not admit of more and less. Therefore, good really differs from being.

On the contrary, Augustine says in his book *De doctrina Christiana* that "we are good inasmuch as we exist."[3]

I answer that good and being are really the same, and they differ only conceptually. And we make this clear as follows. The nature of good certainly consists in the fact that something is desirable, and hence the Philosopher says in the *Ethics* that good is "what everything desires."[4] But everything is evidently desirable as perfect, for everything seeks its own perfection. Everything is perfect, however, insofar as it is actual. And hence something is evidently good inasmuch as it is a being, for existing is the actuality of everything, as is clear from what I have said before.[5] And so it is evident that good and being are really the same, but good expresses the aspect of being desirable, which being does not.

Reply to Obj. 1. Although good and being are really the same, yet we do not say in the same way that something is a being unconditionally and good unconditionally, because good and being are conceptually distinct. For,

57

since being expresses that something is actual in the strict sense, and actuality in the strict sense is related to potentiality, we accordingly call something a being without qualification as we first distinguish it from what is only potential. But the substantial existing of every object distinguishes it from what is potential, and hence we unconditionally call everything a being by reason of its own existence as a substance. We say, however, that something exists in a certain way by reason of added actualities; for example, being white means existing in a certain way, for being white does not take away an existing that is unconditionally potential, since being white comes to something already existing.

But good expresses the aspect of being perfect, that is, of being desirable, and consequently expresses the aspect of something final. And hence we say that something ultimately perfect is unconditionally good. Moreover, we do not say that something that does not possess the final perfection that it ought to have, although it does possess some perfection insofar as it is actual, is nonetheless unconditionally perfect, nor that it is unconditionally good, but that it is perfect and good in a certain way.

We thus call something a being unconditionally and good in a certain way, that is, inasmuch as it is a being, by its first existing, which is substantial existing, but we call something a being in a certain way and good unconditionally by its final actuality. We should thus relate what Boethius says, that "in reality" it is "one characteristic for things to be, and another for them to exist," to being good unconditionally and to existing unconditionally, because something is a being without qualification by its first actuality and good without qualification by its final actuality. And yet an object is in some way good by its first actuality, and it is in some way a being by its final actuality.

Reply to Obj. 2. We call something good when it receives a form, just as we understand it to be unconditionally good by its final actuality.

Reply to Obj. 3. And we likewise need to say in response to the third objection that we call things more and less good by reason of an additional actuality, for example, by reason of knowledge or virtue.

Second Article

Is Good Conceptually Prior to Being?

I proceed in this way to the second article: it seems that good is conceptually prior to being.

Obj. 1. The order of names is according to the order of the things that the names signify. But Denis, among other names of God, posits good before being, as he made clear in his *De divinis nominibus*.[6] Therefore, good is conceptually prior to being.

Obj. 2. What extends to more objects, is conceptually prior to what extends to less objects. But "good" extends to more objects than "being" does, for, as Denis says in his *De divinis nominibus*, "'good' extends to objects that exist, and to objects that do not exist, but 'being' extends only to existing things."[7] Therefore, good is conceptually prior to being.

Obj. 3. The more universal is conceptually prior to the less universal. But good seems to be more universal than being, because good has the aspect of desirable, and yet nonexistence itself is desirable for some. For the Gospel of Matthew says of Judas: "It were better for him if he had not been born," etc.[8] Therefore, good is conceptually prior to being.

Obj. 4. Not only is existing desirable, but life and wisdom and many such things are also, and so it seems that existing is one particular kind of desirable object, and that good is the universal object that is desirable. Therefore, good is without qualification conceptually prior to being.

On the contrary, the *Liber de causis* says that "the first of created things is existing."[9]

I answer that being is conceptually prior to good. The consideration that a term signifies, is what the intellect conceives about something, and the intellect signifies this by the expression. What first falls within the grasp of the intellect, therefore, is conceptually first. But being falls first within the grasp of the intellect, because everything is knowable accordingly as it is actual, as the *Metaphysics* says.[10] Thus being is the proper object of the intellect, and so it is the first object of understanding, just as sound is the first object of hearing. Therefore, being is conceptually prior to good.

Reply to Obj. 1. Denis defines divine names insofar as they imply a causal relationship about God, for we name God from creatures as we name causes from their effects, as Denis says.[11] But good, since it has the nature of desirable, implies the relationship of a final cause, and such causality is first because an efficient cause acts only for the sake of an end, and because an efficient cause moves matter to a form. And hence we call an end the "cause of causes." And so, in causing, good is prior to being as end is prior to form, and, for this reason, he posits good before being in the names signifying the divine causality.

And he also posits good before being because, according to the Platonists, who did not distinguish matter from privation and said that matter is nonbeing, the sharing in good applies to more things than does the sharing in being. For prime matter[12] shares in good, since it seeks the good (although it seeks only what is like itself), but it does not share in being, since the Platonists hold prime matter to be nonbeing. And so Denis says that we "apply 'good' to objects that do not exist."[13]

Reply to Obj. 2. The solution to the second objection is clear from the reply to the first objection. Or we need to say that good extends to what exists and what does not, not by predication but by causality, so that we do not understand by nonexisting things those that are without qualification completely nonexistent, but we understand those that are potential and not actual. This is so because good has the consideration of end, not only the end in which actual things rest, but also the end toward which things not actual but only potential are moved. Being, however, imports only the relationship of a formal cause, whether one that is inherent, or one that is exemplary, and this causality extends only to actual things.

Reply to Obj. 3. Nonexistence is not desirable as such but by accident, namely, insofar as the removal of something bad is desirable, and nonexistence indeed removes such an evil. But the removal of an evil is desirable only inasmuch as an evil deprives something of a certain kind of existence. Therefore, what is desirable of itself, is existence, while nonexistence is desirable only by accident, namely, inasmuch as one seeks the kind of being of which human beings ought not to be deprived. And so we by accident also call nonexistence good.

Reply to Obj. 4. Life and knowledge and other such things are desirable as they are actual, and hence we desire some sort of existing in everyone of them. And so only being is desirable, and, therefore, only being is good.

Third Article

Is Every Being Good?

I proceed in this way to the third article: it seems that not every being is good.

Obj. 1. Good adds something to being, as is clear from what I have said.[14] But things that add something to being, such as substance, quantity, quality, and other such things, constrict being. Therefore, good constricts being, and so not every being is good.

Obj. 2. Nothing bad is good, as the prophet Isaiah says: "Woe to you who call bad good, and good bad."[15] But we call some beings bad. Therefore, not every being is good.

Obj. 3. Good has the nature of desirable. But prime matter does not have the nature of desirable but only the nature of desiring. Therefore, prime matter does not have the nature of good, and so not every being is good.

Obj. 4. The Philosopher says in the *Metaphysics* that good does not exist in mathematical objects.[16] But mathematical objects are certain beings; otherwise, we would not know them. Therefore, not every being is good.

On the contrary, every being other than God is a creature of God. But "every creature of God is good," as the First Letter to Timothy says,[17] and God is good in the highest degree. Therefore, every being is good.

I answer that every being as such is good. For every being as such is actual and perfect in some way, because every actuality is a certain perfection. But perfect has the nature of desirable and good, as is clear from what I have said.[18] And hence it follows that every being as such is good.

Reply to Obj. 1. Substance, quantity, quality, and everything included in them constrict being by applying being to some essence or nature. But this thereby adds nothing good to being except the aspect of being desirable and of perfection, and such is appropriate to existing itself in whatever nature it exists. And hence good does not constrict being.

Reply to Obj. 2. We call no being as such bad, but we call a being bad insofar as it lacks a certain way of existing, as we call human beings bad insofar as they lack virtuous existence, and we call an eye bad insofar as it lacks accuracy of vision.

Reply to Obj. 3. As prime matter is only a potential being, so is prime matter only a potential good. Although, according to the followers of Plato, we can call prime matter nonbeing because of the privation connected with it, prime matter nonetheless shares in something of being, namely, the very ordering toward, or capacity for, good. And so it does not befit prime matter to be desirable, but it does befit prime matter to desire.

Reply to Obj. 4. Mathematical objects do not really subsist as separate things because, were they to subsist, there would be something good in them, namely, their very existing. But mathematical objects exist only conceptually as separate things, as we abstract them from motion and matter, and so we abstract them from the nature of ends, which have the nature of causing motion. Moreover, it is not inappropriate that good or the aspect of good be absent from a conceptual being, because the nature of being is prior to the nature of good, as I have said before.[19]

Fourth Article

Does Good Have the Nature of Final Cause?

I proceed in this way to the fourth article: it seems that good does not have the nature of final cause but rather the nature of other causes.

Obj. 1. "We praise good as beautiful," as Denis says in his *De divinis nominibus*.[20] But beautiful implies the nature of formal cause. Therefore, good has the nature of formal cause.

Obj. 2. Good tends to pour itself out, as we learn from the words of Denis, whereby he says that "good is the source by which everything subsists and exists."[21] But to be diffusive implies the nature of an efficient cause. Therefore, good has the nature of efficient cause.

Obj. 3. Augustine says in his *De doctrina Christiana* that "we exist because God is good."[22] But we exist from God as efficient cause. Therefore, good has the nature of efficient cause.

On the contrary, the Philosopher says in the *Physics* that "that for whose sake something exists, exists as the end and good of other things."[23] There-fore, good has the nature of final cause.

I answer that, since good is what everything desires, good has, moreover, the nature of an end; good clearly implies the nature of end. Nonetheless, however, the aspect of good presupposes the aspect of efficient cause and the aspect of formal cause. For we see that what is first in causing, is last in the effect; fire, for example, heats before it induces the form of fire, although the heat in the fire nonetheless results from its substantial form. But in causing, we first find the good or end that moves the efficient cause; second, we find the action of the efficient cause, which moves to produce the form; third comes the form. And so the converse needs to be the case in the effect: the first thing is the form itself, by which a being exists; second, we consider the efficient power in the form, insofar as the form is something perfect in existing (because anything is perfect when it can make something like itself, as the Philosopher says in the *Meteorology*)[24]; third results the aspect of good, whereby perfection is grounded in being.

Reply to Obj. 1.   Beautiful and good are indeed identical in a subject, be-cause they are grounded on the same thing, namely, the form, and we praise good as beautiful because of this. But beautiful and good differ conceptual-ly, for good properly regards desire, since good is what all things desire. And so good has the nature of end, for desire is a kind of quasi-motion to-ward something. Beautiful, however, regards a cognitive power, for we call objects that please when seen, beautiful. And hence beautiful consists in a due proportion, because the senses are delighted in objects duly pro-portioned, as objects like themselves, for even the senses and all cognitive powers are a kind of reasoning. And because knowledge is achieved by assim-ilation, and likeness regards form, beautiful properly belongs to the con-sideration of formal cause.

Reply to Obj. 2.   We say that good tends to pour itself out in the same way that we say that an end causes motion.

Reply to Obj. 3.   We call whoever have the power to will, good insofar as they have good will, because we make use of everything in us by the will. And hence we do not say that human beings who have a good intellect, are good, but we do say that those who have a good will, are. But the will re-gards an end as its proper object, and so the saying "We exist because God is good" refers to our final cause.

Sixth Article

Do We Appropriately Distinguish Good into the Worthy,
the Useful, and the Pleasurable?

I proceed in this way to the sixth article: it seems that we do not appro-priately distinguish good into the worthy, the useful, and the pleasurable.

Obj. 1. We divide the good into ten predicaments,[25] as the Philosopher says in the *Ethics*.[26] But we can find the worthy, the useful, and the pleasurable in a single predicament. Therefore, we do not appropriately divide good into the worthy, the useful, and the pleasurable.

Obj. 2. Every division is by contraries. But the worthy, the useful, and the pleasurable do not seem to be contrary, for worthy things are pleasurable, and no unworthy thing is useful (although the worthy and the useful would have to be contrary if the division were to be by contraries, as Cicero likewise says in his *De officiis*.)[27] Therefore, the aforementioned division is inappropriate.

Obj. 3. There is only one thing where something is for the sake of something else. But the useful is good only for the sake of something pleasurable or worthy. Therefore, we should not contradistinguish the useful from the pleasurable and the worthy.

On the contrary, Ambrose employs this division of good in his *De officiis*.[28]

I answer that this division seems properly to belong to the human good. If we consider the nature of good more deeply and more generally, however, we find that this division properly belongs to good as such. For an object is good insofar as it is desirable and the term of a movement of desire. And we can reflect upon the term of this motion by considering the movement of a natural body. Now, the movement of a natural body indeed terminates absolutely at its ultimate destination. But such movement also conditionally terminates at the intermediate points through which the material substance moves toward the final goal that terminates the motion. And we call the intermediate points terms of the movement insofar as they terminate part of the movement.

Moreover, we can understand the final term of movement in two ways: either as the object itself toward which movement is directed, such as a place or a form, or as the condition of repose in that object. In appetitive movements, therefore, we call "useful" the desirable objects that in some respect terminate the movement of appetite, as the means whereby the movements of appetite strive for something else. But we call "worthy" the objects that we desire as the final goal that completely terminates movements of appetite, as certain objects toward which, in themselves, the appetites tend, because we call worthy what is in itself desired. And what terminates a movement of appetite as a state of repose in the object desired, is "pleasure."

Reply to Obj. 1. We divide good into the ten predicaments insofar as good is identical with being in a subject, but the division into worthy, useful, and pleasurable belongs to good by the nature of good.

Reply to Obj. 2. This division is not by contrary things but by contrary considerations. We nonetheless properly call things that have no aspect of desirability other than pleasure, pleasurable, although such things are sometimes harmful and unworthy. But we call useful, things that do not possess in themselves the reason why one desires them, but one desires them only as they conduce to something else, as the taking of bitter medicine does. And we call worthy, things that possess in themselves the reason why one desires them.

Reply to Obj. 3.   We divide good into these three classes, not as something univocal that we predicate equally of them, but as something analogous that we predicate by what is prior and what is subsequent. For we first predicate good of what is worthy; second, of what is pleasurable; third, of what is useful.

Notes

1. *De hebdomatibus.* PL 64:1312.
2. *Super Librum de causis expositio,* on props. 21, 23. St. Thomas was one of the first to discover that the *Liber de causis* was not by Aristotle but derived from Proclus.
3. *De doctrina Christiana* I, 32. PL 34:32.
4. *Ethics* I, 1. 1094a3.
5. Q. 3, A. 4.
6. *De divinis nominibus* 3. PG 3:680.
7. *De divinis nominibus* 5. PG 3:816.
8. Mt. 26:24.
9. *Liber de causis,* prop. 4.
10. Aristotle, *Metaphysics* VIII, 9. 1051a29–32.
11. *De divinis nominibus* 1. PG 3:593.
12. See Glossary, s.v. "matter."
13. *De divinis nominibus* 5. PG 3:816.
14. Q. 5, A. 1.
15. Is. 5:20.
16. *Metaphysics* II, 2. 996a35–61.
17. 1 Tim. 4:4.
18. Q. 5, A. 1.
19. Q. 5, A. 2.
20. *De divinis nominibus* 4. PG 3:701.
21. *De divinis nominibus* 4. PG 3:700.
22. *De doctrina Christiana* I, 32. PL 34:32.
23. *Physics* II, 3. 195a24–25.
24. *Meteorology* IV, 3. 380a12–15.
25. See Glossary, s.v. "predicament."
26. *Ethics* I, 6. 1096a19–27.
27. Cicero, *De officiis* II, 3.
28. Ambrose, *De officiis* I, 9. PL 16:31–32.

ST I
Question 6
On the Goodness of God

[This question is divided into four articles, all of which are included here.]

First Article

Is It Appropriate for God to Be Good?

I proceed in this way to the first article: it seems that it is not appropriate for God to be good.

Obj. 1. The nature of good consists in limit, species, and order.[1] But these do not seem to be appropriate for God, since God is unlimited, and he is not ordered to anything. Therefore, it is not appropriate for God to be good.

Obj. 2. Good is what everything desires. But some things do not desire God, because some things do not know him, and nothing is desired unless it is known. Therefore, it is not appropriate for God to be good.

On the contrary, the Book of Lamentations says: "The Lord is good to those who hope in him, to the soul that seeks him."[2]

I answer that it is especially appropriate for God to be good. For an object is good insofar as it is desirable. But everything desires its own perfection. Moreover, the perfection and form of an effect is a certain likeness of the efficient cause, since every efficient cause produces an effect like itself. And hence an efficient cause is desirable and has the nature of good, for the sharing of its likeness is what is desired of it. Since God is the first efficient cause of everything, therefore, the aspect of good and desirable manifestly belongs to him. And hence Denis in his work *De divinis nominibus* attributes good to God as first efficient cause, saying that we call God good "as the source whereby everything subsists."[3]

Reply to Obj. 1. Having limit, species, and order belongs to the nature of a good that is caused. But good exists in God as cause, and hence it belongs to him to set limit, species, and order for other things. And hence these three are in God as their cause.

Reply to Obj. 2. Everything, by desiring its own perfection, desires God

65

himself, inasmuch as the perfections of all things are certain likenesses of the divine existing, as is clear from what I have said.[4] And so some things that desire God, know him as such, and such knowledge belongs to rational creatures. Other things, however, know some participations of his goodness, and such knowledge extends to sense knowledge as well. Still other things have a desire from nature apart from knowledge, as another, higher being endowed with knowledge inclines them toward their ends.

Second Article

Is God the Highest Good?

I proceed in this way to the second article: it seems that God is not the highest good.

Obj. 1.   Highest adds something to good; otherwise, it would be appropriate for every good to be highest. But everything constituted by adding something to something else, is composite. Therefore, the highest good is composite. But God is most simple, as I have shown before.[5] Therefore, God is not the highest good.

Obj. 2.   "Good is what everything desires," as the Philosopher says.[6] But nothing other than God, who is the end of everything, is the object that everything desires. Therefore, nothing other than God is good. And this is also evident by what the Gospel of Matthew says: "No one except God is good."[7] But we call something highest in comparison to other things; for example, we call something hottest in comparison to every hot object. Therefore, God cannot be called the highest good.

Obj. 3.   Highest implies comparison. But things that do not belong to one genus, are not comparable, as we inappropriately call sweetness greater or lesser than a line. Therefore, since God is not in the same genus with other good things, as is clear from what I have said before,[8] it seems that God cannot be called the highest good with respect to those things.

On the contrary, Augustine says in his *De Trinitate* that the Trinity of divine persons "is the highest good, and the most purified minds discern this."[9]

I answer that God is the highest good without qualification and not only in some genus or order of things. For we thus attribute good to God, as I have said before,[10] inasmuch as all desired perfections flow from him as first cause. But they do not flow from him as a univocal efficient cause, as is clear from what I have said before,[11] but from him as an efficient cause that does not agree with its effects either in the aspect of species or in the aspect of genus. Moreover, we indeed find the likeness of an effect uniformly in a univocal cause, but we find the likeness of an effect in an equivocal cause in a more excellent way, as, for example, heat exists in the sun in a more excellent way than it exists in fire. Since good is in God as the first, nonunivocal cause of all things, good is thus necessarily in him in the most excellent way. And we consequently call him the highest good.

Reply to Obj. 1. The highest good does not add to being anything absolute but only a relation. The relation whereby we affirm something about God in relation to creatures, however, does not really exist in God but in creatures, although, according to our conception, the relation exists in God. In the same way, we call an object knowable, not because we relate the object to our knowledge of it, but because we relate our knowledge to the object. And so there need not be any composition in the highest good, but it is only necessary that other things fall short of that good.

Reply to Obj. 2. We do not so understand the saying "Good is what everything desires" as if everything desires every good, but we understand that every object of desire has the aspect of good. But we understand the saying "No one except God is good" about something good by its essence, as I shall subsequently explain.[12]

Reply to Obj. 3. Objects not contained in the same genus are in no way comparable if they are contained in different genera. But we deny that God is in the same genus with other things, not that he should belong to some other genus, but because he is outside genus and the source of every genus. And so we compare him to other things by superfluity, and the highest good implies such a comparison.

Third Article

Does It Belong Exclusively to God to Be Essentially Good?

I proceed in this way to the third article: it seems that it does not belong exclusively to God to be essentially good.

Obj. 1. As "one" and "being" are convertible, so also are "good" and "being," as I have maintained before.[13] But every being is by its essence "one," as the Philosopher makes clear in the *Metaphysics*.[14] Therefore, every being is by its essence good.

Obj. 2. If good is what everything desires, since everything desires existing itself, the very existing of each thing is its good. But each thing is by its essence a being. Therefore, each thing is by its essence good.

Obj. 3. Everything is good by its own goodness. Therefore, if something is not good by its own essence, its goodness will necessarily not be its own essence. Therefore, that goodness, since it is a certain reality, is necessarily good, and if it is indeed good by another goodness, we shall inquire again about that goodness. Therefore, either we shall regress endlessly, or we shall arrive at some goodness that will not be good by another goodness. Therefore, by the same argument, we ought to rest in the first position, that everything is good by its own goodness. Therefore, everything is good by its own essence.

On the contrary, Boethius says in his *De hebdomatibus* that everything other than God is good by participation.[15] Therefore, everything other than God is not essentially good.

I answer that God alone is good by his essence. For we call everything good insofar as it is perfect, and things have three kinds of perfection: the first, indeed, insofar as they are constituted in their existing; the second as some accidental things necessary for the things' complete activity are added to them; the third by things attaining other things as ends. For example, the first kind of perfection of fire consists in existing, which fire possesses by its substantial form; its second kind of perfection consists in heat, buoyance, dryness, and the like; its third kind of perfection consists in resting in its proper place.

But these three kinds of existence belong essentially to God alone and no creature. Only his essence is its existing. And no accidents inhere in him, although what we predicate as accidents about other things, for example, being powerful, wise, and the like, belong to him essentially, as is clear from what I have said.[16] And he himself is not ordered to anything but is the ultimate end of all things. And hence God alone evidently possesses every kind of perfection by his essence. And so he alone is good by his essence.

Reply to Obj. 1. "One" does not imply the aspect of perfection but only the aspect of being undivided, and the latter aspect belongs to each thing by its essence. But the essences of simple things are both actually and potentially undivided, while the essences of composite things are only actually undivided. And so each thing is by its essence necessarily one but is not by its essence good, as I have shown.[17]

Reply to Obj. 2. Although everything is good inasmuch as it possesses existence, yet no essence of a created thing is existence itself. And so it does not follow that a created thing is by its essence good.

Reply to Obj. 3. The goodness of a created thing is not its very essence but something added, either its very existing or an additional perfection or a relation to an end. Nonetheless, we call the very goodness so added, good in the same way that we call it being. But we call it being because it is something, not because it exists by reason of something else. And hence we call it good because it is something good, not because it has some other goodness whereby it may be good.

Fourth Article

Are All Things Good by Reason of God's Goodness?

I proceed in this way to the fourth article: it seems that all things are good by reason of God's goodness.

Obj. 1. Augustine says in his *De Trinitate*: "This and that are good. Take away this and that particular thing, and look at good itself, if you can. You will then look at God, who is not a good by reason of another good but is the good that belongs to every good."[18] But everything is good by reason of its own good. Therefore, everything is good by reason of the very good that is God.

Obj. 2. As Boethius says in his *De Hebdomatibus*, we call all things good inasmuch as they are ordered to God, and this is by reason of God's goodness.[19] Therefore, all things are good by reason of his goodness.

On the contrary, all things are good inasmuch as they exist. But we call all things beings by reason of their own existing, not by reason of God's existing. Therefore, all things are good by reason of their own goodness, not by reason of God's goodness.

I answer that, in the case of things that imply relations, nothing prevents us from designating things by something external; for example, we designate things in a place by the place, and something measured by the measure. But there have been various opinions about things that we predicate absolutely. Plato, for instance, held that there are separate forms of all things,[20] and that we designate individuals by reason of those forms, by individuals sharing in those forms, as it were; just so, for example, we call Socrates a human being by reason of the separate form of human being. And as Plato posited the separate forms of human being and horse, which he called human being as such and horse as such, so he posited the separate forms of being and one, which he called being as such and one as such. And we call everything being or one by reason of its sharing in those forms. Moreover, he held what is being as such and one as such, to be the highest good. And because "good" and "being" are convertible, just as "one" and "being" are, he said that good itself as such is God. And hence he calls all things good by way of participation.

And although this opinion seems contrary to reason insofar as it posited intrinsically subsistent forms of the things of nature, as Aristotle demonstrates in many ways,[21] it is nonetheless absolutely true that there is something first, which is by its essence being and good. And we call this first being God, as is clear from what I said before.[22] Aristotle also agrees with this judgment.

Therefore, we can call everything good and being by reason of the first being, which is by its essence being and good; we can do so inasmuch as everything partakes of the first being by way of a certain imitation, albeit remotely and deficiently, as is clear from what I have said before.[23] Thus we call everything good by reason of God's goodness as the first exemplary, efficient, and final source of all goodness. Nevertheless, we call everything good by reason of the likeness of God's goodness inhering in it, and this is formally each thing's own goodness, which designates it as good. And so there is one goodness that belongs to everything—and also many goodnesses.

Reply to the Objections. The foregoing makes clear the answer to the objections.

Notes

1. Cf. Q. 5, A. 5.
2. Lam. 3:25.
3. *De divinis nominibus* 4. PG 3:700.
4. Q. 4, A. 3.
5. Q. 3, A. 7.
6. *Ethics* I, 1. 1094a3.
7. Mt. 19:17.
8. Q.3, A. 5.
9. *De Trinitate* I, 2. PL 42:822.
10. Q. 6, A. 1.
11. Q. 4, A. 3.
12. Q. 6, A. 3.
13. Q. 5, A. 1.
14. *Metaphysics* III, 2. 1003b22.
15. *De hebdomatibus*. PL 64:1313.
16. Q. 3, A. 6.
17. In the body of the article.
18. *De Trinitate* VIII, 3. PL 42:949.
19. *De Hebdomatibus*. PL 64:1312.
20. See Aristotle, *Metaphysics* I, 6. 987.
21. *Metaphysics* I, 9. 990a34–991b9; II, 6. 1002b12–32; VI, 14–15. 1039a24–1040b4.
22. Q. 2, A. 3.
23. Q. 4, A. 3.

ST I
Question 7
On the Infinity of God

[This question is divided into four articles, the first of which is included here.]

First Article

Is God Unlimited?

I proceed in this way to the first article: it seems that God is limited.

Obj. 1. Everything unlimited is imperfect, since it has the nature of something partial and material, as the *Physics* says.[1] But God is most perfect. Therefore, he is limited.

Obj. 2. Finite and infinite are fitting for quantity, as the Philosopher says in the *Physics*.[2] But there is no quantity in God, since God is not a material substance, as I have said before.[3] Therefore, it does not belong to him to be unlimited.

Obj. 3. Besides, something so in a particular place as not to be somewhere else is limited as to place. Therefore, something so particular as not to be something else is limited as to substance. But God is this particular being and not something else, for he is not stone or wood. Therefore, God is limited as to substance.

On the contrary, Damascene says that God is "infinite and eternal, and limits cannot circumscribe him."[4]

I answer that all ancient philosophers attribute the infinte to a first source, as the *Physics* says,[5] and they reasonably do so when they reflect on the fact that things flow without limit from a first source. But because some of them erred about the nature of the first source, they consequently erred concerning the infinity of that source. For, because they posited a material first source, they consequently attributed a material infinity to the first source, saying that an infinite material substance is the first source of things.

We need to consider, therefore, that we call something infinite because it is not limited. But form limits matter in some way, and matter limits form in

71

another way. Form indeed limits matter, inasmuch as matter has potentiality for many forms before it receives a form, and form limits matter when matter receives a particular form. And matter limits form, inasmuch as form, considered in itself, is common to many things and becomes definitively the form of this particular thing by the fact that it is received in matter.

Moreover, the form that limits matter, perfects it, and so the infinite, as attributed to matter, has the nature of something imperfect, for it is formless matter, as it were. Matter, on the other hand, does not perfect form, but rather matter restricts the fullness of form, and hence the infinite, as possessed by a form that matter does not limit, has the nature of something perfect.

But the most formal of all things is existence itself, as is clear from what I have said before.[6] Therefore, since God's existence is not an existence received in something, but God is his own subsistent existence, as I have shown before,[7] God himself is clearly infinite and perfect.

Reply to Obj. 1.   The foregoing makes clear the response to the first objection.

Reply to Obj. 2.   The limits of quantity are a quasi-form of the same, and an indication of this is that shape, which consists in limiting quantity, is a certain form with respect to quantity. And hence the infinite that belongs to quantity, is the infinite possessed by matter, and we do not attribute such an infinite to God, as I have said.[8]

Reply to Obj. 3.   We distinguish God from everything else, and we separate everything else from him, because his existing, insofar as we call it infinite, is something intrinsically subsistent, unreceived in anything—just as subsistent whiteness, if there were such, would differ from every whiteness existing in a subject by the fact that the subsistent whiteness would not exist in another.

Notes

1. *Physics* III, 6. 207a21–27.
2. *Physics*, I, 2. 185a34–63.
3. Q. 3, A. 1.
4. *De fide orthodoxa* I, 4. PG 94:797.
5. *Physics* III, 4. 203a1–4.
6. Q. 4, A. 1, *ad* 3.
7. Q. 3, A. 4.
8. In the body of the article.

ST I
Question 8
On the Existence of God in the World

[This question is divided into four articles, two of which are included here.]

First Article

Is God in All Things?

I proceed in this way to the first article: it seems that God is not in all things.
Obj. 1.   What is above all things, is not in all things. But God is above all things, as the Psalm says: "Highest above all peoples is the Lord."[1] Therefore, God is not in all things.
Obj. 2.   What is in something, is contained by it. But God is not contained by things; rather, he contains things. Therefore, God is not in things, but rather things are in him. And hence Augustine says in his book *Octoginta trium quaestionum* that "all things are in him rather than he himself is somewhere."[2]
Obj. 3.   The more power an efficient cause possesses, the further the cause's activity reaches. But God is the most powerful efficient cause. Therefore, his action can even reach objects distant from him, and he need not be in all things.
Obj. 4.   Devils are certain things. God, however, is not in devils, for there is not "a compact of light with darkness," as the Second Letter to the Corinthians says."[3] Therefore, God is not in all things.

On the contrary, a thing is wherever it acts. But God acts in all things, according to the saying of Isaiah: "You have worked in us all our works, O Lord."[4] Therefore, God is in all things.

I answer that God is in all things, not indeed as part of their essence, or as an accident, but as an efficient cause is present to the objects on which it acts. For every efficient cause needs to be united to the object on which it acts directly, and hence the *Physics* proves that a moved object and the cause of the object's movement need to exist together.[5] Since God by his essence is existing itself, moreover, created existing is necessarily his own effect, as burning is fire's own effect. But God causes this effect in things,

73

not only when they first begin to exist, but as long as they are preserved in existence, just as the sun causes light in air as long as air stays illumined. Therefore, God needs to be present to things in the way in which they possess existence as long as they do so. Moreover, existing is innermost to, and deeper in, all things, since existing is something formal with respect to everything that really exists, as is clear from what I have said before.[6] And hence God needs to be, and to be innermost, in all things.

Reply to Obj. 1. God is above all things by the excellence of his nature, and yet he is in all things as the one who causes all things to exist, as I have said before.[7]

Reply to Obj. 2. Although we say that corporeal objects are in something inasmuch as something contains them, yet spiritual beings contain the things in which they are present, as, for example, the soul contains the body. And hence God, too, is in things as the being that contains them. Nonetheless, by a certain comparison to corporeal objects, we say that everything is in God, inasmuch as he includes them.

Reply to Obj. 3. The action of no efficient cause, however powerful, reaches a distant object except insofar as the cause acts on such an object through intermediate causes. But it belongs to the consummate power of God that he act on everything apart from intermediate causes. And hence nothing is distant from him, as if it did not have God present within itself. We say, nonetheless, that things are distant from God by the unlikeness of nature or grace, just as he is above everything by the excellence of his nature.

Reply to Obj. 4. We understand that there are in devils both their nature, which is from God, and the deformity of wrongdoing, which is not from him. And so we do not need to admit without qualification that God is in devils, but we need to admit that he is in them with this qualification: "insofar as they are certain beings." Moreover, we need to say unconditionally that God is in things that designate the devils' undeformed nature.

Third Article

Is God Everywhere by His Essence, Presence, and Power?

I proceed in this way to the third article: it seems that we poorly assign the ways that God exists in things when we say that he is in all things by his essence, power, and presence.

Obj. 1. What by essence exists in something else, is essentially in the other. But God is not essentially in things, for he does not belong to the essence of anything. Therefore, we ought not to say that God is in things by his essence, presence, and power.

Obj. 2. To be present to something is not to be absent from it. But for

God to be in things by his essence is for him not to be absent from anything. Therefore, it is identical for God to be in all things by his essence and by his presence. Therefore, it is superfluous to say that God is in things by his essence, presence, and power.

Obj. 3. As God is the source of everything by his power, so is he by his knowledge and will. But we do not say that God is in things by his knowledge and will. Therefore, neither is he in things by his power.

Obj. 4. As grace is a certain perfection added to something's substance, so are many other perfections. Therefore, if we say that God is in certain things in a special way by grace, it seems that we ought to understand a special way of his being in things with regard to every perfection.

On the contrary, Gregory says in his *Super Cantica Canticorum* that "God is in everything in a general way by his presence, power, and substance, but we say that he is in some things in an intimate way by his grace."[8]

I answer that we say in two ways that God is in something: in one way, as efficient cause, and he is thus in everything that he creates; in the second way, as the object of an action is in the one who acts, and this is characteristic in operations of the soul, insofar as a known object exists in a knowing subject, and a desired object exists in the one who desires. In this second way, therefore, God is in a special way in rational creatures that know and love him actually or habitually. And because rational creatures possess this by grace, as I shall make clear later,[9] we say that God is in the saints in this way by grace.

But we need to consider how God is in other things that he creates, from what we say exists in human affairs. For we say that a king is in the whole of his kingdom by his power, although he is not present everywhere. Moreover, we say that something is by its presence in everything within its view, as, for example, we say that everything in a house is present to someone, who nonetheless is not in every part of the house with respect to his substance. And we say that something is substantially or essentially where its substance is confined.

There were then some, namely, the Manicheans, who said that spiritual and incorporeal things are subject to divine power, but they asserted that visible and corporeal things are subject to the power of a contrary source. Against these, therefore, we need to say that God is in all things by his power.

But there were others, who, although they believed that everything is subject to divine power, yet did not extend divine providence to these lower material substances, and the Book of Job says in their person: "He walks around the cardinal points of the heavens, and he does not consider our affairs."[10] And we need to say against these that God is in everything by his presence.

There were still others, who, although they said that everything belongs to God's providence, yet held that God does not create everything without intermediate causes, but that he immediately created the first creatures, and that the latter created the others. And we need to say against these that God is in everything by his essence.

Thus God is in everything by his power, inasmuch as everything is subject to his power. He is in everything by his presence, inasmuch as everything is bare and open to his eyes. He is in everything by his essence, inasmuch as he is present to everything as the cause of its being, as I have said.[11]

Reply to Obj. 1. We say that God is in all things by essence, not indeed as though he should be a part of their essence, but by his essence because his substance is present to all things as the cause of their being, as I have said.[12]

Reply to Obj. 2. We can say that something is present to persons inasmuch as it lies within their sight, although it is distant from them as to their substance, as I have said.[13] And so we need to posit two ways in which God is in things, namely, by his essence and by his presence.

Reply to Obj. 3. It belongs to the nature of knowledge and will that a known object exists in a knowing subject, and that a willed object exists in the subject willing it, and hence, with respect to knowledge and will, things exist in God rather than God exists in things. But it belongs to the nature of power that it be the source of acting on another, and hence, as to power, we relate and apply an efficient cause to an external object. And so we can say that an efficient cause is in another by the cause's power.

Reply to Obj. 4. No other perfection added to substance except grace causes God to be in something as an object known and loved, and so only grace causes an extraordinary way of God existing in things. There is, however, another extraordinary way of God being in human beings by union, and we shall treat of this way in its own place.[14]

Notes

1. Ps. 113:4.
2. *Octoginta trium quaestionum*, Q. 20. PL 40:15.
3. 2 Cor. 6:14.
4. Is. 26:12.
5. Aristotle, *Physics* VII, 2. 243a3–245b2.
6. Q. 4, A. 1, *ad* 3.
7. In the body of the article.
8. Gregory the Great (Pope Gregory I), *Super Cantica Canticorum* 5 (on 5:17). Many authorities question the authenticity of this work. Cf. *Glossa ordinaria*. PL 113:1157.
9. Q. 43, A. 3.
10. Job 22:14.
11. Q. 8, A. 1.
12. Ibid.
13. In the body of the article.
14. ST III, Q. 2.

ST I
Question 9
On the Immutability of God

[This question is divided into two articles, the first of which is included here.]

First Article

Is God Altogether Unchangeable?

I proceed in this way to the first article: it seems that God is not altogether unchangeable.

Obj 1. Whatever moves itself, can somehow change. But, as Augustine says in his *Super Genesim ad litteram:* "The Spirit Creator moves himself neither by time nor by place."[1] Therefore, God can somehow change.

Obj. 2. The Book of Wisdom says of wisdom that it is "more variable than everything variable."[2] But God is wisdom itself. Therefore, God can change.

Obj. 3. To approach and to retreat indicate motion. But Scripture (the Letter of James) says such things about God: "Draw close to God, and he will draw close to you."[3] Therefore, God can change.

On the contrary, the Book of Malachi says: "I am God, and I do not change."[4]

I answer that what I have previously set forth, shows the complete immutability of God. First, indeed, because I have shown before that there is a first being, whom we call God,[5] and that such a first being needs to be pure actuality without admixture of any potentiality, because potentiality is unconditionally secondary to actuality.[6] But everything that is in any way changed, is in some way potential. And it is clear from this that God cannot change in any way.

Second, God is completely unchangeable because everything changed partially remains and partially passes away; for example, an object changed from whiteness to blackness remains the same as to substance. And so we note that in everything changed there is some composition. I have shown before, however, that there is no composition in God, and that he is altogether simple.[7] And hence God evidently cannot be changed.

Third, God is completely unchangeable because everything that is moved, acquires something by its movement and attains what it did not attain before. Since God is without limit, including in himself all the fullness of the perfection of the whole of existing,[8] however, he cannot acquire anything or reach what he did not reach before. And hence motion in no way belongs to him.

And hence some ancient philosophers, compelled by truth itself, as it were, held that the first source cannot change.

Reply to Obj. 1.   Augustine is speaking there in the way that Plato, who called every action a motion, said that the first mover moves himself, as the very acts of understanding and willing and loving are called motions. Therefore, since God understands and loves himself, Augustine and Plato accordingly said that God moves himself, although not as motion and change belong to something that exists as potential, as we are presently speaking about change and motion.

Reply to Obj. 2.   We say metaphorically that wisdom can vary, insofar as wisdom spreads its likeness even on the most distant of things. For nothing can exist that does not come by some kind of imitation from God's wisdom as the thing's first efficient and formal cause, just as artifacts also come from the practical knowledge of a craftsman. Therefore, as the likeness of God's wisdom goes step-by-step from the highest things, which share more likeness, even to the lowest things, which share less likeness, we indeed say that there is a certain course and movement of his wisdom into things; this is as if we should say that the sun comes down to earth, inasmuch as the rays of its light reach even the earth. And Denis explains in this way in his *De coelesti hierarchia*, when he says that "every course of God's manifestation comes to us by the Father of lights being moved."[9]

Reply to Obj. 3.   Such things are said in Scripture about God metaphorically. For, as we say that the sun goes into and out of a house, insofar as its rays reach the house, so we say that God approaches us and retreats from us insofar as we receive the influence of his goodness or rebel against him.

Notes

1. *Super Genesim ad litteram* VIII, 20. PL 34:388.
2. Wis. 7:24.
3. Jas. 4:8.
4. Mal. 3:6.
5. Q. 2, A. 3.
6. Q. 3, A. 1.
7. Q. 3, A. 7.
8. Q. 7, A. 1.
9. *De coelesti hierarchia* 1. PG 3:119.

ST I
Question 10
On the Eternity of God

[This question is divided into six articles, the first two of which are included here.]

First Article

Do We Appropriately Define Eternity as the Simultaneously-Whole and Perfect Possession of Life without End?

I proceed in this way to the first article: it seems that the definition of eternity that Boethius posited in his *On the Consolation of Philosophy*, when he said that "eternity is the simultaneously-whole and perfect possession of life without end,"[1] is inappropriate.

Obj. 1. We express the phrase "without end" negatively. But negation belongs only to the nature of things that lack something, and such does not belong to eternity. Therefore, we ought not posit "without end" in the definition of eternity.

Obj. 2. Eternity means a certain duration. But duration regards existing rather than life. Therefore, we ought to posit "existing" rather than "life" in the definition of eternity.

Obj. 3. We say that a whole is something that has parts. But having parts is not appropriate for eternity, since the latter is simple. Therefore, we inappropriately call eternity "whole."

Obj. 4. Several days cannot exist simultaneously, nor can several periods of time. But we speak in the plural about days and times in eternity, for the Book of Micah says: "His going forth from the beginning, from the days of eternity"[2]; and the Letter to the Romans says: "According to the revelation of the mystery kept secret for enduring times."[3] Therefore, eternity is not "simultaneously whole."

Obj. 5. To be whole is the same thing as to be perfect. Assuming that something is whole, therefore, it is superfluous to add that it is "perfect."

Obj. 6. Possession does not belong to duration. But eternity is a certain duration. Therefore, eternity is not "possession."

I answer that, as we need to come to knowledge of simple things by means of things that are composite, so we need to come to knowledge of eternity by means of time, which is nothing other than the numbering of motion by what comes before and what comes after. For, since there is succession in every motion, and one part comes after another, we apprehend time because we number the before and after in motion, and time is only the number of the before and after in motion. But we do not apprehend before and after in something that lacks motion and is always situated in the same way. As the nature of time consists in the numbering of the before and after in motion, therefore, so the nature of eternity consists in the apprehension of the simplicity of what is entirely outside of motion.

Likewise, we say that time measures what has a beginning and an end in time, as the *Physics* says,[4] and this is so because we apprehend a beginning and an end in whatever is moved. But as something altogether unchangeable can have no succession, so it can have no beginning or end.

We thus know eternity by two characteristics: first, by the fact that the eternal is without end, i.e., without beginning or end (since "end" relates to both beginning and end); second, by the fact that eternity itself is without succession, the whole of it existing simultaneously.

Reply to Obj. 1. We are accustomed to define simple things by negation, as, for example, we define a point as something without any parts. And this is so, not because negation is part of the essence of simple things, but because our intellect, which first apprehends things that are composite, cannot come to knowledge of simple things except by removing the composition.

Reply to Obj. 2. Something truly eternal is not only something real, but something living, and living itself—but not existing—extends in some way to operation.[5] Moreover, we note the length of duration by activity rather than by existing. And so also is time the numbering of motion.

Reply to Obj. 3. We call eternity whole, not because eternity has parts, but inasmuch as it lacks nothing.

Reply to Obj. 4. As Scripture metaphorically names God, although incorporeal, by the names of corporeal objects, so do we designate eternity, although existing simultaneously whole, by temporally successive terms.

Reply to Obj. 5. There are two things to consider in time, namely, time itself, which is successive, and the "now" of time, which is imperfect. Therefore, Boethius says "simultaneously whole" to take away time, and he says "perfect" to exclude the "now" of time.

Reply to Obj. 6. An object possessed is held firmly and with repose. To designate the unchangeability and completeness of eternity, therefore, Boethius used the term "possession."

Second Article

Is God Eternal?

I proceed in this way to the second article: it seems that God is not eternal.

Obj. 1. We can predicate of God nothing that is caused. But eternity is something caused, for Boethius says that "the fluid 'now' causes time, the permanent 'now' causes eternity,"[6] and Augustine says in his work *Octoginta trium quaestionum* that "God is the author of eternity."[7] Therefore, God is not eternal.

Obj. 2. Eternity does not measure what is before eternity and after eternity. But God exists before eternity, as the *Liber de causis* says,[8] and he exists after eternity, for the Book of Exodus says that "the Lord will reign forever and beyond."[9] Therefore, it is not suitable for God to be eternal.

Obj. 3. Eternity is a kind of measure. But it is not appropriate for God to be measured. Therefore, being eternal is not proper to him.

Obj. 4. There is no present, past, or future in eternity, since eternity is simultaneously whole, as I have said.[10] But Scripture predicates present, past, or future time of God. Therefore, God is not eternal.

On the contrary, Athanasius says: "Eternal Father, eternal Son, eternal Holy Spirit."[11]

I answer that the aspect of eternity results from immutability as the aspect of time results from motion, as is clear from what I have said.[12] And hence being eternal is most proper to God, because he is most unchangeable. Not only is he eternal, but he is his eternity, although nothing else is its duration, because nothing else is its existing. Moreover, God is his existing without composition, and hence he is his eternity in the same way that he is his essence.

Reply to Obj. 1. We say that the permanent "now," according to our conception, causes eternity. For, as the apprehension of time results in us because we apprehend the flow of "now" itself, so the apprehension of eternity results in us inasmuch as we apprehend the permanent "now." But we understand the saying of Augustine, that "God is the author of eternity," to be about shared eternity, for God communicates his eternity to some in the same way that he communicates his immutability.

Reply to Obj. 2. The foregoing makes clear the solution to the second objection. For we say that God exists before eternity as shared by immaterial substances. And so the same text says that "understanding is equated with eternity."

But as to what the Book of Exodus says, "The Lord will reign forever and beyond," one needs to realize that "forever" is there understood to mean "for ages," as another translation has it. Thus Exodus says that the Lord will reign beyond eternity because he lasts beyond every age, i.e., beyond every given duration, for age is only the duration of each thing, as the *De coelo* says.[13] Or the Lord is said to reign even beyond eternity because, even if something else were always to exist (such as the motions of the heavens according to certain philosophers), he nonetheless reigns beyond, inasmuch as his reign is simultaneously whole.

Reply to Obj. 3.   Eternity is nothing other than God himself. And hence we do not say that God is eternal as if he is measured in some way, but the nature of measure is there only according to our conception.

Reply to Obj. 4.   We attribute to God expressions denoting different periods of time inasmuch as his eternity includes every period of time, not that he himself is changed by present, past, and future.

Notes

1. *On the Consolation of Philosophy* V, 6. PL 63:858.
2. Mic. 5:2.
3. Rom. 16:25.
4. Aristotle, *Physics* IV, 12. 221b3–5.
5. See Glossary, s.v. "operation."
6. *De Trinitate* 4. PL 64:1253.
7. *Octoginta trium quaestionum*, Q. 23. PL 40:16.
8. *Liber de causis*, prop. 2.
9. Ex. 15:18.
10. Q. 10, A. 1.
11. St. Thomas quotes what is known as the Athanasian Creed, although that work was not composed by Athanasius. PG 28:1581.
12. Q. 10, A. 1.
13. Aristotle, *De coelo* I, 9. 279a22–28.

ST I
Question 11
On the Oneness of God

[This question is divided into four articles, two of which are included here.]

First Article

Does "One" Add Anything to Being?

I proceed in this way to the first article: it seems that "one" adds something to being.

Obj. 1. Everything is in a determined genus by something added to being, which encompasses every genus. But "one" is in a determined genus, for "one" is the source of number, and number is a species of quantity. Therefore, "one" adds something to being.

Obj. 2. What distinguishes something common, is constituted by an addition to it. But "one" and "many" distinguish being. Therefore, "one" adds something to being.

Obj. 3. If "one" does not add anything to being, it would be the same to say "one" as to say "being." But it is trifling to say that being is being. Therefore, it would be trifling to say that being is one, and it is false to say that this is trifling. Therefore, "one" adds something to being.

On the contrary, Denis says in his *De divinis nominibus*: "Nothing exists that does not share in being one."[1] And this would not be so if "one" were to add to being something that would limit being. Therefore, "one" is not constituted by an addition to being.

I answer that "one" does not add anything to being but only negates division, for being one means only being undivided. By this very fact, "one" is clearly convertible with being. For every being is either simple or composite. Moreover, something simple is both actually and potentially undivided. But a composite being does not possess existence when its parts are divided, but it exists after its parts constitute and put the composite itself together. And hence the existing of everything manifestly consists in its lack of division. And so, as everything safeguards its existence, so it safeguards its oneness.

Reply to Obj. 1.   Certain philosophers, who thought that the one that is convertible with being, and the one that is the source of number, are identical, are divided into opposite camps. For example, Pythagoras and Plato, who perceived that the one that is convertible with being, does not add anything to being but signifies a being's substance as undivided, thought that it is the same with respect to the one that is the source of number. And because numbers are made up of units, they were of the opinion that numbers were the substances of everything.

Conversely, however, Avicenna, who considered that the one that is the source of number, adds something to the substance of being (otherwise, numbers made up of units would not be a species of quantity), was of the opinion that the one that is convertible with being, adds something to the substance of being, as white adds something to being human.

But this is evidently false, because each thing is "one" by its substance. For there would be an endless regress if everything were "one" by something else, since the latter would likewise be "one" if it too were "one" by something else. And hence we need to support the first position.

Thus we need to say that the one that is convertible with being, does not add anything to being, but that the one that is the source of number, which "one" belongs to the genus of quantity, adds something to being.

Reply to Obj. 2.   Nothing prevents something distinguished in one way from being undistinguished in another, as things numerically distinguished are specifically the same, and so something happens to be one in one way, many in another. But still, if something is undistinguished absolutely—either because it is undistinguished as to what belongs to the thing's essence, although it is distinguished as to what is outside the thing's essence (e.g., what is one in subject and many as to accidents), or because it is actually undistinguished and potentially distinguishable (e.g., what is one in a whole and many as to parts)—that thing is one absolutely and many in some respect.

Conversely, however, if things are undistinguished in some respect and distinguished absolutely, as things will be many absolutely and one in some respect because they are distinguished as to essence and undistinguished as to their nature or as to their source or cause (e.g., what is many in number and one in species or one in source). Thus is being distinguished by "one" and "many, " by "one" absolutely and by "many" in some respect, as it were. For even the very multitude would not be included in being unless it were somehow included in "one." For Denis says in his *De divinis nominibus* that "there is no multitude that does not share in being one; rather, things many in parts are one in a whole, and things many in accidents are one in subject, and things many in number are one in species, and things many in species are one in genus, and things many in processions are one in source."[2]

Reply to Obj. 3.   It is not thereby trifling to say that being is one, because "one" adds something conceptually to being.

Third Article

Is There Only One God?

I proceed in this way to the third article: it seems that there is not only one God.

Obj. 1.   The First Letter to the Corinthians says: "For there are many gods and many lords."[3]

Obj. 2.   We cannot predicate of God the one that is the source of number, because we cannot predicate any quantity of him. Likewise, neither can we predicate of God the one that is convertible with being, because such predication implies privation, and every privation is an imperfection, and imperfection is not proper for God. Therefore, we should not say that there is only one God.

On the contrary, the Book of Deuteronomy says: "Hear, O Israel, the Lord your God is one God."[4]

I answer that we demonstrate by three arguments that there is only one God. First, indeed, by God's simplicity. For it is evident that the source by which something individual is this particular thing, can in no way be communicated to many things. For the source by which Socrates is human, can be communicated to many things, but the source by which Socrates is this human being, can be communicated only to one thing. Therefore, if Socrates were human by the source whereby he is this human being, just as there could not be many Socrates, so there could not be many human beings. But such uniqueness is appropriate for God, because God is his nature, as I have shown before.[5] Therefore, being God and being this God are identical. Therefore, there cannot be several gods.

Second, moreover, we can demonstrate the oneness of God by the infinity of his perfection. For I have shown before that God includes within himself the whole perfection of existing.[6] Therefore, if there were several gods, they would need to differ. Therefore, something would be appropriate for one that was not appropriate for the other. And if such a thing were a privation, the one deprived would not be absolutely perfect; on the other hand, if such a thing were a perfection, the other would lack it. Therefore, there cannot be several gods. And so even the ancient philosophers, compelled by truth itself, as it were, posited only one source when they posited an infinite source.

Third, we can demonstrate the oneness of God by the oneness of the world. For we find that all existing things are ordered to one another, in-

sofar as some are subordinate to others. But different things would not be
united in one order unless one thing ordered them. For one thing brings
many things into one order better than many things would, since one thing
intrinsically causes one thing, and many beings do so only accidentally,
namely, insofar as the many things are one in some way. Therefore, since
what is first, is most perfect, and such intrinsically, not accidentally, there is
necessarily only one first being that brings everything into one order. And
this first being is God.

Reply to Obj. 1.   The Apostle speaks of many gods with respect to the
error of certain philosophers, who, thinking the planets and other stars, or
even individual parts of the world, to be gods, worshiped many gods. And
hence the Apostle adds: "But for us, there is one God," etc.[7]

Reply to Obj. 2.   We do not predicate the one that is the source of number,
of God but only of things that possess existence in matter. For the one that
is the source of number, belongs to the genus of mathematical objects,
which possess existence in matter but are conceptually abstracted from matter. But the one that is convertible with being, is something metaphysical,
which does not depend on matter as to its existing. And although there is no
privation in God, yet according to the way of our understanding, we know
him only by way of privation and elimination. And so nothing prevents us
from predicating of God expressions that are privative, such as, that he is incorporeal, that he is infinite. And we in like manner predicate of God that
he is one.

Notes

1. *De divinis nominibus* 13. PG 3:977.
2. *De divinis nominibus* 13. PG 3:980.
3. 1 Cor. 8:5.
4. Dt. 6:4.
5. Q. 3, A. 3.
6. Q. 4, A. 2.
7. 1 Cor. 8:6.

ST I
Question 12
How We Know God

[This question is divided into thirteen articles, two of which are included here.]

First Article

Can A Created Intellect Behold the Essence of God?

I proceed in this way to the first article: it seems that no created intellect can behold the essence of God.

Obj. 1. Chrysostom, explaining the text of Jn. 1:18, "No one has ever beheld God," says the following in his *Super Ioannem*: "Neither prophets alone, nor angels or archangels, have beheld God himself. For in what sort of way would anything belonging to creatable nature have been able to behold what is unthinkable?"[1] And Denis, speaking about God, says in his *De divinis nominibus*: "There is neither sense perception nor imagination nor conjecture nor consideration nor knowledge of him."[2]

Obj. 2. Everything unlimited is not as such an object of knowledge. But God is unlimited, as I have shown before.[3] Therefore, God is not as such an object of knowledge.

Obj. 3. A created intellect can know only things that exist, since the first object falling within the grasp of the intellect is being. But God is not something that exists; rather, he is something "above existence," as Denis says.[4] Therefore, God is not an object of understanding; rather, he surpasses every intellect.

Obj. 4. There needs to be some proportion between a knowing subject and a known object, since a known object perfects a knowing subject. But there is no proportion between a created intellect and God, since they are infinitely different. Therefore, no created intellect can behold the essence of God.

On the contrary, the First Letter of John says: "We shall see him as he is."[5]

I answer that, since everything is knowable insofar as it is actual, God, who is pure actuality without any admixture of potentiality, is most knowable as he is in himself. But something most knowable in itself is not knowable for a particular intellect, because the intelligible object surpasses such an intellect. Similarly, bats cannot see the sun, which is most visible, because of the sun's superabundant light. Adverting to this, certain thinkers consequently held that no created intellect can behold God's essence.

But it is improper to affirm such a position. For the ultimate happiness of human beings consists in their highest activity, which is the activity of the intellect; therefore, if no created intellect can ever behold God's essence, either the created intellect will never obtain happiness, or its happiness will consist in something other than God. And this conclusion is foreign to faith. For a rational creature's ultimate perfection rests in the very thing that is the source of the rational creature's existing, since everything is perfect inasmuch as it attains its source.

The position is likewise contrary to reason. For human beings, when they see an effect, have a desire from nature to know the effect's cause, and they consequently start to wonder. Therefore, if the intellect of a rational creature could not attain the first cause of things, this desire from nature will remain unfulfilled. And hence we need to admit without qualification that the blessed behold God's essence.

Reply to Obj. 1. Both authorities are speaking about comprehensive vision. And hence Denis notes this presupposition immediately before the cited words, saying: "He himself is totally incomprehensible to everyone," etc.[6] And Chrysostom, a little after the quoted words, adds: "He [John] calls the most certain vision of the Father as much consideration and comprehension as the Father has of the Son."[7]

Reply to Obj. 2. The unlimited with respect to matter not perfected by form is not as such an object of knowledge, since all knowledge results from forms. But the unlimited with respect to a form not limited by matter is most of all an object of knowledge. And God is unlimited in the latter way and not in the former way, as is clear from what I said above.[8]

Reply to Obj. 3. We do not in such a way call God something that does not exist, as if he is something that in no way exists, but because he is above everything that exists, inasmuch he is his existing. And hence it does not thereby follow that he cannot be known in any way, but that he surpasses all knowledge, and this is to say that his very self is not comprehended.

Reply to Obj. 4. We speak of proportion in two ways. In one way, we call a fixed relationship of one quantity to another a proportion, and double, triple, and equal are specific proportions in this way. In the second way, we call any relationship of one thing to another a proportion. And there can in this way be a proportion between a creature and God, inasmuch as a creature is related to God as effect to cause and as potentiality to actuality. And a created intellect can accordingly be proportioned to know God.

Twelfth Article

Can We Know God in This Life by Natural Reason?

I proceed in this way to the twelfth article: it seems that we cannot know God in this life by natural reason.

Obj. 1. Boethius says in his *On the Consolation of Philosophy* that "reason does not grasp a simple nature."[9] But God is a most simple nature, as I have shown before.[10] Therefore, natural reason cannot arrive at knowledge of him.

Obj. 2. The soul understands nothing by natural reason without a sense image, as the *De anima* says.[11] But there cannot be in us a sense image of God, because he is incorporeal. Therefore, we cannot know God by natural knowledge.

Obj. 3. Both the good and the wicked obtain knowledge by natural reason, just as they have a common nature. But knowledge of God belongs only to the good, for Augustine says in his *De Trinitate* that "the insight of the human mind is not fixed on so excellent a light unless the virtue of faith purify it."[12] Therefore, we cannot know God by natural reason.

On the contrary, the Letter to the Romans says: "What is known of God," that is, what can be known about him by natural reason, "is clearly present in their midst."[13]

I answer that our natural knowledge originates with the senses, and hence our natural knowledge can reach only as far as sensible objects can lead it. Moreover, our intellect cannot reach beyond sensible objects to perceive the divine essence, because sensible creatures are effects of God unequal to the power of their cause. And hence we cannot know the entire power of God from our knowledge of sensible objects, and consequently, neither can we perceive his essence. But because God's effects depend on their cause, we can be led by them to know that he exists, and to know about him what necessarily befits him insofar as he is the first cause of everything, he who surpasses everything that he has caused. And hence we know about him the relationship of himself to creatures, namely, that he causes everything, and the difference of creatures from him, namely, that he is not any part of what he has caused, and his effects are apart from him because he surpasses them superabundantly, not because he lacks anything.

Reply to Obj. 1. Reason cannot attain a simple nature in such a way as to know what that nature is, but reason can know in such a way as to know that it exists.

Reply to Obj. 2. We know God by natural knowledge through sense images of his effects.

Reply to Obj. 3. Knowledge of God by his essence, since it is by his grace, belongs only to the good, but knowledge of him by natural reason can belong to the good and the bad. And hence Augustine says in his *Retracta-tionum*: "I disapprove what I said in the prayer 'O God, you who willed that only the pure know what is true,'[14] for one can rejoin that many people, even those who are not pure, can know many things that are true,"[15] name-ly, by natural reason.

Notes

1. *Super Ioannem, homilia* 15. PG 59:98.
2. *De divinis nominibus* 1. PG 3:593.
3. Q. 7, A. 1.
4. *De divinis nominibus* 4. PG 3:697.
5. 1 Jn. 3:2.
6. See n. 2, *supra*.
7. See n. 1, *supra*. PG 59:99.
8. In the body of the article.
9. *On the Consolation of Philosophy* V, 5. PL 63:849.
10. Q. 3, A. 7.
11. Aristotle, *De anima* III, 7. 431a16–17.
12. *De Trinitate* I, 2. PL 42:822.
13. Rom. 1:19.
14. *Soliloquiorum* I, 1. PL 32:870.
15. *Retractationum* I, 4. PL 32:589.

ST I
Question 13
On the Names of God

[This question is divided into twelve articles, nine of which are included here.]

First Article

Is Any Name Appropriate for God?

I proceed in this way to the first article: it seems that no name is appropriate for God.

Obj. 1. For Denis says in his *De divinis nominibus* that "neither a name nor a conjecture is proper for him."[1] And the Book of Proverbs says: "What is his name, and what is the name of his son, if you know?"[2]

Obj. 2. Every term is expressed abstractly or concretely. But terms that signify concretely are not proper to God because he is simple, and terms that signify abstractly, are not proper to him because such names do not signify a perfect, subsistent being. Therefore, we can predicate no name of God.

Obj. 3. Nouns signify substances qualitatively, while verbs and participles signify substances temporarily, and pronouns signify substances demonstratively or relatively. And none of these is proper to God, because he lacks qualities, every accident, and time, and we cannot perceive him sensibly so as to point him out. Nor can we signify him relatively, because relative pronouns record the aforementioned parts of speech, whether nouns or participles or demonstrative pronouns. Therefore, we can in no way give a name to God.

On the contrary, the Book of Exodus says: "The Lord is as if a warrior; almighty is his name."[3]

I answer that, as the Philosopher says,[4] expressions are the signs of what we understand, and what we understand, are the likenesses of things. And so expressions are clearly related to signifying objects by means of what the intellect conceives. Therefore, we can give a name to something insofar as we can know it intellectually. I have shown before,[5] however, that we cannot in this life perceive God by his essence, but we know him from creatures by his causal relationship to them and by way of eminence and elimination. Thus we can give him names from creatures, although not in such a way that the names signifying him express his essence as it is—as, for example, the term "human being" by its meaning expresses the human essence as it is. For "human being" signifies the definition of human being, and the definition declares its essence, since the nature that the name signifies, is the definition.

Reply to Obj. 1. We say that God has no name, or is above being named, for this reason: because his essence is above what we understand about God and signify by an expression.

Reply to Obj. 2. Because we arrive at knowledge of God from creatures, and we give him names from them, the names that we assign to God, signify in the way that is a proper to material creatures, and the knowledge of such creatures is connatural, as I have said before.[6] And because what is perfect and subsistent, is composite in such creatures, while their form is not a complete subsisting entity but rather the source whereby something exists, every name that we apply to signify a complete subsisting thing, thus signifies the thing in its materiality, as materiality belongs to composite things. But the names that we apply to signify simple forms, do not signify an entity as subsistent but as the source whereby something is such, as whiteness, for example, signifies the source by which something is white. Therefore, because God is both uncomposed and subsistent, we attribute to him both abstract names, to signify his simplicity, and concrete names, to signify his subsistence and perfection, although both such names fall short of his way, inasmuch as our intellect in this life does not know him as he is.

Reply to Obj. 3. To signify a substance qualitatively is to signify an individually existing subject with the determined nature or form in which it subsists. And hence, just as we predicate some names of God in their materiality in order to signify his subsistence and perfection, as I have already said,[7] so do we predicate of him names that signify his substance qualitatively. Moreover, we predicate of him verbs and participles connoting time because eternity includes all time. For, as we can absolutely apprehend and signify absolutely subsistent things only by way of composite things, so we can understand absolute eternity and give expression to it only by way of temporal things and because of the connaturality of our intellect for composite and temporal things. And we predicate demonstrative pronouns of God insofar as they point to what we understand, not to what we sensibly perceive. For something falls within demonstration insofar as we understand it. And so we can also signify God by relative pronouns in the way in which we predicate nouns and participles and demonstrative pronouns of him.

Second Article

Do We Predicate Any Name of God Substantially?

I proceed in this way to the second article: it seems that we do not predicate any name of God substantially.

Obj. 1. Damascene says: "Each name predicated of God needs not to signify what he is substantially, but to show what he is not, or a certain relationship, or one of the things that result from his nature or activity."[8]

Obj. 2. Denis says in his *De divinis nominibus*: "You will find every hymn of holy theologians clearly and praiseworthily distinguishing the names of God by the beneficent processions from the divine source."[9] And the meaning is that the names that the holy teachers appropriate for divine praise are distinguished by the processions from God himself. But what signifies the procession of something, signifies nothing that belongs to the thing's essence. Therefore, we do not substantially predicate the names predicated of God.

Obj. 3. We give a name to something in the way we understand the name. But we do not in this life understand God by his substance. Therefore, neither do we substantially predicate of him any name that we apply.

On the contrary, Augustine says in his *De Trinitate*: "For God, to exist is to be strong or to be wise, and anything whereby his substance is signified, if you should say anything about that simplicity."[10] Therefore, all such names signify his divine substance.

I answer that the names that we predicate of God negatively, or that signify his relation to a creature, evidently in no way signify his substance but signify the elimination of something from him, or his relation to something else—or rather the relation of something to him. But thinkers have held many opinions about the names that we predicate absolutely and affirmatively about God, names such as "good," "wise," and the like.

For certain thinkers said that all these names, although predicated affirmatively about God, are nonetheless devised to eliminate something from him rather than to posit something in him. And hence they say that, when we say that God is a living being, we signify that God does not exist in the same way that nonliving things do, and we should similarly understand this in the case of other names. And Rabbi Moses held this position.[11] Other thinkers, however, say that we apply these names to signify the relation of God to creatures, so that, when we say that God is good, we mean that God causes the goodness in things. And their argument is the same in the case of other names.

But both of those positions seem inappropriate for three reasons. First, indeed, because according to neither of them could we ascribe a reason why we predicate certain names of God rather than other names. For God causes material substances in the same way that he causes good things, and hence, if, when we say that God is good, we indicate nothing else than that he causes good things, we could similarly say that God is a material substance, because he causes material substances. Likewise, by saying that God is a material substance, one does not say that he is not a purely potential being like prime matter. Second, those positions seem inappropriate because we would consequently in a secondary sense predicate every name predicated of God. For example, we predicate "healthy" of medicine in a secondary sense, because "healthy" signifies only what causes health in animals, and we call animals healthy in the primary sense. Third, those positions seem inappropriate because they contradict the intention of those who speak about God. For those who speak about God, when they say that God is a living being, intend to say something other than that he causes our life, or that he differs from nonliving material substances.

And so we should say otherwise, that some names indeed signify the divine substance, and that we predicate them of God substantially, although they deficiently represent him. And this is evident as follows. Names certainly signify God in the way in which our intellect knows him. But our intellect, since it knows God from creatures, knows him in the way in which creatures represent him. I have shown before that God, as absolutely and completely perfect, possesses in himself beforehand all the perfections of creatures.[12] And hence every creature represents him and is like him insofar as it has some perfection, although not in such a way that it represents him as something belonging to the same species or genus but as the pre-eminent source. And the effects fall short of his form, even though they attain a certain likeness to him, just as the forms of lower material substances represent the power of the sun. And I have explained this before, when I treated of the divine perfection.[13] The aforementioned names thus signify the divine substance, albeit imperfectly, just as creatures represent him imperfectly.

Therefore, when we say that God is good, we do not mean that God causes goodness, or that God is not bad, but we mean that what we call goodness in creatures, pre-exists in God, and this indeed in a higher way. And hence it does not follow from this meaning that good belongs to God inasmuch as he causes goodness, but rather the converse, that he pours out goodness to things because he is good, as Augustine says in his *De doctrina Christiana*: "We exist because he is good."[14]

Reply to Obj. 1. Damascene thus says that these names do not signify what God is, because none of them perfectly expresses what God is, but each name imperfectly signifies him, as creatures also imperfectly represent him.

Reply to Obj. 2. In the meaning of terms, the source from which we apply a term in order to signify, sometimes is one thing, and what we apply a term to signify, is something else. For example, we apply the term "stone" from what hurts the foot,[15] not to signify what "hurting the foot" signifies, but to signify a certain kind of material substance; otherwise, everything that hurts the foot would be a stone. We thus need to say that we indeed apply such divine names from processions of the deity. For, as creatures represent God by different processions of perfections, albeit imperfectly, so our intellect knows and names God by each procession. But our intellect, nonetheless, does not apply these names to signify the processions themselves, as if we should mean that life comes from him when we say that he is a living being, but we apply the names to signify the very source of things, as life pre-exists in him, although in a more excellent way than we understand or signify.

Reply to Obj. 3.   We cannot in this life know the essence of God as it is in itself, but we know that essence as represented in the perfections of creatures. And so the names that we apply, signify the essence of God.

Third Article

Do We Predicate Any Name of God in a Proper Sense?

I proceed in this way to the third article: it seems that we predicate no name of God in a proper sense.

Obj. 1.   We take from creatures every name that we predicate of God, as I have said.[16] But we predicate creatures' names of God metaphorically, as when we say that God is stone or lion or any such thing. Therefore, we predicate every name of God metaphorically.

Obj. 2.   We do not predicate any name in a proper sense about something from which the name is more truly removed than it is predicated of that thing. But every such name—"good," "wise," and the like—are more truly removed from God than they are predicated of him, as Denis makes clear in his *De coelesti hierachia*.[17] Therefore, we predicate none of those names of God in the proper sense.

Obj. 3.   We predicate the names of material substances of God only metaphorically, because he is not corporeal. But all such names imply certain corporeal conditions, for the names signify with time and with composition and with other such things, and these are conditions of material substances. Therefore, we predicate all such names of God metaphorically.

On the contrary, Ambrose says in his *De fide*: "There are certain names that evidently show a property of divinity, and certain names that express the clear truth of the divine majesty, but there are others that we predicate metaphorically of God by analogy."[18] Therefore, we do not predicate every name of God metaphorically, but we predicate some names in a proper sense.

I answer that, as I have said,[19] we know God from the perfections that come from him to creatures, and these perfections are indeed in God in a more excellent way than they are in creatures. But our intellect apprehends them in the way in which they are in creatures, and it signifies them by names in the way in which it apprehends them. Therefore, there are two things to consider in the names that we assign to God, namely, the perfections themselves that are signified, such as goodness, life, and like things, and the way of signifying them. Therefore, such names, as to what they signify, belong to God in the proper sense, and more properly than they belong to creatures themselves, and we predicate them of him in the primary sense. But as to the names' way of signifying, we do not predicate them of God in the proper sense, for they have a way of signifying that belongs to creatures.

Reply to Obj. 1. Certain names signify perfections of this kind that come from God to creatures in such a way that the imperfect way itself whereby a creature shares a divine perfection, is included in the very meaning of the name. For example, "stone" signifies something that exists in a material way, and we can assign such names to God only metaphorically. But certain names signify the perfections themselves absolutely, without any mode of sharing being included in their meaning, such as "being," "good," "living," and like names, and we predicate such names of God in the proper sense.

Reply to Obj. 2. Denis in this way says that we deny such names of God because what the name signifies, is not appropriate to him in the way in which the name signifies but appropriate in a more excellent way. And hence Denis says in the same place that God is "above every substance and life."[20]

Reply to Obj. 3. The names that we predicate of God in the proper sense, imply corporeal conditions, not in the very meaning of the names, but by the names' way of signifying. But the names that we metaphorically predicate of God, imply a corporeal condition in their very meaning.

Fourth Article

Are the Names Predicated of God Synonyms?

I proceed in this way to the fourth article: it seems that the names predicated of God are synonyms.

Obj. 1. We call synonyms names that signify entirely the same thing. But names predicated of God signify entirely the same thing in God, because God's goodness is his essence, and likewise, his knowledge is his essence. Therefore, those names are entirely synonymous.

Obj. 2. If anyone should say that those names signify something that is really the same but conceptually different, the rejoinder would be: an idea to which nothing in reality corresponds, is empty. Therefore, if those concepts are many, and the reality is one, it seems that the concepts are empty.

Obj. 3. Something that is one thing really and conceptually, is more one than something that is one thing really and many things conceptually. But

God is one being in the highest degree. Therefore, it seems that he is not one really and many conceptually. And so names predicated of God do not signify different considerations, and they are thus synonymous.

On the contrary, all synonyms, when added to one another, lead to triviality, as if one were to say "clothing garment." Therefore, if all the names predicated of God are synonyms, we could not say in a proper sense that God is good or any such thing, despite the fact that it is written in the Book of Jeremiah: "O most strong, great, mighty one, yours is the name 'Lord of hosts.'"[21]

I answer that such names predicated of God are not synonyms. And this would indeed be easy to see if we were to say that such names were introduced in order to eliminate something or to designate a causal relationship with respect to creatures, for different aspects belong to these names according to the different things denied or according to the different effects connoted. But as I have said that names of this kind signify the divine substance, albeit imperfectly,[22] it is also plainly evident by what I have previously explained, that the names have different considerations.[23] For the consideration that a name signifies, is a conception of the intellect about the reality that the name signifies. But our intellect, since it knows God from creatures, forms concepts proportioned to the perfections that come from God to creatures, in order to understand him. And these perfections indeed pre-exist in God as one and without composition, although they are received in creatures separately and in various ways. Therefore, as the one simple source that the different perfections of creatures represent in many different ways, corresponds to these different perfections, so the one entirely simple being that we imperfectly understand by the many different concepts of our intellect, corresponds to such concepts. And so the names we assign to God, although they signify only one reality, are nonetheless not synonyms, because they signify that reality under many different aspects.

Reply to Obj. 1.   And thus the solution to the first objection is clear, because we call synonyms names that signify the same thing by the same aspect. For names that signify different aspects of the same thing do not first and intrinsically signify one and the same thing, because names signify things only by means of the intellect's concepts, as I have said.[24]

Reply to Obj. 2.   The several aspects belonging to these names are not hollow and empty, because there corresponds to all of these aspects one simple reality that all such considerations represent imperfectly and in many kinds of ways.

Reply to Obj. 3.   The very fact that aspects that exist in many ways and separately in other things, exist without composition and as one in God, belongs to his perfect unity. And so it happens that he is one being really and more than one conceptually, because our intellect apprehends him in many kinds of ways, as things represent him in many kinds of ways.

Fifth Article

Do We Univocally Predicate the Names We Predicate of God and Creatures?

I proceed in this way to the fifth article: it seems that we univocally predicate the names we predicate of God and creatures.

Obj. 1.   We trace everything equivocal back to something univocal, as we trace many things back to one thing. For, if we equivocally predicate the term "dog" of the animal that barks, and of the sea animal, we necessarily predicate the term univocally about some animals, namely, all the animals that bark, for we would otherwise regress endlessly. But we find that certain efficient causes are univocal, those that are one with their effects in name and definition, as, for example, human beings beget human beings. But we find that certain efficient causes are equivocal, as, for example, the sun causes heat, although the sun is hot only equivocally.[25] It seems, therefore, that the first efficient cause, to which we trace back every efficient cause, is something univocal. And so we univocally predicate the names that we predicate of God and creatures.

Obj. 2.   We note no likeness by equivocal terms. Therefore, since there is a likeness of creatures to God, as the Book of Genesis says, "Let us make human beings to our image and likeness,"[26] it seems that we univocally predicate something of God and creatures.

Obj. 3.   A measure is homogeneous with the object it measures, as the *Metaphysics* says.[27] But God is the first measure of every being, as the *Metaphysics* says in the same place. Therefore, God is homogeneous with creatures. And so we can univocally predicate something of God and creatures.

On the contrary, we equivocally predicate of things whatever we predicate of them by the same name but in different respects. But no name is appropriate for God in the sense in which we predicate the name of creatures; wisdom, for example, is an accidental characteristic in creatures but not in God. And a change of genus involves an essential change, since a genus belongs to the definition. And the reasoning is the same in the case of other things. Therefore, we equivocally predicate whatever we predicate of God and creatures.

Besides, God differs more from creatures than any creature does from another creature. But it is a fact that we can univocally predicate nothing of certain creatures, because of their diversity, as in the case of creatures that do not belong to the same genus. Therefore, far less do we predicate anything univocally of God and creatures, but we predicate everything of them equivocally.

I answer that we can predicate nothing of God and creatures univocally. For every effect unequal to the power of its efficient cause does not receive a likeness of the efficient cause in the same way but in a difficient way, so that what exists in the effects separately and in many different ways, exists in the cause simply and in the same way. For example, the sun by its one power produces many different kinds of forms in the beings below. In the same way, as I have said before,[28] all the perfections of things, which exist in creatures separately and in many different kinds of ways, pre-exist in God as one. Thus, when we predicate of creatures any name proper to a perfection of creatures, the name signifies that perfection as distinct from other perfections by reason of its definition; for example, when we predicate the name "wise" of human beings, we signify a perfection distinct from the essence of human beings, and from their power and their existing, and from all such things. But when we predicate this name of God, we do not intend to signify anything distinct from his essence or his power or his existence. And so the name "wise," when predicated of human beings, somehow circumscribes and comprehends the thing signified; the name, when predicated of God, however, does not do so but leaves the thing signified as uncomprehended and surpassing the meaning of the name. And hence we evidently do not predicate the name "wise" of God and human beings by the same consideration. And the reasoning is the same in the case of other names. And hence we do not predicate any name of God and creatures univocally.

But also neither do we predicate any name of God purely equivocally, as some thinkers have said. For according to the latter, we could neither know nor demonstrate anything about him from creatures, but such would always involve the fallacy of equivocation. And this is as contrary to the philosophers who demonstratively prove many things about God, as it is also contrary to the Apostle, who says in his Letter to the Romans that "we perceive the invisible things of God by means of the things that he has made, when we understand those things."[29]

We need to say, therefore, that we predicate such names of God and creatures by analogy, i.e., by a proportion. And this indeed happens in two ways in the case of names: either because many things have a proportion to one thing, as, for example, we predicate "healthy" of medicine and urine insofar as each has a relation and proportion to the health of animals, of which urine is indeed the sign, and medicine the cause; or because one thing has a proportion to another, as, for example, we predicate "healthy" of medicine and animals insofar as medicine causes the health in animals. And we predicate some names analogically of God and creatures in this way, and not purely equivocally or univocally. For we can name God only from creatures, as I have said before.[30] And so whatever we predicate of God and creatures, we predicate insofar as there is some relation of creatures to God, as the source and cause in which all the perfections of things eminently pre-exist.

And that way of commonality is a mean between pure equivocation and absolute univocity. For neither is there one consideration in things predicated analogically, as there is in univocal things, nor are there totally differ-

ent considerations, as there are in equivocal things. But a name so predicated in many different kinds of ways signifies different proportions to some
one thing, as, for example, "healthy," when predicated of urine, signifies as
the sign of animals' health, but when predicated of medicine, signifies as the
cause of their health.

Reply to Obj. 1. Although it is necessary that we trace the equivocal things
in predications back to univocal things, yet, in actions, a nonunivocal
efficient cause is necessarily prior to a univocal efficient cause. For a nonunivocal efficient cause is the universal cause of a whole species, as, for example, the sun causes the generation of all human beings. But a univocal
efficient cause is not the universal cause of a whole species (otherwise, it
would cause itself, since it is contained in the species); rather, a univocal
efficient cause is the particular cause with respect to this particular individual
thing, which it constitutes to partake of the species. Therefore, the universal
cause of a whole species is not a univocal efficient cause. The universal
cause, moreover, is prior to the particular cause.

But this universal efficient cause, although not univocal, is nonetheless not
completely equivocal, because it would thus not produce anything like itself.
Rather, we can call the universal efficient cause analogical, just as we trace
the univocal things in predications back to one first nonunivocal but analogical thing, i.e., being.

Reply to Obj. 2. The likeness of creatures to God is imperfect, because it
does not even represent the same thing generically, as I have said before.[31]

Reply to Obj. 3. God is not a measure proportioned to the things he measures. And hence God and creatures do not need to be included in one
genus. Things to the contrary in fact prove that we do not predicate such
names univocally of God and creatures, although not that we predicate them
equivocally.

Seventh Article

Do We Temporally Predicate of God Names That Imply a Relation to Creatures?

I proceed in this way to the seventh article: it seems that we do not temporally predicate of God names that imply a relation to creatures.

Obj. 1. All such names signify the divine substance, as people generally
say. And so also Ambrose says that the name "Lord" is the name of
power,[32] which is the divine substance, and the name "creator" signifies the
activity of God, which is his essence. But the divine substance is eternal, not
temporal. Therefore, we do not predicate such names of God from time but
from eternity.

Obj. 2. We can say that that for which something temporal is appropriate, has been made; for example, an object that exists temporally as white, has been made white. But it is not appropriate for God to have been made. Therefore, we predicate nothing of God temporally.

Obj. 3. If we predicate some names of God temporally because they imply a relation to creatures, the same reasoning seems to apply about everything that implies a relation to creatures. But we predicate of God from eternity certain names that imply a relation to creatures, for he knew and loved creatures from eternity, as the Book of Jeremiah says: "I have loved you with a love that is everlasting."[33] Therefore, we also predicate other names that import a relation to creatures, like "Lord" and "creator," of God from eternity.

Obj. 4. Such names signify a relation. Therefore, that relation needs to be either something in God or something only in creatures. But it cannot be the case that the relation is only in creatures, because we would thus name "Lord" by the converse relation, the relation that is in creatures, although we name nothing by its opposite. Therefore, we conclude that the relation is also something in God. But nothing from time can be in God, because he himself is above time. Therefore, it seems that we do not predicate such names of God temporally.

Obj. 5. We predicate something relatively by a relation; for example, we predicate lord by lordship and white by whiteness. Therefore, if the relation of lordship is not really but only conceptually in God, then God is not really Lord, and this conclusion is clearly false.

Obj. 6. In relative things that do not by nature exist at the same time, one of them can exist, and the other not, as a knowable object exists when knowledge of it does not, as the *Categories* says.[34] But the relative things predicated of God and creatures do not by nature exist at the same time. Therefore, we can predicate something relatively of God and a creature, even if the creature does not exist. And so we predicate names of this kind, "Lord" and "creator," of God from eternity and not temporally.

On the contrary, Augustine says in his *De Trinitate* that the relative title "Lord" is temporally appropriate for God.[35]

I answer that we temporally, not eternally, predicate of God certain names that imply a relation to creatures.

And for evidence of this, we should note that certain thinkers held relations not to be things of nature but to be purely conceptual. And this is indeed clearly false, because things themselves have a natural order and relationship to one another. Nonetheless, we should recognize that a relation requires two termini and can be related to real things and conceptual things in three ways. For sometimes a relation is purely conceptual on the part of both termini, namely, when there can be an order or relationship among certain things only because reason conceives it; for example, we say that the same thing is identical with itself. For, as the mind conceives a single object twice, it posits that object as two, and so it conceives a certain relationship of the object to itself. And it is likewise in the case of every relation between being and nonbeing, relations that the mind formulates as it conceives nonbeing as a sort of terminus. And it is the same in the case of every relation that is the product of an act of reason, such as genus, species, and the like.

But certain relations are things of nature as to both of their termini, namely, when there is a relationship between two objects as to something really appropriate to each of them. For example, this is clearly so about all relations that result from size, such as big and little, double and half, and the like, for there is size in both termini. And it is similar in the case of relations that result from acting and being acted upon, such as relations between causes of motion and moveable objects, fathers and sons, and the like.

Sometimes, however, a relation is a thing of nature in one terminus and purely conceptual in the other. And this happens whenever the two termini do not belong to a single order. For example, sense perception and knowledge are related to sensible and knowable objects, and the latter, as certain objects that exist in natural existence, indeed exist outside the order of sensible and intelligible existence. And so there is indeed a real relation in knowledge and sense perception, as the latter are related to knowing or sensibly perceiving objects, but those very objects, considered in themselves, exist outside such an order. And hence the objects have no real relation to knowledge and sense perception but a relation that is purely conceptual, as the intellect conceives the objects as termini of the relations of knowledge and sense perception. And hence the Philosopher says in the *Metaphysics* that we do not predicate the objects of knowledge and sense perception by relations because they are related to other things, but because other things are related to them.[36] And similarly, we only predicate "right" of a post as the post is situated on the right side of an animal, and hence such a relation is not really in the post but in the animal.

Therefore, since God exists outside the whole order of creatures, and all creatures are ordered to him, and not vice versa, creatures are evidently really related to God himself, although there is no real relation of him to creatures, but only a conceptual relation insofar as creatures are related to him. And so nothing prevents us from temporally predicating of God such names that imply a relation to creatures, not because of any change in himself, but because of a change in creatures, as we cause a post to be on the right side of an animal without any change existing concerning the post but with the animal transposed.

Reply to Obj. 1. We apply certain relative names to signify relative relationships themselves, such names as "master" and "servant,"[37] "father" and "son," and the like, and we call these names relative with regard to reality. But we apply other relative names to signify the things that result from certain relationships, such as "mover" and "moved," "head" and "body with a head," and the like, and we call these names relative with regard to expression. We thus also need to consider this distinction in the case of God's names. For certain names, like "Lord," signify his very relationship to creatures. And such relations do not signify his substance directly but indirectly, insofar as the relations presuppose that substance, as, for example, lordship presupposes power, which is his substance. But certain names directly signify God's essence and consequently imply a relationship; for example, "savior," "creator," and the like signify his activity, which is his essence. We nevertheless predicate both kinds of names of God temporally as regards the relationship that the name implies by way of source or result, but not so as to signify his essence, either directly or indirectly.

Reply to Obj. 2. As the relations that we predicate of God temporally, exist in him only conceptually, so we predicate "being made" and "having been made" of him only conceptually, with no real change existing in his regard, as in the expression, "O Lord, you have been made a refuge for us."[38]

Reply to Obj. 3. The operations of intellect and will are in the one who knows and wills, and so we predicate of God from eternity names signifying relations that result from the activity of his intellect and will. But we temporally predicate of God names that result from his activity going out (according to our way of understanding) to external effects, such names as "savior," "creator," and the like.

Reply to Obj. 4. Relations signified by such names that we temporally predicate of God, exist only conceptually in him, but the converse relations really exist in creatures. Nor is it inappropriate that we name God by relations that really exist in things, as our intellect at the same time nonetheless understands the converse relations to exist in God. As a result, we so speak of God in relation to creatures because creatures are related to him, as the Philosopher says in the *Metaphysics* that we speak relatively of something as knowable because knowledge is related to what is knowable.[39]

Reply to Obj. 5. God is related to creatures by the consideration whereby creatures are related to him; since the relation of subjection really exists in creatures, God is consequently Lord not only conceptually but really. For we call him Lord in the way in which creatures are subject to him.

Reply to Obj. 6. In order to know whether or not relative things exist by nature at the same time, we do not need to consider the order of the things about which we say relative things, but we do need to consider the meanings of the relative things themselves. For if one thing should include another in its comprehension, and vice versa, then they exist by nature at the same time; for example, double and half, father and son, and the like. But if one thing should include another in its comprehension, but not vice versa, then they do not exist by nature at the same time. And knowledge and a knowable object are related in this way. For we speak of a knowable object as potentially knowable, but we speak of knowledge as habitual or actual.[40] And hence a knowable object, by the way in which knowable signifies, preexists knowledge. But if we understand a knowable object as it is actually known, then it exists as known at the same time as actual knowledge, for nothing is known unless knowledge of it exists. Therefore, although God is prior to creatures, the two relative things, Lord and servant, exist by nature at the same time, because his having servants is nonetheless included in the meaning of Lord, and vice versa. And hence God was not Lord before he had creatures subject to him.

Tenth Article

Do We Univocally Predicate the Name "God" of God by Participation, Nature, and Opinion?

I proceed in this way to the tenth article: it seems that we univocally predicate the name "God" of God by nature, participation, and opinion.

Obj. 1. There is no contradiction between affirming and denying something where there is a difference of meaning, for equivocation prevents contradiction. But the Catholic who says that an idol is not God, contradicts the pagan who says that the idol is. Therefore, "God," as understood in both cases, is predicated univocally.

Obj. 2. As an idol is God by opinion but not in truth, so the enjoyment of carnal pleasures is called happiness by opinion but not in truth. But the name "happiness" is predicated univocally of this supposed happiness and of true happiness. Therefore, the name "God" is also predicated univocally of God in truth and of God by opinion.

Obj. 3. We call terms with a single meaning univocal. But Catholics, when they say that there is only one God, understand by the name of God a being that is almighty and to be venerated above all things, and pagans understand the same when they say that an idol is God. Therefore, the name "God" is predicated univocally in both instances.

On the contrary,[41] what is in the intellect, is a likeness of what is in reality, as the *De interpretatione* says.[42] But we equivocally predicate the term "animal" when we predicate it of a real animal and of a painted animal. Therefore, we equivocally predicate the name "God" when we predicate it of the true God and of a supposed God.

Besides, one cannot mean what one does not know, but pagans do not know the divine nature. Therefore, when pagans say that an idol is God, they do not mean the true deity. But Catholics, who say that there is only one God, mean the true deity. Therefore, Catholics and pagans do not predicate the term "God" univocally, but they predicate God equivocally about the true God and the supposed God.

I answer that we do not understand the name "God," in the three meanings set forth above, univocally or equivocally but analogically. And this is clear because the meaning of univocal terms is entirely the same, the meaning of equivocal terms entirely different, while in the case of analogical terms, we need to posit a term understood by one meaning in the definition of the same term understood by other meanings. For example, we posit the "being" we predicate of substances, in the definition of being as we predicate being of accidents, and we posit the "healthy" we predicate of animals, in the definition of healthy as we predicate healthy of urine and medicine, for urine is the sign, and medicine the cause, of what is healthy in animals.

And so it is in the case of the question at issue. For we understand the name "God," as understood to mean the true God, to include the meaning of God when we predicate God by opinion or participation. For when we call a being God by participation, we understand by the name of God something that has a likeness to the true God. Likewise, when we call an idol God, we understand by the name "God" something that human beings think to be God. And so the meaning of the name is clearly sometimes this and sometimes that, but one of those meanings is included in the other meanings. And hence it is evident that we predicate the name "God" analogically.

Reply to Obj. 1. We do not attend to multiplicity of terms by their predication but by their meaning; for example, we predicate the term "human being" in only one way of whatever we predicate it, whether truly or falsely. But if we were to intend by the term "human being" to signify different things, then we would predicate it in many different ways; for example, if one person were to intend by the term "human being" to signify what a human being truly is, and another person were to intend by the same term to signify stone or something else. And hence the Catholic who says that an idol is not God, clearly contradicts the pagan who says that the idol is God, because each uses the name "God" to mean the true God. For when pagans say that an idol is God, they do not use the name as to mean God by opinion; they would in that way indeed say something true, since Catholics also sometimes use the name in such a sense, as when Scripture says: "All the gods of the nations are evil spirits."[43]

Reply to Objs. 2 and 3. We also need to respond to the second and third objections in a similar way. For those arguments proceed by different predications of the name and not by different meanings.

Reply to Obj. 4.[44] We do not purely equivocally predicate the term "animal" of a true animal and a painted animal; rather, the Philosopher understands equivocal terms in a broad sense as to include intrinsically analogical terms, because "being," which we predicate analogously, is also sometimes said to be predicated equivocally of different categories.[45]

Reply to Obj. 5.[46] Neither the Catholic nor the pagan knows the very nature of God as it is in itself, but each knows it by a consideration of causality or eminence or elimination, as I have said before.[47] And pagans, when they say that an idol is God, can accordingly understand the name "God" in the same sense in which Catholics understand the name when they say that the

idol is not God. But if someone were not to know God by any consideration, neither would that person give God a name, except by chance as we
express words whose meaning we do not know.

Eleventh Article

Is the Name "He Who Is" the Most Proper Name of God?

I proceed in this way to the eleventh article: it seems that the name "He who
is" is not the most proper name of God.
Obj. 1. The name "God" is a name that cannot be shared, as I have said.[48]
But the name "He who is" is a name that can be shared. Therefore, the
name "He who is" is not the most proper name of God.
Obj. 2. Denis says in his *De divinis nominibus* that "naming good manifests everything that comes from God."[49] But it is most appropriate that
God be the universal source of things. Therefore, the name "Good" and not
the name "He who is" is the most proper name of God.
Obj. 3. Every name of God seems to imply a relation to creatures, since
we know God only by creatures. But the name "He who is" implies no relation to creatures. Therefore, the name "He who is" is not the most proper
name of God.
On the contrary, the Book of Exodus says that, when Moses complains,
"If they should say to me, 'What is his name?' what shall I say to them?"
God replies, "You shall speak thus to them: 'He who is' has sent me to
you."[50] Therefore, the name "He who is" is the most proper name of God.
I answer that the name "He who is" is for three reasons the most proper
name of God. First, indeed, because of its meaning, for it does not mean a
particular form but existing itself. And hence, since God's existing is his
very essence, and this is appropriate to no other, as I have shown before,[51] it
is evident that this among other names most properly names God, for we
name everything by its form.
Second, the name "He who is" is the most proper name of God because
of its universality. For all other names are either less general, or, if convertible with it, nonetheless conceptually add something to it and hence somehow give form and set limits to it. But our intellect in its state of passage
cannot know the very essence of God as it is in itself, but whatever way our
intellect determines about what it understands of God, falls short of the way
in which God is in himself. And so the less limited and the more universal
and absolute some names are, the more properly we predicate them of God.
And hence Damascene too says that "'He who is' is quite the foremost of all
the names predicated of God, for he who includes everything in himself,
possesses existing itself as a kind of boundless and undetermined sea of
substance."[52] For every other name limits some way of a thing's substance,

but the name "He who is" does not limit any way of existing and is unlimitedly disposed toward every way of existing, and so "He who is" names the very "unlimited sea of substance."

Third, the name "He who is" is the most proper name of God by its connotation, for "He who is" means presently existing, and we most properly predicate this of God, whose existing knows neither past nor future, as Augustine says in his *De Trinitate*.[53]

Reply to Obj. 1. The name "He who is" is a more proper name of God than the name "God," regarding the source from which we apply it, namely, existing, and regarding its way of denoting and connoting, as I have said.[54] But the name "God," which we apply to signify the divine nature, is the more proper name regarding that to which we apply the name in order to signify. And the still more proper name is the Tetragrammaton,[55] which we apply to signify the very substance of God that cannot be shared and is, if one may so speak, singular.

Reply to Obj. 2. The name "Good" is the chief name of God inasmuch as he is cause, but not the absolutely chief name, since we unconditionally understand existing before we understand cause.

Reply to Obj. 3. Not every name of God need imply a relationship to creatures, but it suffices that we apply names to God from some perfections that come from him to creatures. And the first of these perfections is existence itself, from which we take the name "He who is."

Twelfth Article

Can We Formulate Affirmative Propositions about God?

I proceed in this way to the twelfth article: it seems that we cannot formulate affirmative propositions about God.

Obj. 1. Denis says in his *De coelesti hierarchia* that "negations about God are true, but we do not compose affirmations about him."[56]

Obj. 2. Boethius says in his *De Trinitate* that "a pure form cannot be a subject."[57] But God is a pure form in the highest degree, as I have shown before.[58] Therefore, he cannot be a subject. But everything about which we formulate an affirmative proposition, is taken as a subject. Therefore, we cannot formulate affirmative propositions about God.

Obj. 3. Every act of the intellect that understands an object otherwise than the object exists, is false. But God has existing without any composition, as I have proved before.[59] Therefore, since every affirmative act of the intellect understands an object as composite, it seems that we cannot truly formulate affirmative propositions about God.

On the contrary, nothing subject to faith is false. But certain affirmative propositions, such as that God is threefold and one, and that he is almighty,

are subject to faith. Therefore, we can truly formulate affirmative propositions about God.

I answer that we can truly formulate affirmative propositions about God.
And for evidence of this, we should recognize that the predicate and subject
in any affirmative true proposition need to signify something really the same
in some way, and something conceptually different. And this is evident both
in the case of propositions about accidental predicates and in the case of
propositions about substantial predicates. For being human and being white
are clearly identical in their subject, but they differ conceptually, since the
aspect of being human is one thing, and the aspect of being white another.
And it is likewise the case when I say, "Human beings are animals." For the
very thing that is human, is truly animal, since both the sensory nature, by
which we call human beings animal, and the rational nature, by which we
call them human, exist in the same individually existing subjects. And so
here also the predicate and subject are identical in the individually existing
subjects, although in different respects.

But we in some way find this even in the case of propositions in which we
predicate the same thing of itself. For the intellect ascribes what it posits of
the subject, to the individually existing thing, and what it posits of the predicate, to the nature of the form that exists in the individual thing. This is
according to the saying that "we understand predicates as forms, and subjects as matter." The plurality of predicate and subject indeed corresponds
to this conceptual diversity, and the intellect signifies the identity of the
thing by the very composition of the predicate and subject.

Moreover, God, considered in himself, is entirely one and uncomposed,
and yet our intellect knows him by different conceptions, since it cannot perceive him as he is in himself. But, even though our intellect understands him
under different conceptions, it nonetheless knows that something absolutely
one and the same corresponds to all these conceptions. Therefore, the intellect represents this conceptual plurality by the plurality of predicate and subject, and it represents the oneness of God by their composition.

Reply to Obj. 1.   Denis says that affirmations about God are not composed
(or "not appropriate," according to another translation),[60] inasmuch as no
name belongs to God by its way of signifying, as I have said before.[61]

Reply to Obj. 2.   Our intellect cannot apprehend noncomposite subsistent
forms as they are in themselves, but it apprehends them by the way of composite things, in which there is something that is the subject, and something
that is in the subject. And so our intellect apprehends a noncomposite form
as a subject and attributes something to the subject.

Reply to Obj. 3.   The proposition, "An act of the intellect that understands
an object otherwise than the object exists, is false," is ambiguous, because
the adverb "otherwise" can modify the verb "understands" as regards what
is understood, or as regards the one who understands.

If "otherwise" modifies "understands" as regards what is understood, then the proposition is true, and the meaning is: any act of the intellect that understands something to be otherwise than it is, is false. But this has no place in the argument proposed, because our intellect, when it formulates a proposition about God, does not assert that he is composite, but that he is uncomposed.

If, however, "otherwise" modifies "understands" as regards the one who understands, then the proposition is false, since the intellect's way in understanding differs from the object's way in existing. For our intellect evidently understands in an immaterial way the material objects inferior to itself, not that it understands material objects to be immaterial, but it has an immaterial way in understanding. And likewise, when the intellect understands noncomposite beings superior to itself, it understands them in its own way, namely, in a composite way. And thus the act of our intellect is not false when it forms a composite proposition about God.

Notes

1. *De divinis nominibus* 1. PG 3:593.
2. Prov. 30:4.
3. Ex. 15:3.
4. *De interpretatione* I, 1. 16a13–14.
5. Q. 12, AA. 11–12.
6. Q. 12, A. 4.
7. In the reply to the second objection.
8. *De fide orthodoxa* I, 9. PG 94:836.
9. *De divinis nominibus* 1. PG 3:589.
10. *De Trinitate* VI, 4. PL 42:927.
11. Moses Maimonides, *Guide of the Perplexed*, part 1, chap. 58.
12. Q. 4, A. 2.
13. Q. 4, A. 3.
14. *De doctrina Christiana* I, 32. PL 34:32.
15. St. Thomas here dubiously derives the Latin word for stone ("*lapis*") from "*laedens pedem*" (what hurts the foot).
16. Q. 13, A. 1.
17. *De coelesti hierarchia* 2. PG 3:140–41.
18. *De fide* II (prologue). PL 16:559.
19. Q. 13, A. 2.
20. *De coelesti hierarchia* 2. PG 3:141.
21. Jer. 32:18.
22. Q. 13, A. 1.
23. Q. 13, AA. 1, 2.
24. Q. 13, A. 1.
25. On univocal and equivocal causes, see Glossary, s.v. "cause."
26. Gen. 1:26.
27. Aristotle, *Metaphysics* IX, 1. 1053a24–30.
28. Q. 13, A. 4.
29. Rom. 1:20.
30. Q. 13, A. 1.

31. Q. 4, A. 3.
32. *De fide* I, 1. PL 16:530.
33. Jer. 31:3.
34. Aristotle, *Categories* 7. 7b30–31.
35. *De Trinitate* V, 16. PL 42:922.
36. *Metaphysics* IV, 15. 1021a26–31.
37. The servitude referred to is involuntary rather than contractual. See Glossary, s.v. "slavery."
38. Ps. 90:1.
39. *Metaphysics* IV, 15. 1021a26–31.
40. See Glossary, s.v. "potency," "habit," "act."
41. St. Thomas in this and the succeeding paragraph poses two further objections to the analogical predication of the name "God," but from the perspective of those who would argue that the predication is purely equivocal.
42. Aristotle, *De interpretatione* I, 1. 16a13–14.
43. Ps. 96:5.
44. The fourth objection is posed in the first paragraph of the section "But on the contrary." See n. 41, *supra*.
45. Aristotle, *Categories* 1. 1a1–3.
46. The fifth objection is posed in the second paragraph of the section "But on the contrary." See n. 41, *supra*.
47. Q. 12, A. 12.
48. Q. 13, A. 9.
49. *De divinis nominibus* 3. PG 3:680.
50. Ex. 3:13–14.
51. Q. 3, A. 4.
52. *De fide orthodoxa* I, 9. PG 94:836.
53. *De Trinitate* V, 2. PL 42:912.
54. In the body of the article.
55. The Tetragrammaton is the set of four letters making up the Hebrew word for Yahweh (God). St. Thomas understands it to mean "I am."
56. *De coelesti hierarchia* 2. PG 3:141.
57. *De Trinitate* 2. PL 64:1250.
58. Q. 3, A. 7.
59. Ibid.
60. That of John the Saracen.
61. Q. 13, A. 3

ST I
Question 14
On God's Knowing

[This question is divided into sixteen articles, eight of which are included here.]

First Article

Does God Have Knowledge?

I proceed in this way to the first article: it seems that God has no knowledge.

Obj. 1. Knowing is a habit, and no habit belongs to God, since a habit is midway between potentiality and actuality. Therefore, God has no knowledge.

Obj. 2. Theoretical knowing,[1] because it is knowledge of conclusions, is the kind of knowledge that is caused by something else, namely, by knowledge of principles. But nothing in God is caused. Therefore, God has no theoretical knowledge.

Obj. 3. All knowing is either universal or particular. But there is nothing universal or particular in God, as is clear from what I have said before.[2] Therefore, God has no knowledge.

On the contrary, the Apostle says in the Letter to the Romans: "O the depth of riches of God's wisdom and knowledge."[3]

I answer that one needs to say that God knows most perfectly. And for evidence of this, we should consider that we distinguish knowing beings from things that do not know, in that the latter possess only their own form, while a knowing being is by nature constituted to possess the form of something else as well, for the likeness of a known object exists in a knowing subject. And hence the nature of a being that does not know, is evidently more constricted and limited, while the nature of knowing beings has greater breadth and extension. And because of this, the Philosopher says in his *De anima* that "the soul is somehow everything."[4] The limitation of form, however, is by matter. And hence we have also said before that forms come closer to a kind of infinity as they are more immaterial.[5] Therefore, the immateriality of something is clearly the reason why it is a knowing being, and the way of knowledge is by way of immateriality. And hence the *De anima* says that plants, because of their materiality, do not know.[6] On the other hand, the senses can know because they can receive forms apart from matter, and the intellect can know still more because it is more separate from, and unmixed with, matter, as the *De anima* says.[7] And hence, since God is at the pinnacle of immateriality, as is clear from what I have said before,[8] he is consequently at the pinnacle of knowledge.

Reply to Obj. 1. Because perfections that come from God to creatures, exist in God in a higher way, as I have said before,[9] whenever we assign to God a name taken from any perfection of creatures, we need to exclude from the name's meaning everything that belongs to the imperfect way proper to creatures. And hence knowing is not a qualitative accident or habit in God but substance and pure actuality.

Reply to Obj. 2. What exist separately and in many different kinds of ways in creatures, exist without composition and as one in God, as I have said before.[10] But human beings have different acts of knowing according to the different things that they know, for we say that human beings have understanding insofar as they know principles, but theoretical knowledge insofar as they know conclusions, wisdom insofar as they know the highest cause, counsel or prudence insofar as they know what things are to be done. But God knows all these things by one uncomposed act of knowing, as I shall make clear later.[11] And hence we can designate God's simple knowledge by all those names, but in such a way that we exclude every imperfection from each of them, as they come into predications of God, and we retain every perfection. And the Book of Job accordingly says: "Wisdom and strength are with him; he has counsel and understanding."[12]

Reply to Obj. 3. Knowing is according to the way of the knowing subject, for a known object exists in a knowing subject in the way of the knowing subject. And so, since the way of the divine essence is higher than the way in which creatures exist, God's knowing does not have the way of created knowing, namely, that it be universal or particular, habitual or potential, or disposed in any such way.

Third Article

Does God Comprehend Himself?

I proceed in this way to the third article: it seems that God does not comprehend himself.

Obj. 1. Augustine says in his *Octoginta trium quaestionum* that "what comprehends itself, is limited with respect to itself."[13] But God is not limited in any way. Therefore, he does not comprehend himself.

Obj. 2. If anyone should say that God is not limited with respect to us but is limited with respect to himself, the rejoinder would be: everything is truer as it is in God than as it is in us. Therefore, if God is limited with respect to himself but unlimited with respect to us, it is truer to say that God is limited than to say that he is unlimited. And this is contrary to what I have previously determined.[14] Therefore, God does not comprehend himself.

On the contrary, Augustine says in the same place: "Everything that understands itself, comprehends itself."[15] But God understands himself. Therefore, he comprehends himself.

I answer that God comprehends himself perfectly. And this is made clear in the following way. For we say that we comprehend something when we attain the goal of knowing it, and this is the case when we know the object as perfectly as it is knowable. For example, we comprehend a demonstrable proposition when we know it by demonstration, although not when we know it by a probable argument. God, however, evidently knows himself as perfectly as he is knowable. For everything is knowable by way of its actuality; we indeed do not know anything as potential but know it as actual, as the *Metaphysics* says.[16] Moreover, God's power in knowing is as great as his actuality in existing, because he knows by reason of the fact that he is actual and separate from every matter and potentiality, as I have shown.[17] And hence he evidently knows himself as much as he is knowable. And for this reason, he perfectly comprehends himself.

Reply to Obj. 1. "Comprehending," if understood in the strict sense, means something that possesses and encloses something else. And so everything comprehended is necessarily limited, as is everything that is enclosed. We do not say, however, that God comprehends himself in such a way that his intellect is anything other than himself, or that he contains and encloses himself. Rather, we need to explain such expressions by way of negation. For, as we say that God exists in himself because nothing external contains him, so we say that he comprehends himself because no part of him is hidden to himself. For Augustine says in his *De videndo Deum* that "the seer comprehends everything, and everything is seen in such a way that no part of it is hidden from the seer."[18]

Reply to Obj. 2. When Augustine says, "God is limited with respect to himself," we should understand the saying by a certain analogy of proportion, because God is disposed not to exceed his intellect in the same way that a finite being is disposed not to exceed a finite intellect. But we do not say that God is limited with respect to himself in such a way that he understands himself to be something limited.

Fourth Article

Is God's Very Understanding His Substance?

We proceed in this way to the fourth article: it seems that God's very understanding is not his substance.

Obj. 1. Understanding is a certain operation.[19] But an operation means something that proceeds from the one who operates. Therefore, God's very understanding is not his very substance.

Obj. 2. To understand that one understands, is not to understand anything important or the most important thing understood, but to understand something secondary and supplementary. Therefore, if God should be his very understanding, his understanding himself will be the same as when we understand our understanding. And so God's understanding of himself will be nothing important.

Obj. 3. Every understanding is an understanding of something. Therefore, when God understands himself, if he is identical with his understanding, he understands himself understanding, and he understands himself understanding himself understanding, and so on endlessly. Therefore, God's very understanding is not his substance.

On the contrary, Augustine says in his *De Trinitate*: "For God, to exist is to be wise."[20] But to be wise is to understand. Therefore, for God, to exist is to understand. But God's existing is his substance, as I have shown before.[21] Therefore, God's understanding is his substance.

I answer that we need to say that God's understanding is his substance. For, if God's understanding should differ from his substance, it would be necessary, as the Philosopher says in the *Metaphysics*,[22] that something else be the actuality and perfection of the divine substance, to which the divine substance would be related as potentiality to actuality (and this is altogether impossible), since understanding is a perfection and actuality of one who understands.

We need to consider, however, how this is so. For, as I have said before,[23] understanding is not an action that goes out to something external, but remains in the being that acts, as actuality and perfection, just as existing perfects the being that exists. For understanding results from an intelligible form in the same way that existing results from a form. But there is in God no form other than his existence, as I have shown before.[24] And hence, since God's essence itself is also his intelligible form, as I have said,[25] it necessarily follows that his very understanding is his essence and his existence.

And so it is clear from everything that I have previously explained,[26] that the intellect and the object understood and the intelligible form and the understanding itself are entirely one and the same thing in God. And hence it is clear that we posit no multiplicity in God's substance by saying that he is a being that understands.

Reply to Obj. 1. Understanding is not an action that goes out from the one who acts, but an activity that remains in the one who acts.

Reply to Obj. 2. We understand nothing important when we understand an understanding that is not subsistent, as is the case when we understand our understanding. And so it is not similar in the case of God's understanding, which is subsistent.

Reply to Obj. 3.   And the foregoing makes clear the response to the third objection. For God's understanding, which is in itself subsistent, belongs to his very self and not to something else such that we would then need to regress endlessly.

Fifth Article

Does God Know Things Other than Himself?

I proceed in this way to the fifth article: it seems that God does not know things other than himself.

Obj. 1.   Anything other than God exists outside of him. But Augustine says in his *Octoginta trium quaestionum* that "God does not behold anything outside of himself."[27] Therefore, he does not know things other than himself.

Obj. 2.   Something understood perfects the one who understands. Therefore, if God should understand things other than himself, something else will perfect God and be more excellent than himself, which is impossible.

Obj. 3.   An intelligible object specifies understanding itself, as proper objects specify every other act. And hence the more excellent the object understood, the more excellent the understanding itself also is. But God is his very understanding, as is clear from what I have said.[28] Therefore, if God understands anything other than himself, something other than himself gives form to himself, which is impossible. Therefore, God does not know things other than himself.

On the contrary, the Letter to the Hebrews says: "Everything is bare and open to his eyes."[29]

I answer that God necessarily knows things other than himself. For he evidently understands himself perfectly; otherwise, his existing would not be perfect, since his existing is his understanding. Moreover, if something is perfectly known, its power is necessarily known perfectly. The power of something, however, can be perfectly known only if one knows the things to which the power extends. And hence, since God's power extends to other things, because it is itself the first efficient cause of every being, as is clear from what I have said before,[30] God necessarily knows things other than himself. And this becomes still more evident if we add that the very existing of the first efficient cause, namely, God, is his understanding. And hence it is necessary that whatever effects pre-exist in God as their first cause, be in his very understanding, and that all things be in him in an intelligible way, for everything that exists in something else, is such in the way of the other in which it exists.

In order to know how God knows things other than himself, moreover, we need to consider that we know something in two ways: in one way, in itself; in the second way, in another. We indeed know something in itself when we know it by a special form equivalent to the knowable object itself, as, for example, when the eye sees a human being by the form of a human being. But we see in another what we see by the form of something surrounding it, as, for example, when we see a part in a whole by the form of the whole, or when we see a human being in a mirror by the mirror's form, or in whatever other way we happen to see something in another.

We thus need to say that God sees himself in himself because he sees himself by his essence. But he sees things other than himself, not in themselves, but in himself insofar as his essence contains the likeness of things other than himself.

Reply to Obj. 1. We should not so understand the words of Augustine, when he says that God "beholds nothing outside of himself," as if God beholds nothing that is outside of himself, but we should understand the words to mean that God does not behold anything outside of himself except in himself, as I have said.[31]

Reply to Obj. 2. Something understood perfects the one who understands, not indeed by its substance but by its likeness, by which it is in the intellect as a form and perfection of the intellect, for "a stone is not in the soul, but its form is," as the *De anima* says.[32] But God understands things other than himself insofar as his essence contains their forms, as I have said.[33] And hence it does not follow that something other than the very essence of God is a perfection of the divine intellect.

Reply to Obj. 3. We do not specify understanding itself by what we understand in something else, but by the chief object understood, in which other things are understood. For the proper object of understanding specifies understanding itself, inasmuch as intelligible form is the source of intellectual activity, since every action is specified by the form that is the action's source, as heat specifies heating. And hence the intelligible form that causes the intellect to be active, specifies intellectual activity. And this is the form of the chief object understood, which in God is nothing other than his essence, and he comprehends all the forms of things in that essence. And hence nothing other than the divine essence needs to specify God's very understanding, or rather, God himself.

Eight Article

Does God's Knowledge Cause Things?

I proceed in this way to the eighth article: it seems that God's knowledge does not cause things.

Obj. 1. Origen says in his commentary on the Letter to the Romans: "Something will not be because God knows it will be, but, because it will be, God knows it before it happens to be."[34]

Obj. 2. When we posit a cause, we posit an effect. But God's knowledge is eternal. Therefore, if God's knowledge causes created things, it seems that creatures exist from eternity.

Obj. 3. The knowable is prior to knowledge and measures it, as the *Metaphysics* says.[35] But something subsequent and measured cannot be a cause. Therefore, God's knowledge does not cause things.

On the contrary, Augustine says in his *De Trinitate*: "God does not know all creatures, whether spiritual or corporeal, because they exist, but they exist because he knows them."[36]

I answer that God's knowledge causes things. For God's knowledge is related to all created things just as a craftman's knowledge is related to the things he crafts. But a craftsman's knowledge causes the things he crafts, because a craftsman acts by means of his intellect. And hence a form in the intellect necessarily causes action, just as heat causes heating. But we need to note that forms belonging to nature, as forms remaining in the things on which they bestow existing, do not denote sources of action except as the forms have a tendency to produce effects. And intelligible forms likewise do not denote sources of action simply as the forms exist in those who understand but in conjunction with an inclination to produce effects, and such an inclination results from the will. For intelligible forms are disposed toward contraries, since to know one contrary is to know the other; therefore, intellectual forms would produce no fixed effects unless the appetite were to determine them to produce particular effects, as the *Metaphysics* says.[37] And God evidently causes things by means of his intellect, since his existing is his understanding. And hence his knowledge necessarily causes things insofar as his knowledge is linked to his will. And hence we are accustomed to call God's knowledge, insofar as it causes things, a knowledge of assent.

Reply to Obj. 1. Origen was speaking about the aspect of knowledge to which the nature of causality belongs only in conjunction with the will, as I have said.[38]

But we need to understand Origen's statement that God knows some things because they will be, to refer to the cause of logical inference, not the cause of existing. For it follows logically that God will know some things if they will be, but the things that will be, do not cause God to know them.

Reply to Obj. 2. God's knowledge causes things as things are part of his knowledge. But it was not part of his knowledge that things would be from eternity. And hence, although God's knowledge is eternal, it nonetheless does not follow that creatures would exist from eternity.

Reply to Obj. 3. Things of nature stand halfway between God's knowledge and ours, for we receive our knowledge from the things of nature, and God causes them by his knowledge. And hence, as the knowable things of nature are prior to our knowledge and measure our knowledge, so God's knowledge is prior to the things of nature and measures the things themselves. Similarly, a particular house stands halfway between the knowledge of the builder who built it, and the knowledge of those who get their knowledge of the house from the house itself after it has been built.

Ninth Article

Does God Know Nonbeings?

I proceed in this way to the ninth article: it seems that God does not know nonbeings.

Obj. 1. God knows only things that are true. But true and being are convertible. Therefore, God does not know nonbeings.

Obj. 2. Knowing requires a likeness between the one who knows and the object known. But things that do not exist, cannot have a likeness to God, who is existing itself. Therefore, God cannot know things that do not exist.

Obj. 3. God's knowing causes the objects that he knows. But he does not cause nonbeings, because a nonbeing does not have a cause. Therefore, God does not know nonbeings.

On the contrary, the Apostle says in the Letter to the Romans: "God, who calls [into existence] things that do not exist, as if they were things that do exist."[39]

I answer that God knows all things, whatever they are, in whatever way they are. But nothing prevents things that do not exist absolutely, from existing in a way. For things that are actual, exist absolutely. Things that are not actual, however, exist in the power either of God himself or a creature, whether in an active power or in a passive power, or in the power of conjecturing or imagining or any way of signifying. Therefore, whatever a creature can cause or think or say, and also whatever God himself can cause, all these things God knows even if they are not actual. And we can say to this extent that he knows even nonbeings.

But we need to note a certain difference about things that are not actual. For although certain things are not now actual, they nonetheless either have existed or will exist, and we say that God knows all these things by a knowing of vision. For, since eternity, which exists without succession and includes the whole of time, measures God's understanding, which is his existing, his present contemplation is carried to all time and to everything that exists in any time, as things presently subject to him. But there are certain things in the power of God or a creature that, nonetheless, neither exist nor will exist nor have existed. And with respect to these, we do not say that God has a knowing of vision but one of pure understanding. And we say this in this way because the things that we see around us, have a separate existence outside the seer.

Reply to Obj. 1. Things that are not actual, have truth insofar as they are potential, for it is true to say that they are potential. And God knows them in this way.

Reply to Obj. 2.   Since God is existing itself, everything exists as much as it shares some likeness of God, just as everything is hot as much as it shares in heat. Thus God also knows things that are potential, even though they are not actual.

Reply to Obj. 3.   God's knowing causes things when his will is added to his knowing. And hence it is not necessary that whatever God knows, exist or have existed or will exist, but only the beings that he wills to exist or allows to exist. And also, God does not know that those things exist, but that they can exist.

Eleventh Article

Does God Know Individual Things?

I proceed in this way to the eleventh article: it seems that God does not know individual things.

Obj. 1.   The divine intellect is more immaterial than the human intellect. But the human intellect, because of its immateriality, does not know individual things; rather, as the *De anima* says, "Reason treats of universal things, but the senses of singular things."[40] Therefore, God does not know individual things.

Obj. 2.   Only those human powers that receive forms mixed with the conditions of matter, know individual things. But things in God are most of all removed from every materiality. Therefore, God does not know individual things.

Obj. 3.   Every knowledge is by some likeness. But there does not seem to be any likeness of individual things as such in God, because the source of individuality is matter, and matter, as merely potential being, is entirely unlike God, who is pure actuality. Therefore, God cannot know individual things.

On the contrary, the Book of Proverbs says: "All the ways of human beings lie open to his eyes."[41]

I answer that God knows individual things. For all the perfections found in creatures pre-exist in God in a higher way, as is clear from what I have said before.[42] But to know individual things belongs to our perfection. And hence God necessarily knows individual things. For the Philosopher likewise holds it to be unfitting that we should know something that God does not know. And hence he argues against Empedocles, in the *De anima*[43] and the *Metaphysics*,[44] that, were God not to know of discord, he would consequently be very stupid. But perfections that are separate in lesser things, exist in God without composition and as one. And hence, although we know by one power what is universal and immaterial, and know by another power

what is individual and material, yet God knows both by his simple understanding.

But some thinkers, who wish to show how this can be, have said that God
knows individual things through general causes,[45] for there is nothing in any
part of individual things that does not arise from a general cause. And they
posit this example: an astronomer would be able to predict all future
eclipses were he to know all the general movements of the heavens. But
this does not suffice, because individual things receive from general causes
certain forms and powers that only individual matter individuates,
howevermuch the forms and powers are joined to one another. And hence
one who might know Socrates because he is white, or the son of Sophronis-
cus or anything else said in this way, would not know Socrates as he is this
particular human being. And hence God would not in the aforementioned
way know individual things in their individuality.

Other thinkers, however, have said that God knows individual things by
connecting general causes to particular effects. But this is no explanation,
because no one can connect something to something else unless one should
know the other thing beforehand, and hence the connection mentioned cannot be the reason for knowing particular things but presupposes knowledge
of individual things.

And we need, therefore, to say otherwise, that, since God causes things
by his knowing, as I have said,[46] his knowing reaches as far as his causality.
And hence, since the active power of God extends not only to the forms by
which a common nature is received, but also to matter, as I shall show
later,[47] God's knowing necessarily extends even to individual things, which
matter individuates. For, since God knows things other than himself by his
own essence, inasmuch as he is the likeness of things as their efficient
source, his essence is necessarily the sufficient source for him to know all the
things that he has made, not only in general but in particular. And it would
be similar in the case of a craftsman's knowing if the craftsman were to produce the entire artifact and not only its form.

Reply to Obj. 1.   Our intellect abstracts an intelligible form from individuating sources, and hence the intelligible form of our intellect cannot be a
likeness of the individuating sources. And so our intellect does not know individual things.[48] But the divine intellect's intelligible form, which is God's
essence, is not immaterial by abstraction but by itself, which is the source of
all the sources that enter into the composition of something, whether
sources of the species or of the individual thing. And hence God by that
form knows not only what is universal but also what is individual.

Reply to Obj. 2.   Although the divine intellect's form as to the form's own
existing has no material conditions, as do the forms received in our imagination and senses, yet the divine intellect's form by its power extends to
immaterial and material things, as I have said.[49]

Reply to Obj. 3.   Although matter by its potentiality departs from a likeness of God, matter still retains a certain likeness to God's existing inasmuch as matter has existence even in this way.

Thirteenth Article

Does God Know Future Contingent Things?[50]

I proceed in this way to the thirteenth article: it seems that God does not know future contingent things.

Obj. 1. A necessary effect comes from a necessary cause. But God's knowing causes the objects he knows, as I have said before.[51] Therefore, since God's knowing is necessary, the objects he knows, are necessary. Therefore, God does not know contingent things.

Obj. 2. Absolutely necessary is the consequent of every conditional proposition whose antecedent is absolutely necessary. For antecedents are related to consequents as principles to conclusions, but only necessary conclusions result from necessary principles, as the *Posterior Analytics* proves.[52] But the proposition, "If God knew that this particular thing will be, it will be," is a true conditional proposition, because God knows only things that are true. The antecedent of this conditional proposition, moreover, is absolutely necessary, both because it is eternal, and because it is denoted as something past. Therefore, the consequent as well is absolutely necessary. Therefore, whatever God knows, is necessary. And so God does not know future contingent things.

Obj. 3. Everything that God knows, necessarily exists, because every object that we know, necessarily exists, and God's knowing is still more certain than ours. But no future contingent thing necessarily exists. Therefore, God does not know any future contingent thing.

On the contrary, the Psalm calls God "he who fashioned their hearts one by one, he who understands all their deeds,"[53] namely, the deeds of human beings. But the deeds of human beings, as subject to free choice, are contingent. Therefore, God knows future contingent things.

I answer that, since I have shown before that God knows all things, not only those that actually exist but also those that exist in his power or that of creatures,[54] and since some of these things are future things contingent on us, it follows that God knows future contingent things.

And for evidence of this, we need to consider that we can in two ways regard something as contingent. In one way, intrinsically, insofar as it already actually exists. And so we do not regard it as future but as present, nor do we regard it as something contingent to one of several outcomes but as something determined to one outcome. And consequently, it can thus be subject to indisputable knowledge, as, for example, to the sense of sight when I see that Socrates is sitting. In the other way, we can regard something as contingent as it exists in its cause. And so we regard it as something future and something contingent not yet determined to one outcome, because a contingent cause is disposed toward contrary effects. And so a contingent thing is not subject to any certain knowledge. And hence whoever knows a contingent effect only in its cause has only conjectural knowledge about it. But God knows all contingent things, not only as they exist in their causes, but also as each of them actually exists in itself.

And although contingent things become actual successively, yet God does not know contingent things successively, as they are in their own existing, as we do, but he knows them at the same time. This is so because eternity measures his knowledge, as also his existing, and eternity, which exists simultaneously whole, embraces the whole of time, as I have said before.[55] And hence everything that exists in time, is present to God from eternity, not only because he has the natures of things present with him, as certain thinkers say, but because his sight is borne from eternity over all things as they exist in their presence to him.

And hence God evidently knows contingent things unerringly, as they are subject to his inspection by their presence, and yet they are future contingent things in relation to their own causes.

Reply to Obj. 1.   Although the highest cause is necessary, an effect can nonetheless be contingent because of a proximate contingent cause, as the budding of a plant is contingent because of a proximate contingent cause, although the motion of the sun, which is the first cause, is necessary. And likewise, things that God knows, are contingent because of proximate causes, although God's knowing, which is the first cause, is necessary.

Reply to Obj. 2.   Certain thinkers claim that the antecedent, "God knew that this particular contingent thing will be," is not necessary but contingent, because the antecedent, although something past, nonetheless implies a regard for the future. But this does not take necessity away from the antecedent, because what had a regard for the future, necessarily had that regard, even though the future thing sometimes does not result.

Other thinkers, however, say that the antecedent is contingent, because it is made up of the necessary and the contingent, just as the statement "Socrates is a white man" is contingent. But this is also nonsense, because, when we say, "God knew that this particular contingent thing will be," we posit "contingent" there only as the subject matter of the expression and not as the chief function of the proposition. And hence the contingency or necessity of "contingent" relates not at all to whether the proposition is necessary or contingent, true or false. For it can in this way be as true that I said that a human being is an ass as I said that Socrates is running, or that God exists, and the reasoning is the same about the necessary and the contingent.

And so we need to say that the antecedent is absolutely necessary. Still, it does not follow, as certain thinkers say, that the consequent is absolutely necessary because the antecedent is the remote cause of the consequent, which is contingent by reason of a proximate cause. This, however, is nonsense. For a conditional proposition whose antecedent were a remote necessary cause, and its consequent a contingent effect, would be false, as if, for example, I were to say, "If the sun is in motion, grass will grow."

And so we need to say otherwise, that when we posit something in the antecedent that belongs to an act of the soul, we ought not to understand the consequent as it is in itself, but as it exists in the soul, for the existing of an object in itself is one thing, and the existing of the object in the soul another. For example, if I should say, "If the soul understands something, that object is immaterial," I need to understand that the object is immaterial as it exists in the intellect, not as it is in itself. And likewise, if I should say, "If God knew something, it will be," we need to understand the consequent as it is subject to God's knowing, namely, as it is in its presence to him. And so the consequent is just as necessary as the antecedent; "For everything that exists, while it exists, necessarily exists," as the *De interpretatione* says.[56]

Reply to Obj. 3. We know successively things brought into actuality in time, but God knows such things in eternity, which transcends time. And hence we cannot be certain of future contingent things, because we know them as such, while God, whose understanding is in eternity, which transcends time, alone can be certain of them. For example, one who proceeds along a road, does not see those coming behind him, but one who sees the whole road from a height, sees at the same time all those going along the road. And so the things that we know, need to be necessary, indeed as they are in themselves, because we cannot know things that are in themselves future contingent things. But the things that God knows, need to be necessary in the way in which they are subject to his knowing, as I have said,[57] but not absolutely, as they are considered in relation to their particular causes.

And hence we are accustomed also to distinguish the proposition, "Everything that God knows, necessarily exists." This is so because the proposition can be about the thing or about the statement. If we understand the proposition to be about the thing, the proposition is a simple proposition and false, and its meaning is, "Everything that God knows, is necessary." Or we can understand the proposition to be about the statement, and then the proposition is a composite proposition and true, and its meaning is, "The statement, 'The things that God knows, exist,' is necessary."

But certain thinkers object, saying that that distinction is appropriate for forms that can be separated from subjects, as if, for example, I should say, "Something white can be black." And this is indeed false about the statement while true about the thing, for a thing that is white, can be black, while the statement, "Something white is black," can never be true. For forms inseparable from subjects, however, the aforementioned distinction is improper, as if, for example, I should say, "A black raven can be white," because the proposition is false in both senses. Moreover, being known by God is inseparable from things, because things that God knows, cannot not be known.

Still, this objection would hold if the words, "known thing," were to imply some disposition inherent in the subject. But since the words imply an act of knowing, we can attribute to the known thing as such, even if it be always known, something that we do not attribute to it insofar as it falls within the act of knowing. For example, we attribute material existence to a stone as such, and we do not attribute material existence to it as intelligible.

Notes

1. On St. Thomas's understanding of science, see Glossary, s.v. "science."
2. Q. 3, A. 9, *ad* 2.
3. Rom. 11:33.
4. *De anima* III, 8. 431b21.
5. Q. 7, AA. 1, 2.
6. Aristotle, *De anima* II, 12. 424a32–b3.
7. Aristotle, *De anima* III, 4. 429a18–27.
8. Q. 7, A. 1.
9. Q. 4, A. 2.
10. Q. 13, A. 4.
11. Q. 14, A. 7.
12. Job 12:13.
13. *Octoginta trium quaestionum*, Q. 15. PL 40:14–15.
14. Q. 7, A. 1.
15. See n. 13, *supra*.
16. Aristotle, *Metaphysics* VIII, 9. 1051a29–33.
17. Q. 14, AA. 1, 2.
18. *De videndo Deum*, Letter 147, 9. PL 33:606.
19. See Glossary, s.v. "operation."
20. *De Trinitate* VII, 2. PL 42:936.
21. Q. 3, A. 4.
22. *Metaphysics* XI, 9. 1074b17–21.
23. Q. 14, A. 2.
24. Q. 3, A. 4.
25. Q. 14, A. 2.
26. In this article and article two of this question.
27. *Octoginta trium quaestionum*, Q. 46. PL 40:30.
28. Q. 14, A. 3.
29. Heb. 4:13.
30. Q. 2, A. 3.
31. In the body of the article.
32. Aristotle, *De anima* III, 8. 431b28–432a3.
33. In the body of the article.
34. *In Epistolam ad Romanos* VII, on 8:30. PG 14:1126.
35. Aristotle, *Metaphysics* IX, 1. 1053a31, b3.
36. *De Trinitate*, XV, 13. PL 42:1076.
37. Aristotle, *Metaphysics* VIII, 5. 1048a8–16.
38. In the body of the article.

39. Rom. 4:17.
40. Aristotle, *De anima* II, 5. 417b22–23.
41. Prov. 16:2.
42. Q. 4, A. 2.
43. *De anima* I, 5. 410b4–6.
44. *Metaphysics* II, 4. 1000b3–11.
45. See Avicenna, *Metaphysics*, tract. 8, chap. 6.
46. Q. 14, A. 8.
47. Q. 44, A. 2.
48. Except indirectly. See Q. 86, A. 1.
49. In the body of the article.
50. For a fuller treatment, see St. Thomas's *Commentary on the Sentences* I, dist. 38, Q. 1, A. 5.
51. Q. 14, A. 8.
52. Aristotle, *Posterior Analytics* I, 6. 75a4–6.
53. Ps. 33:15.
54. Q. 14, A. 9.
55. Q. 10, A. 2, *ad* 4.
56. Aristotle, *De interpretatione*, I, 9. 9a23–24.
57. In this article, *ad* 1.

ST I
Question 15
On the Ideas

[This question is divided into three articles, all of which are included here.]

First Article

Are There Ideas¹ in the Divine Mind?

I proceed in this way to the first article: it seems that there are no ideas in the divine mind.

Obj. 1. For Denis says in his *De divinis nominibus* that God does not know things by ideas.[2] But we posit ideas for no other reason than that things be known by them. Therefore, there are no ideas in the divine mind.

Obj. 2. God knows everything in himself, as I have said before.[3] But he does not know himself by an idea. Therefore, neither does he know other things by ideas.

Obj. 3. We posit an idea as the source of knowing and acting. But the divine essence is the sufficient source of knowing and doing everything. Therefore, it is not necessary to posit ideas in the divine mind.

On the contrary, Augustine says in his work *Octoginta trium quaestionum*: "Such power is constituted in the ideas that one could not be wise if one did not understand them."[4]

I answer that we need to posit ideas in the divine mind. For the Greek word *"idea"* is called *"forma"* in Latin, and hence we understand by ideas the forms of different things, forms that exist in addition to the things themselves. But the form of a thing, the form that exists in addition to the thing itself, can serve two purposes: either to be the exemplar of the object of which we call it the form, or to be the source of knowing the object itself, as we say that the forms of knowable objects exist in the knower. And we need to posit ideas in the divine mind to serve both purposes.

And we make this clear in the following way. In everything not coming to be by chance, a form is indeed necessarily the end of each thing's coming to be. But an efficient cause would only act for the sake of a form inasmuch as

126

a likeness of the form exists in the efficient cause. And this indeed happens in two ways. For in the case of certain efficient causes, the form of the thing to be made pre-exists by natural existing, as in the case of things that act by nature; for example, human beings beget human beings, and fire produces fire. But in the case of certain other efficient causes, the form of the thing to be made pre-exists by intelligible existing, as in the case of things that act by means of their understanding; for example, the likeness of a house pre-exists in the mind of its builder. And we can call the latter likeness an idea of the house, because the builder intends the house to be like the form that he conceives in his mind.

Therefore, because the world has not been made by chance but by God acting by means of his understanding, as I shall make clear later,[5] there necessarily is a form in the divine mind, to the likeness of which he has made the world. And the nature of an idea in the divine mind consists in this.

Reply to Obj. 1.   God does not understand things by an idea that exists outside of himself. And so also Aristotle[6] rejects the opinion of Plato[7] about the ideas, insofar as the latter held the ideas to exist in themselves, not in an intellect.

Reply to Obj. 2.   Although God knows himself and other things by his essence, his essence is nonetheless the active source of other things, although not of himself, and so his essence, as related to other things but not to himself, has the nature of an idea.

Reply to Obj. 3.   One needs to say that God is the likeness of everything by his essence. And hence an idea in God is only his essence.

Second Article

Are There Several Ideas in the Divine Mind?

I proceed in this way to the second article: it seems that there are not several ideas in the divine mind.

Obj. 1.   An idea in God is his essence. But there is only one essence of God. Therefore, there is also only one idea.

Obj. 2.   As ideas are sources of knowing and acting, so are theoretical and practical knowledge. But there are not several kinds of theoretical and practical knowledge in God. Therefore, neither are there several ideas.

Obj. 3.   If anyone should say that there are as many ideas as there are relations to different creatures, the rejoinder would be: The plurality of ideas exist from eternity. Therefore, if there are several ideas, and creatures are temporal, the temporal will cause the eternal.

Obj. 4.   Those relations really exist either in creatures alone or in God as well. If the relations exist only in creatures, the plurality of ideas will not be eternal if the ideas are many only by such relations, because creatures are not eternal. But if the relations really exist in God, there consequently would be a real plurality in God other than the plurality of Persons, and the latter conclusion is contrary to Damascene, who says that everything in God is one and the same except "nongeneration, generation, and procession."[8] Thus there are not several ideas in the divine mind.

On the contrary, Augustine says in his work *Octoginta trium quaestionum*: "The ideas are certain original forms, or fixed and incommunicable essences of things, because the ideas are not fashioned, and for this reason, they are eternal and always disposed in the same way. And God's understanding includes the ideas. But although they themselves neither come to be nor pass away, yet we say that they fashion everything that can come to be and pass away, and everything that does come to be and pass away."[9]

I answer that we need to posit several ideas in the divine mind. For evidence of this, we need to consider that the chief efficient cause of any effect strives in the strict sense for what is the final end, as a commander strives to arrange his army. But what is in fact best in the world, is the good of the universe's order, as the Philosopher makes clear in the *Metaphysics*.[10] Therefore, God intends the order of the universe in the strict sense and not as something that results by chance from a succession of efficient causes. In the latter way, certain thinkers said that God created only the first creature, and the latter created a second creature, and so on, until so sizable a multitude of things was produced, and God according to this opinion would have only an idea of the first creature that he created.[11]

But if God has created and intended the universe's very order as such, he necessarily has an idea of the universe's order. One cannot, however, consider the nature of any whole without considering the peculiar natures of the things out of which the whole is constituted; for example, a builder could not conceive the form of a house unless there were to be in his mind the peculiar nature of each of its parts. There thus needs to exist in the divine mind the peculiar natures of everything. And hence Augustine says in his work *Octoginta trium quaestionum* that "God created each thing with its own nature."[12] And hence several ideas consequently exist in the divine mind.

It is, moreover, easy to see how this is compatible with God's simplicity if we should consider that the idea of a product exists in the producer's mind as the object he understands, and not as the form by which he understands, the form that causes actual understanding. For example, the form of a house in the mind of a builder is something that he understands, and he fashions the house in matter to the likeness of this form. But it is not contrary to the simplicity of God's intellect that it understand many things, although it would be contrary to its simplicity if it were informed by several forms. And hence several ideas exist in God's mind as objects of his understanding.

And we can see this in the following way. For God knows his essence perfectly, and hence he knows it by every way in which it is knowable. Moreover, God's essence can be known, not only as it is in itself, but as it can be shared by creatures by any kind of likeness. Every creature, however, has its own form, as it shares a likeness to the divine essence in some way. Thus God knows his essence as the peculiar nature and idea of this creature, inasmuch as he knows his essence as imitable in this way by such a creature. And it is likewise in the case of other things. And so God evidently understands the several peculiar natures of the several things, and these natures are several ideas.

Reply to Obj. 1. An idea in God does not denote his essence as such but as a likeness or nature of this or that thing. And hence we say that there are as many ideas as there are natures understood from his one essence.

Reply to Obj. 2. We signify theoretical and practical knowledge as the means by which God understands, but we signify the ideas as the objects that God understands. Moreover, God by one thing understands many things, not only in themselves but also as understood, and this is to understand the several natures of things. Similarly, we say that a builder understands a house when he understands the form of a house in matter, and that he understands the idea or nature of a house when he understands the house's form as conceived by him, because he understands that he understands the form. Now, God not only understands many things by his essence, but he also understands that he understands them by his essence. And this is to understand the several natures of things, or that there are several ideas in his intellect as objects understood by him.

Reply to Obj. 3. Things do not cause such relations, whereby there are many ideas, but God's intellect does so by relating his essence to things.

Reply to Obj. 4. The relations that cause the ideas to be many, are not in created things but in God. And yet they are not real relations, as are those by which the Persons are distinguished, but relations that God understands.

Third Article

Does God Have Ideas of Everything that He Knows?

I proceed in this way to the third article: it seems that God does not have ideas of everything that he knows.

Obj. 1. God has no idea of evil, because there would consequently be evil in God. But God knows things that are evil. Therefore, God does not have ideas of everything that he knows.

Obj. 2. God knows things that neither exist nor will exist nor have existed, as I have said before.[13] But God has no ideas of such things, because Denis says in his *De divinis nominibus* that "exemplars are divine decrees that determine and cause things."[14] Therefore, God does not have ideas of everything that he knows.

Obj. 3. God knows prime matter,[15] which cannot have an idea, because it has no form. Therefore, the same conclusion follows as before.

Obj. 4. God evidently knows not only species but also genera and individuals and accidents.[16] But there are no ideas of the latter in the view of Plato, who was the first to introduce the ideas, as Augustine says.[17] Therefore, God does not have ideas of everything that he knows.

On the contrary, the ideas are natures existing in the divine mind, as Augustine makes clear.[18] But God possesses the peculiar natures of everything that he knows. Therefore, he has an idea of everything that he knows.

I answer that, since Plato posited the ideas as sources of knowing things and of their coming to be,[19] an idea, as posited in the divine mind, is related to both. And we can call an idea an "exemplar" insofar as an idea is the source of producing things, and an idea as exemplar belongs to practical knowledge. As an idea is a source of knowledge, however, we call an idea a "nature" in the strict sense, and an idea as nature can belong to theoretical knowledge as well. Therefore, the ideas as exemplars are related to everything that God makes in any period of time. But the ideas as sources of knowledge are related to everything that God knows, even if the things at no time come to be, and to everything that God knows in its own nature, and as he knows it in a theoretical way.

Reply to Obj. 1. God does not know evil by its own nature but by the nature of good. And so God has no idea of evil, either as an exemplar or as a nature.

Reply to Obj. 2. Only by his power does God have practical knowledge of things that neither exist nor will exist nor have existed. And hence God has no idea of those things insofar as idea means exemplar, but only insofar as idea means nature.

Reply to Obj. 3. Plato, according to some, held matter to be uncreated, and so he did not hold that there is an idea of matter, but that the ideas and matter are joint causes.[20] But because we hold that God created matter, although not without form, matter indeed has an idea in God, although only the idea of a composite. For matter as such neither has existence nor is knowable.

Reply to Obj. 4. Genera can have only the idea of a species insofar as idea means exemplar, because a genus never comes to exist except in a species. It is also the same in the case of accidental characteristics that inseparably accompany a subject, because they come to exist at the same time as the subject. But accidental characteristics added to a subject have a particular idea. For example, a builder by the form of a house produces all the accidental characteristics that are originally connected with the house, but he by another form produces things that are added to the house after the latter has been completed, such things as paintings or something else. But individuals, according to Plato, had only the idea of the species.[21] He was of this opinion both because individuals are individuated by matter, which he held to be uncreated (as some say) and a joint cause with the ideas, and because nature's aim consists in the species, and nature produces individuals only in order that the species be preserved in them. But divine providence extends both to species and to individuals, as I shall affirm later.[22]

Notes

1. See Glossary, s.v. "idea."
2. *De divinis nominibus* 7. PG 3:869.
3. Q. 14, A. 5.
4. *Octoginta trium quaestionum*, Q. 46. PL 40:29.
5. Q. 47, A. 1.
6. *Metaphysics* I, 9. 991a.
7. *Phaedo* 48. 99E.
8. *De fide orthodoxa* I, 10. PG 94:837. Damascene refers to the Persons of the Trinity: the Father is the ungenerated source, the Son is generated by the Father, and the Spirit proceeds from the Father through the Son.
9. *Octoginta trium quaestionum*, Q. 46. PL 40:30.
10. *Metaphysics* XI, 10. 1075a11–15.
11. See Avicenna, *Metaphysics*, tract. 9, chap. 4.
12. *Octoginta trium quaestionum*, Q. 46. PL 40:30.
13. Q. 14, A. 9.
14. *De divinis nominibus* 5. PG 3:824.
15. See Glossary, s.v. "matter."
16. See Glossary, s.v. "accident."
17. *Octoginta trium quaestionum*, Q. 46. PL 40:29.
18. Ibid.
19. *Phaedo* 48, 49. 100–101. *Timaeus*. 28A–29B, 50B–E.
20. *Timaeus*. 50D–52D.
21. *Phaedo* 49. 100B–101E. *Timaeus*. 50D–52D.
22. Q. 22, A. 2.

ST I
Question 16
On Truth

[This question is divided into eight articles, six of which are included here.]

First Article

Is Truth Only in the Intellect?

I proceed in this way to the first article: it seems that truth is not only in the intellect but rather in things.

Obj. 1. Augustine in his work *Soliloquiorum* rejects this definition of the true, "The true is what is seen," since stones in the deepest bowels of the earth would accordingly not be true stones, because they are not seen.[1] He also rejects this definition, "The true is what is so disposed as to be perceived by a witness willing and able to know," because it would accordingly follow that nothing would be true if no one were able to know it.[2] And he defined the true in this way: "The true is what exists."[3] And so it seems that truth is in things and not in the intellect.

Obj. 2. Everything true is true by reason of truth. If truth is only in the intellect, therefore, nothing will be true except as it is understood, and this is the error of the ancient philosophers who said that everything that seems to be, is true.[4] And contradictory propositions are consequently true at the same time, because different persons at the same time perceive contradictory propositions to be true.

Obj. 3. "What causes anything to be, exists in a still higher degree," as the *Posterior Analytics* makes clear.[5] But "opinion or speech is true or false because something exists or does not exist," according to the Philosopher in the *Categories*.[6] Therefore, truth is in things rather than in the intellect.

On the contrary, the Philosopher says in the *Metaphysics* that "true and false are not in things but in the intellect."[7]

I answer that, as "good" denotes the object toward which an appetite tends, so "true" denotes the object toward which the intellect tends. Moreover, there is this difference between appetite and intellect, or any knowledge, that there is knowledge insofar as the known object is in the knower, while there is appetite insofar as the one who desires, tends toward the desired object itself. And so the object of appetite, which is the good, is in the desirable object, but the object of knowledge, which is the true, is in the intellect itself.

Moreover, as there is good in something inasmuch as something is related to an appetite, and the consideration of goodness is consequently shifted from the desirable object to the appetite, insofar as we call an appetite good as its object is good, so, since there is truth in the intellect as the latter is conformed to the object understood, the consideration of truth is necessarily shifted from the intellect to the object understood. As a result, we also call the understood object true, insofar as the object has a relation to the intellect.

An object understood, moreover, can be related to an intellect either intrinsically or by chance. The object indeed intrinsically has a relation to the intellect on which it depends as to its existing, while it by chance has a relation to an intellect by which it can be known. This is as if we should say that a house is intrinsically related to the intellect of its builder but related by chance to an intellect on which it does not depend. Moreover, we understand a judgment about an object by what intrinsically belongs to the object, and not by what belongs to the object by chance. And hence we call each thing absolutely true by its relation to the intellect on which it depends. And so it is that we call man-made objects true by their relation to our intellect; for example, we call true a house that attains the likeness of the form that is in the mind of the builder, and we call speech true insofar as speech is the sign of a true intellect. And likewise, we call things of nature true insofar as they attain the likeness of the forms that are in the divine mind; for example, we call true a stone that attains the proper nature of stone, as God's intellect preconceives the nature of stone.

Truth is thus primarily in the intellect and secondarily in things, as things are related to an intellect as their source.

And truth is accordingly denoted in different ways. For example, Augustine says in his work *De vera religione* that "truth is the means whereby what exists, is manifested."[8] And Hilary says that "the true declares or manifests being."[9] And this belongs to truth as it is in the intellect.

But the definition of Augustine in his work *De vera religione* "Truth is the best likeness of its source, a likeness without any unlikeness"[10] belongs to the object's truth by the object's relation to the intellect. And there is a certain definition by Anselm: "Truth is the correctness that the mind alone can perceive,"[11] for what agrees with its source, is correct. And there is a certain definition by Avicenna: "The truth of everything is the special way of its existing that has been fixed for it."[12]

And the statement that "truth is the equation of an object with an intellect"[13] can belong to both ways.

Reply to Obj. 1. Augustine is speaking about the truth of the object, and he excludes relation to our intellect from the nature of truth in this sense. For we exclude from every definition what exists by chance.

Reply to Obj. 2.   Ancient philosophers did not say that the forms of things of nature come from an intellect, but that such forms result by chance. And they were compelled to constitute the truth of things in the relation of things to our intellect because they noted that the true implies a relation to an intellect. And from this followed the inappropriate things that the Philosopher attacked in the *Metaphysics*.[14] And these, indeed inappropriate, things do not arise if we hold that the truth of things consists in their relation to the divine intellect.

Reply to Obj. 3.   Although objects cause the truth of our intellect, yet the essence of truth need not be found first in things, just as we do not find the essence of health in medicine before we find the essence of health in animals. For example, the power of medicine, not its health, causes health, since medicine is not a univocal efficient cause.[15] And likewise, the existence of a thing, not its truth, causes the intellect's truth. And hence the Philosopher says that an opinion or speech is true "because something exists," not "because something is true."[16]

Second Article

Does Truth Consist in the Intellect Composing and Dividing?[17]

I proceed in this way to the second article: it seems that truth does not consist only in the intellect composing and dividing.

Obj. 1.   The Philosopher says in the *De anima* that, as sense perception of what is properly sensible, is always true, so also is the understanding of "what something is."[18] But there is no composition or division either in the senses, or in the intellect when it knows "what something is." Therefore, truth does not consist only in the intellect's composition and division.

Obj. 2.   Besides, Isaac says in his work *De definitionibus* that truth is the equation of an object and an intellect.[19] But as the intellect that concerns judgments, can be equated to things, so can the intellect that concerns simple concepts—and also the senses sensibly perceiving things as they exist. Therefore, truth does not consist only in the intellect's composition and division.

On the contrary, the Philosopher says in the *Metaphysics* that neither in the intellect nor in objects is there truth about simple things and "what something is."[20]

I answer that truth, in its primary aspect, is in the intellect, as I have said.[21] Moreover, since everything is true insofar as it has the proper form of its own nature, the intellect, as knowing, is necessarily true insofar as it possesses the likeness of the object known, which likeness is the form of the intellect as the intellect knows the object. And we consequently define truth by the conformity of the intellect to the object. And hence to know that conformity is to know the truth.

But the senses in no way know their conformity to objects; sight, for example, although it possesses the likeness of a visible object, nonetheless, does not know the relation between the object seen and what sight apprehends about the object. Moreover, the intellect can know its conformity to an intelligible object, but it nonetheless does not apprehend the conformity insofar as it knows about something "what something is"; when, however, the intellect judges that something is disposed in the same way as the form of the object that it apprehends, the intellect then first knows and expresses something true. And it does this by composing and dividing, for the intellect in every proposition either adds a form that the predicate signifies, to what the subject signifies, or takes such a form away from what the subject signifies. And thus we rightly find that the senses are true about some things, or that the intellect is true by knowing "what something is," but not such that the intellect knows or expresses what is true. And it is likewise in the case of composite or simple expressions.

Truth, therefore, can indeed be in the senses, or in the intellect knowing "what something is," as in something true, but not as the object known is in the knower—which the term "true" implies, since the intellect's perfection consists in the true as known. And so, properly speaking, truth rests in the intellect composing and dividing but not in the senses or in the intellect knowing what something is.

Reply to the Objections.   And this explanation makes clear the solution to the objections.

Third Article

Are "True" and "Being" Convertible Terms?

I proceed in this way to the third article: it seems that "true" and "being" are not convertible terms.

Obj. 1.   What is true in the strict sense, is in the intellect, as I have said.[22] But being in the strict sense is in things. Therefore, "true" and "being" are not convertible terms.

Obj. 2.   What extends to being and nonbeing, is not convertible with "being." But the true extends to being and nonbeing, for it is true that what exists, exists, and that what does not exist, does not exist. Therefore, "true" and "being" are not convertible terms.

Obj. 3.   Things that are ordered by before and after, do not seem to be exchangeable. But the true seems to be prior to being, since we understand being only under the aspect of the true. Therefore, "true" and "being" do not seem to be convertible terms.

On the contrary, the Philosopher says in the *Metaphysics* that the order of things in existence and truth is identical.[23]

I answer that the true has a relation to knowledge in the same way that good has the nature of desirable. Everything, moreover, is capable of being known inasmuch as it possesses some existence. And for this reason, the *De anima* says that "the soul is somehow everything" by means of the senses and the intellect.[24] And thus as "good" is convertible with "being," so is "true." Nonetheless, however, as good adds the aspect of desirable to being, so also true adds a relation to an intellect.

Reply to Obj. 1.   There is truth in things and in the intellect, as I have said.[25] The true in things, however, is substantially convertible with "being," while the true in the intellect is convertible with "being" as something manifesting with something manifested. For this is the nature of truth, as I have said.[26]

And yet it could be said that being as well as truth exist in things and in the intellect, although the true chiefly exists in the intellect, and being chiefly exists in things. And the latter happens because the true and being differ conceptually.

Reply to Obj. 2.   Nonbeing in itself has nothing whereby it may be known, but we know nonbeing inasmuch as the intellect makes it knowable. And hence truth is grounded in being, inasmuch as nonbeing is a purely conceptual being, namely, one that the mind conceives.

Reply to Obj. 3.   We can understand in two ways the expression that we cannot apprehend being apart from the aspect of the true. In one way, we can understand the expression so that we apprehend being only if the aspect of truth results from the apprehension of being. And the expression is true in this way. In the other way, we could understand the expression in such a way that we could apprehend being only if we were to apprehend the aspect of truth. And this is false. But we cannot apprehend the true unless we apprehend the aspect of being, because being falls within the aspect of the true. And it is similarly the case if we should relate the intelligible to being. For we cannot understand being apart from being being intelligible, although we can nonetheless understand being apart from understanding its intelligibility. And likewise, being as understood is true, while we do not understand the true by understanding being.

Fourth Article

Is the Good Conceptually Prior to the True?

I proceed in this way to the fourth article: it seems that the good is conceptually prior to the true.

Obj. 1.   What is more general, is conceptually prior, as the *Physics* makes clear.[27] But the good is more general than the true, for the true is a certain kind of good, namely, the good of the intellect. Therefore, the good is conceptually prior to the true.

Obj. 2.   The good exists in things, but the true exists in the composition and division of the intellect, as I have said.[28] But what really exists, is prior to what exists in the intellect. Therefore, the good is conceptually prior to the true.

Obj. 3.   Truth is a certain kind of virtue, as the *Ethics* makes clear.[29] But virtue is included in the good, since virtue is a good quality of the mind, as Augustine says.[30] Therefore, the good is prior to the true.

On the contrary, what is in more things, is conceptually prior. But the true is in certain things in which the good is not, namely, mathematical objects. Therefore, the true is prior to the good.

I answer that, although "good" and "true" are convertible with "being" regarding an individually existing substance, they nonetheless differ conceptually. And the true, absolutely speaking, is accordingly prior to the good. And this is clear from two considerations. First, indeed, because the true is related more closely to being—which is first—than the good is. For the true without qualification and immediately regards existing itself, while the aspect of good results from existing, as somehow perfect, for it is thus desirable. Second, the true is prior to the good because knowledge by nature precedes appetite. And hence the true is conceptually prior to the good because the true regards knowledge, while the good regards appetite.

Reply to Obj. 1.   The will and the intellect mutually include one another, for the intellect understands the will, and the will wills the intellect to understand. Thus even things that belong to the intellect, are included in things related to the will's object, and vice versa. And hence, in the order of desirable objects, the good is disposed as something general, and the true is disposed as something particular, while it is the converse in the order of intelligible objects. Because the true is a certain kind of good, therefore, it follows that the good is prior in the order of desirable objects, but not that it is prior without qualification.

Reply to Obj. 2.   What first falls within the intellect, is accordingly conceptually prior. But the intellect apprehends being itself first of all, and apprehends secondly that it understands being, and apprehends thirdly that it desires being. And hence there is first the consideration of being, second the consideration of the true, third the consideration of the good, although the good is in things.

Reply to Obj. 3.   The virtue that we call "truth" is not truth in general but a certain kind of truth by which human beings reveal themselves in word and deed as they are. Moreover, we speak in a particular way of the "truth" of a life as human beings fulfill in their life the goal to which the divine intellect orders them, just as I have said that truth exists in other things.[31] And there is the "truth" of justice as human beings observe what is due to others

according to the legal order. And hence we should not go from these particular kinds of truth to truth in general.

Fifth Article

Is God Truth?

I proceed in this way to the fifth article: it seems that God is not truth.
Obj. 1. Truth consists in the intellect's composition and division. But there
is no composition or division in God. Therefore, truth does not exist in him.
Obj. 2. According to Augustine in his work *De vera religione*, truth is "a
likeness to its source."[32] But there is no likeness of God to a source. Therefore, truth does not exist in him.
Obj. 3. Whatever we predicate of God, we predicate of him as the first
cause of everything, as his existing causes every existing, and his goodness
causes every good. If truth should be in God, therefore, everything true will
be from God himself. But it is true that someone sins. Therefore, this truth
will be from God. And such a conclusion is evidently false.
    On the contrary, the Lord says: "I am the way, the truth, and the life."[33]
    I answer that, as I have said,[34] we find truth in the intellect as the intellect
apprehends things as they exist, and we find truth in an object as the object
has existing conformable to the intellect. But we find such in God in the
highest degree. For God's existing is not only conformed to his intellect but
is also his very understanding, and his understanding is the measure and
cause of every other existing and understanding, and God is his existing and
understanding. And hence it follows not only that there is truth in him, but
that he himself is the very truth that is highest and first.
Reply to Obj. 1. Although there is no composition or division in the divine
intellect, God nonetheless judges about everything and knows all judgments
by his simple understanding. And so there is truth in his intellect.
Reply to Obj. 2. The truth of our intellect consists in our intellect being
conformed to its source, namely, the things from which our intellect gets its
knowledge. There is also the truth of the things as they are conformed to
their source, namely, the divine intellect. But we cannot, properly speaking,
say the latter in the case of God's truth, except perchance as truth is
appropriated to the Son, who has a source. If we speak about the truth that
we predicate of God essentially, however, we can only understand that truth
if we convert an affirmative proposition into one that is negative, as when
we say that the Father is from himself because he is not from another. And
we can likewise call divine truth "a likeness of its source" inasmuch as his
existing is not unlike his intellect.
Reply to Obj. 3. Nonbeing and privations do not have truth of themselves

but by the intellect's conception. But every conception of our intellect is from God, and hence any truth there is in the statement, "It is true that this individual commits fornication," is entirely from God. But if one should argue, "Therefore, it is from God that this individual commits fornication," such reasoning is the fallacy of accident.[35]

Eighth Article

Is Truth Unalterable?

I proceed in this way to the eighth article: it seems that truth cannot be altered.

Obj. 1. Augustine says in his work *De libero arbitrio* that truth does not correspond to the mind, because truth would be just as variable as the mind is.[36]

Obj. 2. What remains after every change, is unchangeable; for example, prime matter does not come to be and cannot pass away, because it remains after every coming-to-be and every passing away.[37] But truth remains after every change, because it is true to say after every change that something exists or does not. Therefore, truth cannot vary.

Obj. 3. If the truth of a statement varies, it varies most of all when the object changes. But truth does not vary in this way. For, according to Anselm, truth is a certain correctness, inasmuch as something fulfills what is in the divine mind about the thing.[38] But the proposition "Socrates is sitting" gets from the divine mind the meaning that Socrates is sitting, and this is its meaning even when Socrates is not sitting. Therefore, the truth of a proposition in no way varies.

Obj. 4. Where the cause is the same, the effect is also the same. But the same thing causes the truth of these three propositions: "Socrates is sitting," "Socrates will sit," and "Socrates has sat." Therefore, the truth of these propositions is the same. But one or another of these things needs to be true. Therefore, the truth of these propositions abides without change. And by the same reasoning, so does the truth of any other proposition.

On the contrary, the Psalm says: "The sons of men belittle the truth."[39]

I answer that truth in the strict sense is in the intellect alone, while we call things true by the truth that is in some intellect, as I have said before.[40] And hence we need to consider the mutability of truth with respect to the intellect. And the intellect's truth, in fact, consists in this, that the intellect should have a conformity to the things it understands. And this conformity as well as any other likeness can indeed change in two ways, from a change of one or the other terminus. And hence, in one way, truth varies on the part of the intellect because someone takes a different opinion about something disposed in the same way; in the other way, truth varies if the thing changes while one's opinion remains the same. And either way, there is a change from what is true to what is false.

If, therefore, there should be an intellect in which there can be no change of opinion, or from whose grasp nothing can escape, the truth in that intellect cannot vary. But such is the divine intellect, as is clear from what I have said before.[41] And hence the truth of the divine intellect cannot vary, while the truth of our intellect can. Not that truth itself is subject to change but inasmuch as our intellect changes from truth to falsity, for we can in this way call the intellect's forms variable. But the truth of the divine intellect is the truth by which we call things of nature true, and this truth is altogether invariable.

Reply to Obj. 1.   Augustine is speaking about divine truth.

Reply to Obj. 2.   "True" and "being" are convertible terms. And hence, as being neither comes to be nor passes away intrinsically, but does so by chance, insofar as this or that particular being passes away or comes to be, as the *Physics* says,[42] so truth varies, not that no truth remains, but that the truth that existed previously, does not remain.

Reply to Obj. 3.   A proposition not only has truth as we say that other things have truth, inasmuch as things fulfill what the divine intellect has ordained about them, but we say that a proposition has truth in a certain special way, inasmuch as a proposition indicates the truth of the intellect. And this truth indeed consists in the conformity of the intellect to the thing. When that conformity is taken away, the truth of an opinion indeed changes, and consequently the truth of the proposition. Thus the proposition "Socrates is sitting" is true while Socrates is sitting, both by reason of the thing's truth, inasmuch as there is some sort of significative expression, and by reason of the truth of the meaning, inasmuch as the proposition signifies a true opinion. But when Socrates gets up, the first truth remains, while the second changes.

Reply to Obj. 4.   Socrates' sitting, which causes the truth of the proposition "Socrates is sitting," is not posited in the same way while Socrates sits, and after he has sat, and before he might sit. And hence the truth that Socrates' sitting causes, is posited in different ways, and the propositions about the present, past, and future variously signify his sitting. And hence it does not follow that the same truth should remain invariable, although one or another of the three propositions is true.

Notes

1. *Soliloquiorum* II, 5. PL 32:888–89.
2. Ibid.
3. Ibid.
4. Cf. Aristotle, *Metaphysics* III, 5, 6. 1009a6–1011b22.
5. Aristotle, *Posterior Analytics* I, 2. 72a29–30.

6. *Categories* 5. 4b8–10.
7. *Metaphysics* V, 4. 1027b25–29.
8. *De vera religione* 36. PL 34:151–52.
9. Cf. *De Trinitate* V, 14. PL 10:137.
10. *De vera religione 36. PL 34:151–52.*
11. *De veritate* 12. PL 158:480.
12. *Metaphysics*, tract. 8, chap. 6.
13. On the derivation of this citation, see St. Thomas Aquinas, *Summa theologiae*, ed. Pietro Caramello (Turin-Rome: Marietti, 1952), I, Q. 16, A. 2, note a, p. 571.
14. See n. 4, *supra*.
15. On univocal and equivocal causes, see Glossary, s.v. "cause."
16. See n. 6, *supra*.
17. I.e., in the intellect judging. Affirmative judgments compose, and negative judgments divide, the subject and the predicate.
18. *De anima* III, 6. 430b27–29.
19. Isaac ben Solomon Israel. On the derivation of the citation, see n. 13, *supra*.
20. *Metaphysics* V, 4. 1027b25–29.
21. Q. 16, A. 1.
22. Ibid.
23. *Metaphysics* Ia, 1. 993b30–31.
24. Aristotle, *De anima* III, 8. 431b21.
25. Q. 16, A. 1.
26. Ibid.
27. Aristotle, *Physics* I, 5. 188b30–189a10.
28. Q. 16, A. 2.
29. Aristotle, *Ethics* IV, 7. 1127a20–25.
30. Cf. *De libero arbitrio* II, 18. PL 32:1267–68.
31. Q. 16, A. 1.
32. *De vera religione* 36. PL 34:151–52.
33. Jn. 14:6.
34. Q. 16, A. 1.
35. The fallacy of accident is committed when one attempts to draw a particular conclusion from a general proposition without regard to necessary qualifications of the general proposition. God causes the truth of the proposition "This individual commits fornication" without causing the individual to commit fornication.
36. *De libero arbitrio* II, 12. PL 32:1259.
37. See Glossary, s.v. "matter."
38. *De veritate* 7. PL 158:475. Also 11. PL 158:480.
39. Ps. 12:2.
40. Q. 16, A. 1.
41. Q. 14, A. 15.
42. Aristotle, *Physics* I, 8. 191a34–b27.

ST I
Question 17
On Falsity

[This question is divided into four articles, three of which are included here.]

First Article

Is There Falsity in Things?

I proceed in this way to the first article: it seems that there is no falsity in things.

Obj. 1. Augustine says in his work *Soliloquiorum*: "If the true is what exists, one will conclude that the false is nowhere, whatever may be to the contrary."[1]

Obj. 2. We derive the word "false" from the verb "to deceive."[2] But things do not deceive, as Augustine says in his work *De vera religione*, "because they manifest only their own form."[3] Therefore, we do not find the false in things.

Obj. 3. We say that there is truth in things by relating them to the divine intellect, as I have said before.[4] But everything, insofar as it exists, imitates God. Therefore, everything is true, without falsity. And so nothing is false.

On the contrary, Augustine says in his work *De vera religione* that "every material substance is a true material substance but a false oneness," because it imitates oneness and is not oneness.[5] But everything imitates the divine goodness and falls short of it. Therefore, there is falsity in all things.

I answer that, since true and false are contraries, and contraries concern the same thing, we need to look first for falsity where we first find truth, that is, in the intellect. In things, moreover, there is neither truth nor falsity except in relation to the intellect. And we denote everything without qualification by what is intrinsically appropriate for it, while we denote everything only with qualification by what is by chance appropriate for it. Consequently, we could call things false without qualification by relation to the intellect on which they depend, to which they are intrinsically related, while we could

142

call them false only in one respect, in relation to another intellect, to which they are related by chance.

But things of nature depend on the divine intellect, just as man-made objects depend on a human intellect. Therefore, we call man-made objects false without qualification and as such insofar as they fall short of the form of a craft, and hence we say that a craftsman produces a false work when the work falls short of the workings of the craft. We cannot, however, thus find falsity in things that depend on God, by their relation to the divine intellect. This is so because whatever happens in things, comes by ordination of the divine intellect—except, per chance, in the case of self-determining efficient causes, in whose power it is to withdraw themselves from the ordination of the divine intellect, and the evil of wrongdoing consists in such withdrawal. And the Scriptures in this way call sins themselves "untruths" and "lies," as the Psalm says: "Why do you love vanity and seek after lying?"[6] Conversely, we likewise call virtuous activity "the truth of a life," insofar as such activity is subjected to the order of the divine intellect, as the Gospel of John says: "He who does the truth, comes to the light."[7]

But we call things of nature false, not without qualification but in one respect, by their relation to our intellect, to which they are related by accident. And this is so in two ways. In one way, by the nature of what is signified, as one may say that what speech or false understanding signifies or represents, is objectively false. And we can say that everything is false in this way regarding what does not belong to it, as we may say that a diameter is a false commensurable, as the Philosopher says in the *Metaphysics*,[8] and that "a tragedian is a false Hector," as Augustine says in his work *Soliloquiorum*.[9] Conversely, just so can we call everything true regarding what belongs to it.

In the second way, we can call things of nature false in a causal way. And so we call things false that by their nature cause false opinions about themselves. And because it is natural for us to judge about things by what appears outwardly, because our knowledge has its source from the senses, whose first and intrinsic objects are external accidents, so we say that things that in their external accidents have a likeness to other things, are false regarding those things, as, for example, that gall is false honey, and that tin is false silver. And Augustine accordingly says in his work *Soliloquiorum* that "we call false those things that we conceive to be like true things."[10] And the Philosopher says in the *Metaphysics* that we call false "anything that is by its nature disposed to appear either such as it is not, or what it is not."[11] And we call human beings false in this way insofar as they are enamoured of false opinions or expressions—although not because human beings can hypothesize false opinions or expressions, since we could thus call false even those who are wise and knowing, as the *Metaphysics* says.[12]

Reply to Obj. 1. We call things true that are related to the intellect as to what exists, and we call things false that are related to the intellect as to what does not exist. And hence "the true tragedian is a false Hector," as the *Soliloquiorum* says.[13] Therefore, as we find a kind of nonexistence in things that exist, so we find a certain aspect of falsity in such things.

Reply to Obj. 2. Things do not intrinsically deceive but by happenstance. For they provide an opportunity for falsity, because they bear a likeness to those things whose existence they do not possess.

Reply to Obj. 3. We do not call objects false by their relation to the divine intellect, which would be for them to be false without qualification, but by their relation to our intellect, which is for them to be false in one respect.

Reply to Obj. 4, which is posed in a contrary way.[14] A defective likeness or representation leads to an aspect of falsity only insofar as the likeness or representation lends an opportunity for false opinion. And hence we do not call something false wherever there is a likeness, but wherever there is such a likeness that by its nature causes a false opinion, not for everyone but for rather many persons.

Second Article

Is There Falsity in the Senses?

I proceed in this way to the second article: it seems that there is no falsity in the senses.

Obj. 1. Augustine says in his work *De vera religione*: "If all the bodily senses report in the way in which they are affected, I do not know what more we ought to require of them."[15] And so the senses seem not to deceive us. And so there is no falsity in the senses.

Obj. 2. The Philosopher says in the *Metaphysics* that "falsity does not belong to the senses but to the imagination."[16]

Obj. 3. There is no true or false in simple concepts but only in judgments. But composing and dividing do not belong to the senses. Therefore, there is no falsity in the senses.

On the contrary, Augustine says in his work *Soliloquiorum:* "An enticing likeness appears to deceive us in every sense perception."[17]

I answer that we should look for falsity in the senses only in the way in which truth is there. Truth, moreover, is not in the senses in such a way that the senses know truth, but insofar as they truly apprehend the sensible, as I have said before.[18] And this indeed happens because they apprehend things as the things exist. And hence falsity occurs in the senses because they apprehend or judge things otherwise than the things exist.

Thus, moreover, the senses are disposed to know things inasmuch as the senses possess the likeness of the things. But a thing's likeness is in the senses in three ways. In one way, primarily and intrinsically, as, for example, there is in vision the likeness of colors and of the other sensible things that it specially perceives. In the second way, the senses are intrinsically but not primarily disposed to know things, as, for example, there is in vision the likeness of shape and size and other sensible things that several senses can perceive. In the third way, the senses are neither primarily nor intrinsically but by accident disposed to know things, as, for example, there is in vision the likeness of a human being, not as such but insofar as this particular colored object happens to be a human being. And the senses do not have false knowledge about what they can peculiarly perceive, except by accident and in a rather few cases, namely, because the senses, due to an organic disorder, do not suitably receive the sensible form, as also other things acted upon, because of their indisposition, defectively receive the imprint of efficient causes. And so, because of an impairment of the tongue, sweet things seem bitter to the sick. But there can be a false judgment even in a well-disposed sense about the sensible things that several senses can perceive, and that are by chance, because no sense is related to those things directly but by accident, or by what results, as the sense is related to other things.

Reply to Obj. 1.   The senses are affected in their very act of perceiving. And hence, because the senses report in the way in which they are affected, we are consequently not deceived in the judgment whereby we affirm that we perceive something. But because the senses are sometimes affected otherwise than things exist, the senses at times may consequently report things to us otherwise than the things exist. And the senses thereby deceive us about things, not about the senses' very act of perceiving.

Reply to Obj. 2.   We say that falsity does not belong to the senses because the senses are not deceived about their proper objects. And hence another translation says more plainly that "the perception of what can be peculiarly perceived, is not false." But we attribute falsity to the imagination because imagination represents the likeness of something even when the thing is absent, and hence, when one directs one's attention to the likeness of something as if to the thing itself, falsity results from such an apprehension. And so too the Philosopher says in the *Metaphysics* that we call shadows and pictures and dreams false insofar as the things whose likeness they possess, do not exist.[19]

Reply to Obj. 3.   That argument shows that there is no falsity in the senses as in a faculty that knows the true and the false.

Third Article

Is There Falsity in the Intellect?

I proceed in this way to the third article: it seems that there is no falsity in the intellect.

Obj. 1. Augustine says in his work *Octoginta trium quaestionum*: "Everyone who is deceived, does not understand that in which he or she is deceived."[20] But we say that there is falsity in some knowledge insofar as such knowledge deceives us. Therefore, there is no falsity in the intellect.

Obj. 2.   The Philosopher says in the *De anima* that "the intellect is always correct."[21] Therefore, there is no falsity in the intellect.

On the contrary, the *De anima* says that "the true and the false exist where there is a composition of things understood."[22] But the composition of things understood exists in the intellect. Therefore, the true and the false exist in the intellect.

I answer that, as a thing has existence by its own form, so a cognitive power has knowledge by a likeness of the thing known. And hence, as things of nature do not fall short of the existing that belongs to them by their form, although they can lack some things that are accidental to, or resulting from, that form (as, e.g., human beings can fail to have two feet but not what it is to be human), so a cognitive power does not fail to know regarding the thing whose likeness informs the power, although a cognitive power can fail to know regarding something resulting from, or accidental to, that thing. For example, I have said that vision is not deceived about its proper sensible object but about sensible things that several senses can perceive—and these sensible things are consequently related to the proper object—and about things sensible by chance.[23]

Moreover, as the likeness of proper sensible objects directly gives form to the senses, so the likeness of a thing's essence gives form to the intellect. And hence the intellect is not deceived about what a thing is, as neither are the senses about what they can peculiarly perceive. But the intellect, in composing or dividing, can be deceived when it attributes to a thing whose essence it understands, something that does not result from, or is contrary to, that essence. For the intellect is thus disposed to judge about things of this kind as the senses are to judge about what several senses can perceive, or by accident. Nonetheless, there is this difference to be observed, about which I have spoken before concerning truth,[24] that there can be falsity in the intellect both because the intellect's knowledge is false, and because the intellect knows falsity, as it also knows truth, while no falsity as known exists in the senses, as I have said.[25]

But because the intellect's falsity as such concerns only the intellect's composition, there can by chance be falsity even in the activity of the intellect whereby the latter knows what something is, inasmuch as the intellect's composition involves such knowledge. And this can be in two ways. In one way, as the intellect applies the definition of one thing to another thing, as, for example, if the intellect should apply the definition of a circle to human beings. And hence the definition of one thing is false about another. In the second way, as the intellect joins to one another as parts of a definition things that cannot at the same time be associated, for the definition is thus false both with respect to a particular thing and intrinsically. For example, if the intellect should form such a definition as "Rational animals are four-footed," the intellect is false in so defining, because it falsely forms the composition "Some rational animal or other is four-footed." And the intellect consequently cannot be false in knowing simple essences, but either the intellect is true or it knows nothing at all.

Reply to Obj. 1. Because the essence of a thing is the intellect's proper object, we consequently say that we understand something when we trace it back to "what it is" and so judge about it, as happens in the case of demonstrations, in which there is no falsity. And we so understand the words of Augustine, that "everyone who is deceived, does not understand that in which he or she is deceived," but not in such a way that one is deceived in none of the intellect's activities.

Reply to Obj. 2. The intellect is always correct as it regards first principles, and it is not deceived about them for the same reason that it is not deceived about "what something is." For self-evident principles are ones that we immediately know when we understand their terms, because we posit the predicate in the definition of the subject.

Notes

1. *Soliloquiorum* II, 8. PL 32:892.
2. *"Falsum"* ("false") is the past participle of *"fallere"* ("to deceive").
3. *De vera religione* 36. PL 34:152.
4. Q. 16, A. 1.
5. *De vera religione* 34. PL 34:150.
6. Ps 4:2.
7. Jn. 3:21.
8. *Metaphysics* IV, 29. 1024b19–24.
9. *Soliloquiorum* II, 10. PL 32:893.
10. *Soliloquiorum* II, 6. PL 32:890.
11. *Metaphysics* IV, 29. 1024b19–24.
12. Aristotle, *Metaphysics* IV, 29. 1025a2–4.
13. *Soliloquiorum* II, 10. PL 32:893.
14. I.e., a hypothetical objection that everything is false.
15. *De vera religione* 33. PL 34:149.
16. *Metaphysics* III, 5. 1010b1–3.
17. *Soliloquiorum* II, 6. PL 32:890.
18. Q. 16, A. 2.
19. *Metaphysics* IV, 29. 1024b19–26.
20. *Octoginta trium quaestionum*, Q. 32, PL 40:22.
21. *De anima* III, 10. 433a28–29.
22. Aristotle, *De anima* III, 6. 430a27–28.
23. Q. 17, A. 2.
24. Q. 16, A. 2.
25. Q. 17, A. 2.

ST I
Question 18
On God's Life

[This question is divided into four articles, all of which are included here.]

First Article

Does Living Belong to All the Things of Nature?

I proceed in this way to the first article: it seems that living belongs to all the things of nature.

Obj. 1. The Philosopher says in the *Physics* that motion is "like a kind of life for everything that exists by nature."[1] But all the things of nature share motion. Therefore, all the things of nature share life.

Obj. 2. We say that plants live, inasmuch as they intrinsically possess a source of movement to increase and decrease. But locomotion is by nature more perfect than, and prior to, the movement of increase and decrease, as the *Physics* proves.[2] Therefore, since all the material substances of nature possess a source of locomotion, it seems that they live.

Obj. 3. The elements are among the less perfect material substances of nature.[3] But we attribute life to them; for example, we speak of "living waters." Therefore, much more do other material substances of nature have life.

On the contrary, Denis says in his *De divinis nominibus* that "plants possess life by the last echo of life,"[4] whereby we can understand that plants possess the lowest grade of life. But inorganic material substances are inferior to plants. Therefore, inorganic material substances do not have life.

I answer that we can understand to which things life belongs, and to which things life does not belong, by those that are evidently alive. And life evidently belongs to animals, for the *De plantis* says that "life in the case of animals is evident."[5] And hence we need to distinguish living things from nonliving things by that by which we call animals living things. Moreover, such is that in which life is first evident and last remains. Now, we say that animals first live when they begin to move themselves, and we judge that

148

animals live as long as such movement is evident in them. But we say that animals are dead, by want of life, when they no longer move themselves at all but are moved only by another. And thus it is clear that things that move themselves by any kind of motion, are living things in the proper sense. This is so whether we understand motion in the proper sense, as we call motion the actuality of something imperfect, that it, the actuality of something that has potentiality, or we understand motion in a general sense, as we call motion the actuality of something perfect, as, for example, we call understanding and sense perception movements, as the *De anima* says.[6] As a result, we in this way call living everything that stirs itself to movement or any activity, while we can only metaphorically call living those things that do not have a nature to do so.

Reply to Obj. 1. We can understand those words of the Philosopher either of the first motion, namely, that of heavenly bodies, or of motion generally. And either way, we call motion the life, as it were, of the material substances of nature metaphorically and not in the proper sense. For the movement of the heavens is in the universe of natural material substances like the movement of the heart in animals, which movement preserves the life of animals. Also, in like manner, every movement of nature is so related to the things of nature, by a certain metaphor of vital activity. And hence, were the corporeal universe a single animal, so that its movement would be from an intrinsic cause of motion, as certain thinkers have indeed held, motion would consequently be the life of every natural material substance.

Reply to Obj. 2. Motion does not belong to heavy and light material substances except as those substances are situated out of their natural disposition, as when they are out of their own position, for they are at rest when they are in their proper and natural position. But vital motion moves plants and other living things as they are situated in their natural disposition, not in their approaching, or receding from, that disposition; rather, living things recede from their natural disposition insofar as they recede from such movement.

And besides, an extrinsic cause of motion moves heavy and light material substances, either by causing them to come to be, which gives them form, or by removing obstacles to their coming-to-be, as the *Physics* says.[7] And so they do not move themselves, as living bodies do.

Reply to Obj. 3. We call waters living that have a continuous flow, for we call waters dead that are not connected to a continuously flowing source, such as the waters of cisterns and ponds. And we say this metaphorically, for living waters have a likeness to life inasmuch as they seem to move themselves. And yet they do not have the true nature of life, because they do not have this movement from themselves but from the cause that produces them, as happens in the case of the movement of other heavy and light material substances.

Second Article

Is Life a Certain Activity?

I proceed in this way to the second article: it seems that life is a certain activity.

Obj. 1. We distinguish something only by things that belong to its genus. But we distinguish living by certain activities, as the Philosopher makes clear in the *De anima*, and he distinguishes living by four activities, namely, nutrition, sense perception, locomotion, and understanding.[8] Therefore, life is a certain activity.

Obj. 2. We say that the active life differs from the contemplative life. But we distinguish those who are contemplative, from those who are active, only by certain activities. Therefore, life is a certain activity.

Obj. 3. Knowing God is a certain activity. But knowing God is life, as the Gospel of John makes clear: "Now, this is life eternal, that they know you, the only true God."[9] Therefore, life is certain activity.

On the contrary, the Philosopher says in the *De anima*: "For living things, living is existing."[10]

I answer that, as is clear from what I have said,[11] our intellect, which in the proper sense knows the essence of a thing as its own object, takes its knowledge from the senses, whose own objects are external accidents. And hence we come to know the essence of something from its external appearances. And because we give a name to something in the way in which we know it, as is clear from what I have said before,[12] so we often apply words by external characteristics to signify the essences of things. And hence we sometimes understand such words in a proper sense to denote the very essences of things, and we apply the words chiefly to signify the essences, but we sometimes understand words to mean the characteristics by which we apply the words, and we do so in a less proper sense. For example, we evidently apply the word "body" to signify a certain kind of substance, because we find three dimensions in such substances. And so we sometimes posit the word "body" to signify three dimensions, as we posit body as a species of quantity.

Thus do we also need to speak about life. For we take the word "life" from something external that is apparent about the reality, that is, self-movement. Nonetheless, we do not apply the word to signify this but to signify the substance to which, by its own nature, it belongs to move itself or to rouse itself somehow to activity. And living is accordingly nothing other than existing in such a nature, and life signifies this very thing, but abstractly, as the noun "running" means the verb "running" in the abstract. And hence "living" is not an accidental predicate but one that is substantial.

Nonetheless, we sometimes understand life less accurately to denote the vital activities from which we derive the word, as the Philosopher says in the *Ethics* that "living consists chiefly in sense perception or understanding."[13]

Reply to Obj. 1. The Philosopher there understands "living" to denote vital activities. Or we should say in a better way that we at times understand sense perception and understanding and such like to denote certain activities, while we at times understand them to denote the very existing of the beings that operate in this way. For example, the *Ethics* says that "the existing" of living beings "consists in sense perception or understanding,"[14] that is, having a nature capable of sense perception or understanding. And it is in this way that the Philosopher by those four activities distinguishes living. For there are four kinds of living things in things here below. And certain of these living things have a nature capable only of nutrition and its consequences, that is, growth and reproduction. Others are further capable of sense perception, as is evident in the case of such immobile animals as oysters. Others, however, in addition to the above powers, have the further capacity of locomotion, such perfect animals as quadrupeds and birds and the like. Still others have the further capacity to understand, as human beings do.

Reply to Obj. 2. We call activities vital whose sources are within the things that are active, such that those things bring themselves to such activities. But there happen to be in human beings not only sources from nature of certain actions, such as powers from nature, but also certain added sources, such as the characteristic dispositions that incline human beings toward certain kinds of activities in a natural way, as it were, and cause those activities to be pleasurable. And thus, by a certain metaphor, as it were, we call activity that is pleasurable to a human being, and to which a human being is inclined, and in which a human being is engaged, and to which a human being arranges his or her life, the life of that human being. And hence we say that some human beings live a dissolute life, others a worthy life. And we distinguish the contemplative life from the active life in this way. And we also in this way call knowing God eternal life.

Reply to Obj. 3. And the foregoing makes clear the solution to the third objection.

Third Article

Is Life Appropriate for God?

I proceed in this way to the third article: it seems that life is not appropriate for God.

Obj. 1. We call some things living as they move themselves, as I have said.[15] But being moved does not belong to God. Therefore, neither does life.

Obj. 2.   We understand a source of life in every living thing, and hence the *De anima* says that "the soul is the cause and source of a living body."[16] But God does not have a source. Therefore, life does not belong to him.

Obj. 3.   The source of life in the living things in our world is a soul capable of nutrition, growth, and reproduction. But such a soul exists only in corporeal beings. Therefore, life does not belong to incorporeal beings.

On the contrary, the Psalm says: "My heart and my flesh have rejoiced in the living God."[17]

I answer that life in the most proper sense exists in God. And for evidence of this, we need to consider that, when we call some things living insofar as they act by themselves and not as if moved by other beings, we find life more perfectly in something the more perfectly we find that self-movement belongs to it. Moreover, we find three things in order in the causes of motion and the things they move. For, first, an end moves an efficient cause, and the chief efficient cause acts by its own form. And the chief cause sometimes does so through an instrumental cause, one that does not act by the power of its own form but by the form of the chief efficient cause, and only the execution of the action belongs to the instrumental cause.

We thus find certain things that move themselves, not with regard to a form or end that is by nature inherent in them, but only with regard to executing movement; rather, nature determines for them the form by which they act, and the end for the sake of which they act. And such things are plants, which move themselves to increase and decrease by the form implanted in them by nature.

But certain things further move themselves, not only with regard to executing motion, but also with regard to the form that is the source of motion, which form they acquire by themselves. And such things are animals, the source of whose motion is a form that is not implanted in them by nature but received through the senses. And hence the more perfect the senses they possess, the more perfectly do they move themselves. For example, things that possess only the sense of touch, such as oysters, move themselves only by movements of expansion and contraction, and they hardly surpass the movements of plants. Things that have perfect powers of sense perception, however, move themselves over a distance by forward motion, not only to know objects that are connected to them or touch them, but also to know objects separated from them.

Although such animals receive by the senses the forms that are the sources of their movements, they nonetheless do not intrinsically prescribe for themselves the end of their activity or movement, but nature has implanted this end in them. And a sensibly apprehended form moves them by an impulse of nature to do something. And hence, superior to such animals are those things that move themselves even with regard to ends that they prescribe for themselves. And this indeed occurs only by means of reason and intellect, to which belong knowing the relation between an end and the means thereto, and ordering the one to the other. And hence the more perfect way of life belongs to those things that have intellect, for they move themselves more perfectly. And this is indicated by the fact that, in one and the same human being, the power of intellection moves the sense powers, and the sense powers at the intellect's command move the bodily organs, and the bodily organs execute the movements. So also in skills, we see that the skill to which the use of ships belongs, namely, the skill of piloting, instructs the skill of designing ships, and the latter skill instructs the skill that orders only the execution of the design, in arranging the building materials.

But although our intellect moves itself to some things, nature nonetheless prescribes some things for the intellect, for example, the first principles, about which the intellect cannot be otherwise disposed, and our final end, which the intellect cannot not will. And hence, although it moves itself with respect to some things, it nonetheless needs to be moved by something else with respect to other things. Thus the thing whose own nature is its very understanding, and for whom another thing does not determine what it by nature possesses, has the highest degree of life. And such a thing is God. And hence there is life in God in the highest degree. And so the Philosopher in the *Metaphysics*, after showing that God is a being with intelligence, concludes that God possesses the most perfect and everlasting life, because his intellect is most perfect and always actual.[18]

Reply to Obj. 1. As the *Metaphysics* says,[19] actions are of two kinds: one kind that passes into external matter, such actions as heating or sawing; the other, a kind that remains in the active cause, such actions as understanding, sense perception, and willing. But there is this difference between them, that the first kind of action perfects the object moved, not the cause that moves the object, while the second kind of action perfects the cause that acts. And hence, because motion is the actuality of a moveable object, we call the second kind of action, as the actuality of the cause that acts, the cause's motion by the following analogy: such action is the cause's actuality as motion is the actuality of a moveable object. Granted that motion is the actuality of something imperfect, that is, something that has potentiality, the second kind of action, however, is the actuality of something perfect, that is, something that has actuality, as the *De anima* says.[20] Therefore, in the way in which understanding is motion, we say that what understands itself, moves itself. And Plato as well held that God moves himself in this way, not in the way in which motion is the actuality of something imperfect.[21]

Reply to Obj. 2. As God is his very existing and understanding, so is he his life. And consequently, he lives in such a way that he has no source of life.

Reply to Obj. 3. Life in things here below is received in a nature that can pass away, a nature that needs both generation to preserve the species, and nutrition to conserve the individual. And consequently, we do not find life here below apart from a soul capable of nutrition, growth, and reproduction. But this has no place in the case of things that cannot pass away.

Fourth Article

Are All Things Life in God?

I proceed in this way to the fourth article: it seems that some things are not life in God.

Obj. 1. The Acts of the Apostles says: "We live, move, and exist in him."[22] But some things in God are not movement. Therefore, some things in him are not life.

Obj. 2. Everything is in God as its first exemplar. But likenesses ought to be conformed to their model. Therefore, since some things in themselves are not living beings, it seems that some things in God are not life.

Obj. 3. A living substance is better than any nonliving substance, as Augustine says in his *De vera religione*.[23] Therefore, if things that in themselves are not living beings, in God are life, it seems that things more truly exist in God than in themselves. And yet this seems to be false, since things in themselves are actual but in God are potential.

Obj. 4. As God knows things that are good, and things that temporally come to be, so God knows things that are evil, and things that he can make but never does. Therefore, if all things are life in God, inasmuch as he knows them, it seems that even things that are evil, and things that he never makes, are life in God inasmuch as he knows them. And this seems to be inappropriate.

On the contrary, the Gospel of John says: "What was made, was life in him."[24] But everything except God was made. Therefore, all things are life in him.

I answer, as I have said, that God's life is his understanding.[25] But in God, his intellect, and what he understands, and his very understanding are identical. And hence everything that is in God as something understood, is his very living or his life. And hence, since everything made by God exists in him as something understood, everything in him is consequently his divine life itself.

Reply to Obj. 1. We say in two ways that creatures exist in God. In one way, inasmuch as God's power includes and preserves them, as, for example, we say that things in our power exist in us. And we thus say that creatures exist in God even as they exist in their own natures. And we need to understand in this way the words of the Apostle when he says, "We live, move, and exist in him," since God causes our living and our existing and our movement. In the second way, we say that things exist in God as a knowing subject. And thus they exist in God by their special exemplars, which are nothing other in God than his essence. And hence things, as they thus exist in God, are the divine essence. And because the divine essence is life but not movement, so it is that things, in this way of speaking, in God are life but not movement.

Reply to Obj. 2.   Likenesses need to be conformed to their model by way of form but not by way of existing. For a form sometimes has different kinds of existing in the exemplar and a likeness. For example, the form of house in the mind of its builder has an immaterial and intelligible existence, but the form in the house that exists outside the soul, has a material and sensibly perceptible existence. And hence even the natures of things that are not in themselves living, are life in God's mind, because they have divine existence in his mind.

Reply to Obj. 3.   If matter were not to belong to the essence of the things of nature, but only form were to, the things of nature would in every respect more truly exist in God's mind by his ideas than they would exist in themselves. Consequently, Plato also held that the separate human being is the true human being, while the material human being is human by participation.[26] But because matter belongs to the essence of things of nature, we need to say that those things, absolutely speaking, have truer existence in God's mind than they have in themselves, because they have uncreated existence in his mind, while they have created existence in themselves. On the other hand, they more truly have their particular existence, for example, as a human being or a horse, in their own nature than in God's mind, because material existence, which things do not have in his mind, belongs to the true reality of being human. Similarly, a house has a more excellent existence in the mind of its builder than it has in matter. But we nonetheless call the house in matter truer than the house in the mind of the builder, because the material house is actual, while the house in the builder's mind is potential.

Reply to Obj. 4.   Although things that are evil, exist in God's knowing, inasmuch as they are included in his knowledge, yet they are not in him as created or preserved by him, nor as having exemplars in him. For God knows them by exemplars of things that are good. And hence we cannot say that things that are evil, are life in God. But we can say that things that never exist, are life in God, insofar as living denotes only understanding, inasmuch as God understands them, but not insofar as life implies a source of activity.

Notes

1. *Physics* VIII, 1. 250b11–13.
2. Aristotle, *Physics* VIII, 7. 260a26–b29.
3. Elements have no mixture of any other material substance. The four elements of ancient and medieval cosmology were earth, water, air, and fire.
4. *De divinis nominibus* 6. PG 3:856.
5. Aristotle, *De plantis* I, 1. 815a10–11.
6. Aristotle, *De anima* III, 4. 429b22–430a9.
7. Aristotle, *Physics* VIII, 4. 255b31–256a3.
8. *De anima* II, 2. 413a20–25.

9. Jn. 17:3.
10. *De anima* II, 4. 415b13.
11. Q. 17, AA. 1, 3.
12. Q. 13, A. 1.
13. *Ethics* IX, 9. 1170a16–19.
14. Aristotle, *Ethics* IX, 9. 1170a30–b1.
15. Q. 18, AA. 1, 2.
16. Aristotle, *De anima* II, 4. 415b13–14.
17. Ps. 84:2.
18. *Metaphysics* XI, 7. 1072b26–30.
19. Aristotle, *Metaphysics* VIII, 8. 1050a23–b2.
20. Aristotle, *De anima* III, 7. 431a6–7.
21. *Phaedrus* 24. 245C–E.
22. Acts 17:28.
23. *De vera religione* 29. PL 34:145.
24. Jn. 1:3–4. St. Thomas's punctuation differs from that of the Vulgate.
25. Q. 18, A. 3.
26. *Phaedo* 49. 100B–101E.

ST I
Question 19
On God's Will

[This question is divided into twelve articles, ten of which are included here.]

First Article

Is There a Will in God?

I proceed in this way to the first article: it seems that there is no will in God.
Obj. 1. The object of the will is an end and a good. But we are not to attribute any end to God. Therefore, there is no will in God.
Obj. 2. Will is one kind of appetite. But since appetites are ordered to things not possessed, they denote imperfection, and imperfection does not belong to God. Therefore, there is no will in God.
Obj. 3. The will is a cause of motion that is moved, as the Philosopher says in the *De anima*.[1] But God is the first cause of motion, one that cannot be moved, as the *Physics* proves.[2] Therefore, there is no will in God.

On the contrary, the Apostle in the Letter to the Romans urges us to "give proof of what is the will of God."[3]

I answer that there is a will in God, just as there is an intellect in him, for the will results from the intellect. For, as things of nature have actual existing by their form, so the intellect is actually understanding by its intelligible form. Moreover, everything has such a disposition toward its natural form that it strives for the form when it does not possess the form, and it is at rest when it possesses the form. And it is the same in the case of every natural perfection, which is the good of nature. And we call this disposition toward good in beings that lack knowledge, an appetite of nature. And so also an intellectual nature has a like disposition toward the good apprehended by an intelligible form, namely, that the intellect be at rest in such a good when possessed, and seek after such a good when not possessed. And both resting in the good possessed and seeking after the good not possessed belong to the will. And hence there is a will in everything that has an intellect, just as there are animal appetites in everything that has senses. And so there needs to be a will in God, since there is an intellect in him. And as his understanding is his existing, his willing is also.

Reply to Obj. 1. Although only God is his end, he himself is nonetheless the end with respect to everything that he makes. And he is such by his essence, since he is good by his essence, as I have shown before,[4] for an end has the nature of good.

Reply to Obj. 2. The will in us belongs to the appetitive part of our soul. And although we denote the will by desiring, the will nonetheless not only has such actuality as to seek after what it does not possess, but also such actuality as to love what it possesses, and to take delight in the same. And we posit a will in God in this way, a will that always possesses the good that is its object, since it does not essentially differ from that good, as I have said.[5]

Reply to Obj. 3. The will whose chief object is a good outside the will, needs to be moved by another. But the object of God's will is his own goodness, which is his essence. And hence, since God's will is his essence, his will is not moved by anything other than himself, to speak in the way we call understanding and willing, motions. And Plato in this way said that the first cause of motion moves itself.[6]

Second Article

Does God Will Things Other than Himself?

I proceed in this way to the second article: it seems that God wills nothing other than himself.

Obj. 1. God's willing is his existing. But he is only himself. Therefore, he wills only himself.

Obj. 2. A willed object moves the will, as a desirable object moves any appetite, as the *De anima* says.[7] Therefore, if God should will anything other than himself, something else will move his will, and this is impossible.

Obj. 3. No will for which some willed object suffices, seeks anything beyond that object. But God's goodness suffices for him, and it satiates his will. Therefore, God wills nothing other than himself.

Obj. 4. There are as many acts of the will as there are objects willed. Therefore, if God should will things other than himself, the acts of his will would consequently be many, and, therefore, his existing, which is his willing. But this is impossible. Therefore, he wills nothing other than himself.

On the contrary, the Apostle says in his First Letter to the Thessalonians: "This is the will of God, your sanctification."[8]

I answer that God wills not only himself but things other than himself. This is evident by the comparison previously introduced.[9] For things of nature not only have an inclination from nature with respect to their own good, to acquire that good when they do not possess it, and to be at rest in it when they do possess it, but also to pour their own good into other things as much as possible. And hence we see that every efficient cause, inasmuch as it is actual and perfect, produces something like itself. And so also does it belong to the nature of the will, that it, as much as possible, communicate to others the good that it possesses. And this especially belongs to the divine will, from which every perfection is derived by a certain likeness. And hence, if the things of nature, insofar as they are perfect, communicate their good to other things, much more does it belong to the divine will, as much as possible, to communicate its good to other beings by likeness. God thus wills both himself and other things to exist. But he wills himself as the end, while he wills other things as means to that end, inasmuch as it befits his goodness that other things also share in his goodness.

Reply to Obj. 1. Although God's willing is really his existing, the two nonetheless differ conceptually by the different ways that we understand and signify them, as is clear from what I have said before.[10] For when I say that God exists, I do not imply a relationship to anything, as I do when I say that God wills. And so, although God is nothing other than himself, he nonetheless wills something other than himself.

Reply to Obj. 2. In things that we will because of an end, the whole reason why we are moved, is the end, and this is what moves our will. And this is most evident in the case of things that we will only for the sake of an end. For example, those who will to consume a bitter potion, will only their health when they do so, and this alone is what moves their will. But it is otherwise in the case of those who consume a sweet potion, which one can will not only for the sake of health but also for its own sake. And hence, although God wills things other than himself only for the sake of the end that is his goodness, as I have said,[11] it does not follow that anything other than his goodness moves his will. And so, as he understands things other than himself by understanding his own essence, so he wills things other than himself by willing his own goodness.

Reply to Obj. 3. It does not follow that, because God's goodness suffices for his will, he wills nothing else, but it does follow that he wills nothing else except by reason of his goodness. Similarly also, God's intellect, although complete because it knows his essence, nonetheless knows other things in that essence.

Reply to Obj. 4. As God's understanding is one, because he sees many things in only one thing, so God's willing is one and uncomposed, because he wills many things by only one thing, which is his goodness.

Third Article

Does God Necessarily Will Everything That He Wills?

I proceed in this way to the third article: it seems that God necessarily wills everything that he wills.

Obj. 1. Everything eternal is necessary. But God eternally wills everything that he wills, for his will would otherwise be variable. Therefore, he necessarily wills everything that he wills.

Obj. 2. God wills things other than himself inasmuch as he wills his own goodness. But God necessarily wills his goodness. Therefore, he necessarily wills things other than himself.

Obj. 3. Everything that belongs to God by nature, is necessary, because God is intrinsically necessary and the source of every necessity, as I have shown before.[12] But it belongs to him by nature that he will everything that he wills, because nothing besides his nature can exist in him, as the *Metaphysics* says.[13] Therefore, he necessarily wills everything that he wills.

Obj. 4. To say that something need not be, is equivalent to saying that it is possible for it not to be. Therefore, if it is not necessary that God will something that he wills, it is possible that he not will it, and it is possible that he will what he does not will. Therefore, his will is contingent with respect to either. And so his will is imperfect, because everything contingent is imperfect and variable.

Obj. 5. No action eventuates from what is disposed to each of several things unless something else inclines it toward one of them, as the Commentator on the *Physics* says.[14] Therefore, if God's will is disposed toward each of several things, something else consequently determines it to an effect. And so God's will has a prior cause.

Obj. 6. God necessarily knows everything that he knows. But as God's knowing is his essence, so is his will. Therefore, God necessarily wills everything that he wills.

On the contrary, the Apostle says in his Letter to the Ephesians: God "does everything according to the counsel of his will."[15] But we do not will necessarily what we do by the counsel of the will. Therefore, God does not will necessarily everything that he wills.

I answer that we call something necessary in two ways, namely, absolutely and hypothetically. We judge something absolutely necessary by the relationship of the terms, as when the predicate term is contained in the definition of the subject term (e.g., human beings are necessarily animals), or when the subject term belongs essentially to the predicate term (e.g., numbers are necessarily even or odd). But it is not thus necessary that Socrates be sitting. And hence the latter is not absolutely necessary, but we can call it hypothetically necessary, because, if Socrates happens to be sitting, it is necessarily the case that he is sitting as long as he does so.

With respect to what God wills, therefore, we need to consider that it is absolutely necessary that God will something, but this is not true about everything that he wills. For God's will has a necessary relationship to his goodness, which is his will's proper object. And hence God necessarily wills that his goodness exist, just as our will necessarily wills our happiness. Similarly, too, every other power has a necessary disposition toward its peculiar and chief object, such as the disposition the power of sight has toward color, because it belongs to a power's nature to tend toward such an object.

But God wills things other than himself inasmuch as they are related to his goodness as their end. Moreover, when we will an end, we do not necessarily will things that are means to that end unless they be such that the end cannot be attained without them; for example, we will to take food when we wish to preserve our life, and we will to take a ship when we wish to cross a sea. We do not in this way, however, necessarily will means not required to attain an end, for example, a horse to travel by land, since we can travel by land without a horse. And the reasoning is the same in the case of other things. And hence, since God's goodness is perfect and can exist without other things, because no perfection accrues to him from anything else, it is consequently not absolutely necessary that he will things other than himself. And yet it is hypothetically necessary that he do so. For, if he should will something, he cannot not will it, because his will cannot vary.

Reply to Obj. 1.   Because God eternally wills something, it does not follow that it is necessary for him to will it, except hypothetically.

Reply to Obj. 2.   Although God necessarily wills his goodness, yet he does not necessarily will the things that he wills because of his goodness, for his goodness can exist without other things.

Reply to Obj. 3.   It does not belong to God by nature to will any of the other things that he does not will necessarily. And yet such willing is not unnatural to him or contrary to nature; rather, it is freely willed.

Reply to Obj. 4.   A necessary cause sometimes does not have a necessary disposition to an effect, and this is due to something lacking in the effect and not to something lacking in the cause. For example, the sun's power has a contingent disposition to produce some contingent results on earth, not because of a deficiency in the sun's power, but because of a deficiency in the effect that results contingently from the cause. And likewise, God happens not to will necessarily some of the things that he wills, not from any deficiency in his will, but from a deficiency belonging essentially to the object willed, namely, because the object is of such a kind that the perfect goodness of God can exist without the object. And this deficiency indeed accompanies every created good.

Reply to Obj. 5.   Something external needs to determine an intrinsically contingent cause to an effect. But the divine will, which intrinsically has necessity, determines itself to a willed object to which it does not have a necessary disposition.

Reply to Obj. 6.   As God's existing is intrinsically necessary, so also are his willing and knowing. But God's knowing has a necessary relationship to the objects he knows, while God's willing does not have such a relationship to the objects he wills. And this is so because knowledge concerns things as they exist in the knower, while the will is related to things as they exist in themselves. Thus, since all other things have a necessary existence as they exist in God, while they have no absolute necessity to be intrinsically necessary as they exist in themselves, it follows that God necessarily knows everything that he knows, but he does not will necessarily everything that he wills.

Fourth Article

Does God's Will Cause Things?

I proceed to the fourth article in this way: it seems that God's will does not cause things.

Obj. 1.   Denis says in his *De divinis nominibus*: "As our sun, not reasoning or choosing but by its very existing, enlightens everything to share its powerful light, so also the divine good by its very essence emits rays of its goodness to everything that exists."[16] But everything that acts by will, acts by reasoning and choosing. Therefore, God's will does not cause things.

Obj. 2.   What is by its essence in any order, is first in that order; for example, what is fire by its essence, is first in the order of burning material. But God is the first efficient cause. Therefore, he is an efficient cause by his essence, that is, his nature. Therefore, he causes by his nature and not by his will. Therefore, God's will does not cause things.

Obj. 3.   Everything that causes something because the cause is of such a kind, causes by nature and not by will. For example, fire causes heat because fire is hot, but a builder causes a house because he wills to produce it. But Augustine says in his *De doctrina Christiana* that "we exist because God is good."[17] Therefore, God causes things by his nature and not by his will.

Obj. 4.   There is only one cause of one effect. But the cause of created things is God's knowledge, as I have said before.[18] Therefore, we ought not to posit God's will as a cause of things.

On the contrary, the Book of Wisdom says: "How could anything perdure, were you not to have willed it"?[19]

I answer that we need to say that God's will causes things, and that he acts by his will, not by a necessity of nature, as some thinkers have thought. And we can show this in three ways. First, indeed, by the very order of efficient causes. For, since both intellect and nature act for the sake of an end, as the *Physics* proves,[20] a higher intellect needs to predetermine the end, and the means necessary to the end, for causes that act by nature; for example, an archer predetermines the target and fixed path of an arrow. And hence a cause that acts by means of intellect and will, necessarily precedes a cause that acts by nature. And hence, since God is first in the order of efficient causes, he needs to cause by means of intellect and will.

Second, that God acts by his will, we can show from the nature of a natural efficient cause, to which cause it belongs to produce one kind of effect, since nature, unless hindered, causes in one and the same way. And this is so because the cause acts insofar as it is of such a kind, and hence causes only such an effect as long as the cause is of such a kind. For everything that acts by nature, has limited existing. Therefore, since God's existing is not limited but includes in itself the whole perfection of existing, he cannot act by a necessity of nature unless he were by chance to cause something boundless and unlimited in existing. And this is impossible, as is clear from what I have said before.[21] Therefore, he does not cause by a necessity of nature, but limited effects come from the unlimited perfection of himself as his will and intellect determine.

Third, we can show that God acts by his will by the relationship of effects to causes. For effects come from an efficient cause in the way in which they pre-exist in it, because every efficient cause produces an effect like itself. Moreover, effects pre-exist in their cause in the manner of the cause. And hence, since God's existing is his very understanding, effects pre-exist in him in an intelligible way. And so they also come from him in the same way. And so, consequently, they come from him by means of his will, for his inclination to produce what his intellect has conceived, belongs to his will. Therefore, God's will causes things.

Reply to Obj. 1. By these words, Denis does not intend to exclude choice by God absolutely but in one respect, namely, inasmuch as God communicates his goodness not only to certain things but to all of them, as choice implies a certain differentiation.

Reply to Obj. 2. Because God's essence is his understanding and willing, it follows from the fact that he causes by his essence that he causes by way of his intellect and will.

Reply to Obj. 3. Good is the object of the will. Therefore, Augustine so says, "We exist because God is good," inasmuch as his goodness is the reason why he wills everything else, as I have said before.[22]

Reply to Obj. 4. Even in us, the knowledge that directs an action, the knowledge whereby the knower conceives the form of a work, and the will that commands the action, cause one and the same effect. The will causes the effect because only the will determines that the form, as it exists in the intellect alone, should or should not actually exist. And hence the theoretical intellect settles nothing about action. But powers cause effects by carrying out the will's choice, since a power denotes the immediate source of action. And all these things are one in God.

Fifth Article

Are We to Ascribe Any Cause to God's Willing?

I proceed in this way to the fifth article: it seems that we are to ascribe a cause to God's willing.

Obj. 1. Augustine says in his work *Octoginta trium quaestionum*: "Who would dare to say that God has not made everything according to reason?"[23] But for an efficient cause that freely wills, the reason for its acting is also the cause of its willing the action. Therefore, God's willing has a cause.

Obj. 2. In things that are made by one who wills something due to no cause, we need ascribe no other cause than the will of the one who wills them. But God's will causes everything, as I have shown.[24] Therefore, if there is no cause of his willing, we will not need to seek in all the things of nature a cause other than his will. And so all theoretical ways of knowing, which attempt to ascribe the causes of particular effects, would be superfluous. And this seems inappropriate. Therefore, we are to ascribe a cause to God's willing.

Obj. 3. What is made by one who does not will on account of any cause, depends only on that person's absolute will. Therefore, if God's willing should have no cause, it follows that everything that he makes, depends only on his absolute will and has no other cause. And this is inappropriate.

On the contrary, Augustine says in his work *Octoginta trium quaestionum*: "Every efficient cause is greater than its effect. But nothing is greater than the will of God. Therefore, we ought not to look for a cause of his willing."[25]

I answer that God's willing in no way has a cause. And for evidence of this, we need to consider that, since willing follows understanding, causing one who wills, to will, and causing one who understands, to understand, happen in the same way. And in the case of intellect, when it understands principle and conclusion separately, understanding the principle causes knowledge of the conclusion. But if the intellect were to perceive a conclusion in the principle itself, grasping both principle and conclusion at one and the same glance, understanding the principle would not cause the intellect's knowledge of the conclusion, because the same thing does not cause itself. And yet, the intellect would understand that the principle causes the conclusion.

It is likewise on the part of the will, and ends are related to means in the case of the will in the same way that principles are related to conclusions in the case of the intellect. And hence, if one should will an end in one act and a means to the end in another act, willing the end will cause willing the means. But if one should will an end and a means to the end in a single act, such could not be the case, because the same thing does not cause itself. And yet it will be true to say that one wills to ordain the means to the end.

Moreover, as God in one act understands everything in his essence, so he in one act wills everything in his goodness. And hence, as God's understanding causes does not cause his understanding effects, but he understands effects in their causes, so his willing ends does not cause his willing means to ends, but he wills that means be ordained to ends. Therefore, he wills that one thing exist because of something else, but he does not will the one because of the other.

Reply to Obj. 1. God's will is rational, not that anything should cause his willing, but inasmuch as he wills that one thing exist because of something else.

Reply to Obj. 2. Since God wills effects to be such that they come from fixed causes in order to preserve an order among things, it is not superfluous to look for other causes even in addition to his will. But it would be superfluous if we were to look for other causes as first causes and causes independent of God's will. And so Augustine says in his *De Trinitate*: "It also pleased the vanity of philosophers to attribute contingent effects to still other contingent causes, since they were altogether unable to perceive a cause superior to all others, that is, the will of God."[26]

Reply to Obj. 3. Since God wills that effects exist because of causes, every effect that presupposes some other effect, does not depend only on the will of God but on something else. But the first effects depend on his will alone. This is as if we should say that God willed human beings to have hands in order that the latter might serve the intellect by performing various actions, and he willed human beings to have an intellect in order that they be human, and he willed human beings to be human in order that they might enjoy himself or complete the universe. And we indeed cannot trace these back to further created ends. And hence such effects depend only on the absolute will of God, but other effects depend on the disposition of other causes as well.

Sixth Article

Is God's Will Always Fulfilled?

I proceed in this way to the sixth article: it seems that God's will is not always fulfilled.

Obj. 1. The Apostle says in the First Letter to Timothy that God "wills that every human being be saved and come to recognition of the truth."[27] But this does not turn out to be so. Therefore, God's will is not always fulfilled.

Obj. 2. As knowledge is related to the true, so is the will to the good. But God knows everything true. Therefore, he wills everything good. But not every good comes to be, for many good things can come to be that do not. Therefore, God's will is not always fulfilled.

Obj. 3. Although God's will is the first cause, it does not exclude intermediate causes, as I have said.[28] But deficiencies of secondary causes can prevent the effect of a primary cause; for example, a defective tibia prevents the effect of the power of locomotion. Therefore, the deficiency of secondary causes can also prevent the effect of God's will. Therefore, his will is not always fulfilled.

On the contrary, the Psalm says: "God has accomplished everything whatsoever that he willed."[29]

I answer that God's will is necessarily always fulfilled. And for evidence of this, we need to consider that, since an effect is conformed to an efficient cause by its form, there is the same reckoning in the case of efficient causes that there is in the case of formal causes. But, we reckon in the case of forms that things can fall short of a particular form but not at all of the universal form; for example, something can be nonhuman or nonliving, but it cannot be nonbeing. And so the same also needs to happen in the case of efficient causes. For something can happen outside the order of a particular efficient cause but not outside the order of the universal cause, in which all particular causes are included. This is so because, if a particular cause fails of its effect, this is due to hindrance by another particular cause, which cause is included in the order of the universal cause. And hence in no way can an effect depart from the order of the universal cause. And this is also evident in the case of corporeal things. For example, a star can be prevented from bringing about its effect, but every effect that results in corporeal things because of hindrance by a bodily cause, needs to be traced through some intermediate causes back to the universal power of the heavenly bodies that are first.

Therefore, since God's will is the universal cause of everything, his will cannot not achieve its effect. And hence what seems to recede from the divine will in one order, slips back under the divine will in another order; for example, the sinner, who retreats from the divine will by sinning, insofar as this lies within the sinner's power, falls under the order of God's will when God's justice punishes the sinner.

Reply to Obj. 1. We can in three ways understand the words of the Apostle, that God "wills that every human being be saved," etc. In one way, that its distribution be adapted in this sense, "God wills everyone of the saved to be saved," "not because there is no human being whom he would not wish to be saved, but because none is saved whom he would not wish to be saved," as Augustine says.[30]

Second, we can understand the words of the Apostle such that the distribution regards types of individuals and not individuals of the types, in this sense, "God wills that some human beings of every condition be saved, men and women, Jews and Gentiles, little and big, but not everyone of every condition."

Third, following Damascene, we can understand the words of the Apostle to be about God's antecedent will, not about his consequent will.[31] And we indeed do not understand this distinction to be on the part of the divine will itself, in which there is nothing prior or subsequent, but on the part of the things that God wills. And to understand this, we need to consider that God wills everything insofar as it is good. Moreover, something can be good or bad in its primary aspect, as we consider it absolutely, and yet it has the contrary character as we consider it with something added, which is its secondary aspect. For example, it is good, absolutely considered, that human beings live, and bad that they be killed, but if we add about a particular human being that he is a murderer or one who, while alive, is a threat to the community, it is then good that such a human being be killed, and bad that such a human being live. And hence we can say that a just judge wills antecedently that every human being live, but that he wills consequently that a murderer be hanged. In like manner, God wills antecedently that every human being be saved, but he wills consequently, by what his justice requires, that certain individuals be damned.

And yet we do not will absolutely what we will antecedently, but we will such in some respect. This is so because we relate the will to things as they exist in themselves, and they exist in themselves in particular ways. And hence we will something absolutely as we will it with all its particular circumstances taken into consideration, and this is to will consequently. And hence we can say that a just judge wills absolutely that a murderer be hanged, but he would in one respect will that the murderer live, namely, insofar as the murderer is a human being. And hence we can call such a qualified willing an inclination rather than an absolute will.

And so it is clear that whatever God wills absolutely, occurs, even if what he wills antecedently, does not occur.

Reply to Obj. 2. The act of a power to know exists in the way that a known object exists in the knower, while the act of an appetitive power is ordered to things as they exist in themselves. But everything capable of possessing the nature of being and truth exists in the power of God, while not all such exist in created things. And God, therefore, knows everything that is true, but he wills everything good only inasmuch as he wills himself, in whose power everything good exists.

Reply to Obj. 3. A primary cause can be thwarted of its effect by the deficiency of a secondary cause when the primary cause is not universally first, including within itself every cause, since an effect could then in no way avoid its order. And it is thus in the case of God's will, as I have said.[32]

Seventh Article

Can God's Will Vary?

I proceed in this way to the seventh article: it seems that God's will can vary.

Obj. 1. The Lord says in the Book of Genesis: "I repent that I made human beings."[33] But whoever repents what he has done, has a variable will. Therefore, God has a variable will.

Obj. 2. Jeremiah says out of the mouth of the Lord: "I speak against a people and against a kingdom, to root out and pull down and destroy it, but if that people should repent of its evil, I also shall repent of the evil that I have planned to do to it."[34] Therefore, God has a variable will.

Obj. 3. God does freely whatever he does. But God does not always do the same things, for he has sometimes prescribed, sometimes forbidden, legal observances. Therefore, he has a variable will.

Obj. 4. God does not need to will what he wills, as I have said before.[35] Therefore, he can will and not will the same thing. But everything that has potentiality for contrary things, can change what it wills, just as what can exist and not exist, can change substantially, and as what can be here and not here, can change locally. Therefore, God, as regards his will, can change.

On the contrary, the Book of Numbers says: "God is not like human beings that he should lie, nor like human offspring that he should change his mind."[36]

I answer that God's will cannot vary at all. But on this matter, we need to consider that it is one thing to change one's will, and another to will that some things change. For one can, with the same will unalterably perduring, will that this thing be done now, and that its contrary be done later. But if one were to begin to will what one has not previously willed, or if one were to cease to will what one has willed, one's will would then be changed. And this indeed can happen only if we presuppose a change either on the part of one's knowledge or with respect to the substantial disposition of the one willing. For, since the will's object is the good, one can in two ways begin anew to will something. In one way, as something begins anew to be good for someone. And this does not exist without the person's condition being altered; for example, when the cold of winter arrives, it begins to be good to sit by a fire, something that was not previously good. In the other way, one begins to will something as one newly recognizes that something is good for oneself, although one did not know this before, for we deliberate in order to know what is good for us. But I have shown before that both God's substance and his knowing cannot change at all.[37] And hence his will is necessarily altogether invariable.

Reply to Obj. 1. We need to understand those words of the Lord in a metaphorical sense, by analogy to ourselves, for we destroy what we have produced when we regret having made it. And yet this could be without any change of will, since human beings, without changing their will, sometimes will to produce something even when they at the same time intend to destroy it later. Thus does the Book of Genesis say that God repented having made human beings, by analogy to our actions, inasmuch as he by the flood wiped from the face of the earth the human beings whom he had made.

Reply to Obj. 2.   Although God's will is the first and universal cause, it does not exclude intermediate causes, which have the power to produce some effects. But since all intermediate causes have less power than the first cause, there are many things in God's power and knowledge and will that are not included in the order of lower causes, and an instance of such is the resurrection of Lazarus. And hence one who regards inferior causes, could say, "Lazarus will not rise again," but one who regards the divine first cause, could say, "Lazarus will rise again." And God wills both of these, namely, that something will sometimes come to be by inferior causes, and that it not exist by a superior cause, or he wills the converse. Thus we need to say that God sometimes declares that something will come to be, insofar as the thing is included in the order of inferior causes, as, for instance, nature or merits so dispose, and yet it does not come to be, because it is otherwise in the case of the superior divine cause. For example, God foretold to Hezekiah, "Put your household in order, because you will die and not live," as Isaiah declares,[38] and yet it does not turn out thus, because it was from eternity otherwise in God's knowledge and will, and his will cannot change. And so Gregory says that "God changes his sentence, but he does not change his plan," namely, the plan of his will.[39]

Therefore, we understand in a metaphorical way his saying, "I shall repent." For human beings seem to repent when they do not carry out what they have threatened to do.

Reply to Obj. 3.   We cannot conclude by that argument that God has a changeable will, but we can conclude that he wills that things change.

Reply to Obj. 4.   Although it is not absolutely necessary that God will something, yet it is hypothetically necessary that he do so, because God's will cannot vary, as I have said before.[40]

Eighth Article

Does God's Will Impose Necessity on the Things He Willed?

I proceed in this way to the eighth article: it seems that God's will imposes necessity on the things he willed.

Obj. 1.   Augustine says in his *Enchiridion*: "No one is saved except those whom God has willed to be saved. And so he should be asked to will it, because it necessarily happens if he has willed it so."[41]

Obj. 2.   Every cause that cannot be thwarted, necessarily produces its effect, because even nature produces the same effect if nothing hinders it, as the *Physics* says.[42] But God's will cannot be thwarted, for the Apostle says in the Letter to the Romans: "For who resists his will"?[43] Therefore, God's will imposes necessity on the effects he willed.

Obj. 3.   What has necessity from something prior, is absolutely necessary;

it is necessary, for example, that animals die, because they are made up of contrary parts. But things God creates, are related to his will as something prior to them, by which they have necessity. For the conditional proposition, "If God wills something, it exists," is true, and every true conditional proposition is necessary. It follows, therefore, that everything that God wills, is absolutely necessary.

On the contrary, God wills every good to come to be that comes to be. Therefore, if his will should impose necessity on the things he wills, it follows that everything good comes to be by necessity. And so free choice and deliberation and all such things are destroyed.

I answer that God's will imposes necessity on certain things that he willed, but not on everything. And some have chosen to assign the reason for this to intermediate causes, because things that God produces by necessary causes, are necessary, while things that he produces by contingent causes, are contingent.

But this does not, for two reasons, seem to be a sufficient explanation. First, indeed, because the effect of a primary cause is contingent due to a secondary cause, since the deficiency of a secondary cause thwarts the effect of a primary cause; for example, the deficiency of a plant thwarts the sun's power. But no deficiency in a secondary cause can prevent God's will from producing its effect.

Second, the aforementioned explanation is insufficient because, if the difference between contingent and necessary causes relates only to secondary causes, that difference is consequently outside God's design and will. And this is inappropriate.

And so we need rather to say that such happens contingently because of the efficacy of God's will. For, when a cause has been effective in causing, the effect results from the cause not only as to what comes to be but also as to its way of coming to be or existing. For example, a child may be born dissimilar to its father in accidental characteristics, which belong to the way of existing, because the efficient power in the father's seed is weak. Therefore, since God's will is most efficacious, it follows not only that the things that he wills to come to be, come to be, but that they come to be in the way in which he wills them to come to be. Moreover, God wills that certain things come to be necessarily, and that certain other things come to be contingently, so that there may be an order among things to make the universe complete. And so, for certain effects, he has prepared causes that are necessary and cannot fail, and effects necessarily result from such causes. But for other effects, he has prepared fallible, contingent causes, and effects contingently come to be from such causes. Thus effects willed by God do not contingently come to be because their proximate causes are contingent, but he prepared contingent causes for those effects because he willed that the effects contingently come to be.

Reply to Obj. 1.   We need to understand by the words of Augustine that there is in things willed by God a necessity that is not absolute but hypothetical. For the conditional proposition, "If God wills this, it necessarily exists," is necessarily true.

Reply to Obj. 2. Because nothing resists God's will, it follows not only that things that he wills to come to be, come to be, but that things he wills to come to be contingently or necessarily, come to be in such a way.

Reply to Obj. 3. Consequent things have necessity from prior things in the way of the prior things. And so the things that God's will produces, also have the kind of necessity that God wills them to have, namely, either absolute necessity or only hypothetical necessity. And so some effects are not absolutely necessary.

Ninth Article

Does God Will Evils?

I proceed in this way to the ninth article: it seems that God wills evils.

Obj. 1. God wills everything good that exists. But it is good that evils exist, for Augustine says in his *Enchiridion*: "Although evils as evils are not good, yet it is good not only that good things exist, but also that evil things do."[44] Therefore, God wills evils.

Obj. 2. Denis says in his *De divinis nominibus*: "Evil contributes to the perfection of everything," i.e., the universe.[45] And Augustine says in his *Enchiridion*: "Out of everything consists the universe's wonderful beauty, wherein even what we call evil, when rightly ordered and properly disposed, more excellently recommends what is good, so that good things may be more pleasing and more praiseworthy when compared to evils."[46] But God wills everything that belongs to the perfection and beauty of the universe, because this is what God most of all wills in creatures. Therefore, God wills evils.

Obj. 3. There is contradictory opposition between the proposition "Evils exist" and the proposition "Evils do not exist." But God does not will that evils not exist, because his will would thus not always be fulfilled, since certain evils do exist. Therefore, God wills that evils exist.

On the contrary, Augustine says in his work *Octoginta trium quaestionum*: "No wise human being makes another worse. But God is more excellent than any wise human being. Therefore, much less does God as cause make anyone worse. Moreover, when we say that God causes something, we say that he wills it."[47] Therefore, a human being is not made worse by God's willing. But every evil evidently makes something worse. Therefore, God does not will evils.

I answer that, since the good and the desirable are essentially the same, as I have said before,[48] while evil is the contrary of good, nothing evil as such can be sought either by a natural appetite or by an animal appetite or by an intellectual appetite, that is, the will. But something evil is sought by accident, inasmuch as something evil results from something good. And this is evident in every appetite. For example, a natural efficient cause does not aim at privation and passing away, but strives for one form, which involves the deprivation of another form, and the coming-to-be of one thing, which is the passing away of another. Also, when a lion kills a stag, the lion aims to feed itself, and this involves killing the stag. Likewise, a fornicator intends his pleasure, and this involves the deformity of wrongdoing.

Moreover, the evil that accompanies a particular good, is the deprivation of another good. Thus evil would never be sought, not even by accident, unless the good that involves evil, were to be sought more than the good that evil takes away. But God wills no good more than his own goodness, although he wills one particular good more than another. And hence God in no way wills the evil of wrongdoing, which takes away the order toward the divine good. But he wills the evil of a natural deficiency or the evil of punishment when he wills a particular good that involves such an evil. For example, he wills punishment when he wills justice, and he wills that certain things by nature pass away when he wills that the order of nature be observed.

Reply to Obj. 1.   Certain thinkers said that, although God does not will evils, he nonetheless wills that evils exist or come to be. They said this because, although evils are not good, it is nonetheless good that evils exist or come to be. And so they said this because intrinsically evil things are ordered to some good, and they indeed believed this order to be implied in the clause, "that evils exist or come to be." But this statement is not correct, because evil is not ordered to good intrinsically but by accident. For it is outside the intention of a sinner that any good result from his sinning; for example, it was no part of the intention of tyrants that the patience of martyrs become evident by the tyrants' persecution of the martyrs. And so we cannot say that the statement, that it is good that evils exist or come to be, implies such an ordering to good, because we do not judge anything by what belongs to it by accident, but we judge something by what intrinsically belongs to it.

Reply to Obj. 2.   Evil works for the perfection and beauty of the universe only by accident, as I have said.[49] And so also the statement of Denis, that evil contributes to the perfection of the universe, argues by drawing attention to an improper conclusion, as it were.

Reply to Obj. 3.   Although the propositions "Evils exist" and "Evils do not exist" are contradictorily opposed, yet the propositions "God wills evils to exist" and "God wills evils not to exist" are not opposed in that way, since both of the latter two propositions are affirmative. God thus neither wills that evils exist, nor that they not exist, but he wills to permit evils to exist. And this is good.

Tenth Article

Does God Have Free Choice?

I proceed in this way to the tenth article: it seems that God has no free choice.

Obj. 1. Jerome says in his homily on the prodigal son: "God is the only one in whom sin does not occur nor can occur; others can be inclined to sin or not to sin, because they have free choice."[50]

Obj. 2. Free choice is the power of reason and will by which good and evil are chosen. But God does not will evil, as I have said.[51] Therefore, God has no free choice.

On the contrary, Ambrose says in his work *De fide*: "The Holy Spirit distributes things to individuals as he wills, that is, according to the choice of his free will, not by submitting to necessity."[52]

I answer that we have free choice with respect to things that we do not will by necessity or an impulse of nature. For example, it does not belong to free choice but to an impulse of nature that we will to be happy. And so also we do not say that free will moves other animals, whom an impulse of nature moves to something. Therefore, since God necessarily wills his own goodness, but he does not will other things necessarily, as I have shown before,[53] he has free choice with respect to the things that he does not will necessarily.

Reply to Obj. 1. Jerome seems not to exclude free choice from God absolutely but only with respect to being inclined to sin.

Reply to Obj. 2. Since we say that the evil of wrongdoing consists in turning away from God's goodness, whereby he wills everything, as I have shown before,[54] God evidently cannot will the evil of wrongdoing. And yet he is disposed toward contrary things inasmuch he can will that this particular thing exist or not exist. In like manner, we also can, without sinning, will to sit and not will to sit.

Notes

1. *De anima* III, 10. 433b14–18.
2. Aristotle, *Physics* VIII, 4–6. 254b7–260a19.
3. Rom. 12:2.
4. Q. 6, A. 3.
5. This article, *ad* 1.
6. *Phaedrus* 24. 245C–E.
7. Aristotle, *De anima* III, 10. 433a14–26.
8. 1 Thess. 4:3.
9. Q. 19, A. 1.
10. Q. 13, A. 4.
11. In the body of the article.
12. Q. 2, A. 3.

13. Aristotle, *Metaphysics* IV, 5. 1015b14–15.
14. Averroes, *In libros Physicorum* II, comm. 48.
15. Eph. 1:11.
16. *De divinis nominibus* 4. PG 3:693.
17. *De doctrina Christiana* I, 32. PL 34:32.
18. Q. 14, A. 8.
19. Wis. 11:26.
20. Aristotle, *Physics* II, 5. 196b18–22.
21. Q. 7, A. 2.
22. Q. 19, A. 2.
23. *Octoginta trium quaestionum*, Q. 46. PL 40:30.
24. Q. 19, A. 4.
25. *Octoginta trium quaestionum*, Q. 28. PL 40:18.
26. *De Trinitate* III, 2. PL 42:871.
27. 1 Tim. 2:4.
28. Q. 19, A. 5.
29. Ps. 115:3.
30. *Enchiridion* 103. PL 40:280.
31. *De fide orthodoxa* II, 29. PG 94:968.
32. In the body of the article.
33. Gen. 6:7.
34. Jer. 17:7, 8.
35. Q. 19, A. 3.
36. Num. 23:19.
37. Q. 9, A. 1. Q. 14, A. 15.
38. Is. 38:1.
39. *Moralia* XVI, 10. PL 75:1127.
40. Q. 19, A. 3.
41. *Enchiridion* 103. PL 40:280.
42. Aristotle, *Physics* II, 8. 199b15–26.
43. Rom. 9:19.
44. *Enchiridion* 96. PL 40:276.
45. *De divinis nominibus* 4. PG 3:717.
46. *Enchiridion* 10, 11. PL 40:236.
47. *Octoginta trium quaestionum*, Q. 3. PL 40:11.
48. Q. 5, A. 1.
49. This article, *ad* 1.
50. *Epistola* 21, *ad Damasum*. PL 22:393.
51. Q. 19, A. 9.
52. *De fide* 6. PL 16:569.
53. Q. 19, A. 3.
54. Q. 19, A. 2.

ST I
Question 20
On God's Love

[This question is divided into four articles, three of which are included here.]

First Article

Does God Love?

I proceed in this way to the first article: it seems that God does not love.

Obj. 1. God has no capacity to be acted upon. Love is a capacity to be acted upon. Therefore, God does not love.

Obj. 2. We contradistinguish love, anger, sadness, and the like from one another. But we predicate sadness and anger of God only metaphorically. Therefore, we also predicate love of God only in that way.

Obj. 3. Denis says in his *De divinis nominibus*: "Love is a unifying and binding force."[1] But there cannot be such in God, because he is uncomposed. Therefore, God does not love.

On the contrary, the First Letter of John says: "God is love."[2]

I answer that we need to posit love in God, since the first movement of the will and of every appetitive power is love. For acts of the will and of every appetitive power tend toward good and evil as the powers' proper object, good being principally and intrinsically their object, while evil is their object secondarily and by something else, namely, as contrary to good; consequently, acts of will and appetite that regard good, are by nature necessarily prior to those that regard evil. For example, joy is prior to sadness, and love prior to hate. For what intrinsically exists, is always prior to what exists by something else.

Again, something more general is by nature prior, and so also the intellect has a relation to truth in general before it has a relation to certain particular truths. Moreover, there are certain acts of will and appetites that regard good under a special condition; for example, joy and pleasure concern a good that is present and possessed, while desire and hope concern a good

175

not yet possessed. But love concerns good in general, whether possessed or not. And hence love is by nature the first act of the will and appetites.

And for this reason, all other appetitive movements presuppose love, their first source, as it were. For no one desires, or rejoices in, anything except as a good that is loved. Hate, too, concerns only what is contrary to something loved. And likewise, sadness and other such things are evidently related to love as their first source. And hence love needs to exist in everything in which there is will and appetite, for other things are taken away if the thing that is first, is taken away. But I have shown that God has a will.[3] And hence we need to posit love in him.

Reply to Obj. 1. A cognitive power moves only by means of an appetitive power. And just as universal reason causes motion in us by means of particular reason,[4] as the *De anima* says,[5] so the intellectual appetite, which we call the will, causes motion in us by means of the sense appetites. And hence the proximate powers of bodily motion in us are the sense appetites. And hence a bodily change always accompanies the act of a sense appetite, and most of all a bodily change in the case of the heart, which is the first source of motion in animals. We thus call acts of the sense appetites, inasmuch as they have accompanying bodily changes, capacities to be acted upon, while we do not so call acts of the will. Therefore, love and joy and pleasure, as these signify acts of the sense appetites, are capacities to be acted upon, but not as they signify acts of the intellectual appetite. And we thus posit them in God. And hence the Philosopher says in the *Ethics* that "God rejoices by activity that is one and uncomposed."[6] And for the same reason, he loves without a capacity to be acted upon.

Reply to Obj. 2. In the capacities of the sense appetites to be acted upon, we need to consider something quasi-material, namely, a bodily change, and something quasi-formal, which is on the part of the sense appetites. For example, in the case of anger, as the *De anima* says,[7] the material element is the increased circulation of blood around the heart, or some such thing, while the formal element is the appetite for revenge. And also, on the part of the formal element, we signify an imperfection in certain appetites; for example, in the case of desire, what regards a good not possessed, and in the case of sadness, what regards an evil that one has. And there is the same consideration in the case of anger, which presupposes sadness. But certain appetites, such as love and joy, signify no imperfection. Therefore, since no appetite is fitting for God insofar as it contains a material element, as I have said,[8] appetites that imply an imperfection even in a formal way, can be appropriate for God only metaphorically, because of an analogy of effect, as I have said before.[9] But we predicate of God in a proper sense appetites that imply no imperfection, such as love and joy, although without him having a capacity to be acted upon, as I have said.[10]

Reply to Obj. 3. An act of love always tends toward two things, namely, the good that one wills for someone, and the person for whom one wills the good. For willing good for someone is, in the proper sense, to love that person. And hence, insofar as persons love themselves, they will good for themselves. And so they seek to unite that good to themselves as much as they can. And we accordingly call love a unifying force even in the case of God, although without him being composed, since the good that he wills for himself, is only himself, who is good by his essence, as I have shown before.[11]

Indeed, in loving another, one wills good for that person. And so one rejoices in the other as if oneself, judging the good for the other as good for oneself. And we accordingly call love a binding force, because love, being disposed toward the other as to oneself, unites the other to oneself. And so also God's love is a binding force, inasmuch as he wills good for others, without composition existing in him.

Second Article

Does God Love Everything?

I proceed in this way to the second article: it seems that God does not love everything.

Obj. 1. Love puts the lover outside himself and somehow transposes him into the beloved, as Denis says in his *De divinis nominibus*.[12] But it is inappropriate to say that God is posited outside himself and transposed into other things. Therefore, it is inappropriate to say that God loves things other than himself.

Obj. 2. God's love is eternal. But other things than God do not exist from eternity except in God. Therefore, God loves things other than himself only in himself. But things are not other than God as they exist in him. Therefore, God does not love things other than himself.

Obj. 3. There are two kinds of love, namely, the love of desire, and the love of friendship. But God does not love creatures that lack reason, by a love of desire, because he needs nothing outside himself. Nor does God love such creatures by a love of friendship, because one cannot have the love of friendship toward things that lack reason, as the Philosopher makes clear in the *Ethics*.[13] Therefore, God does not love everything.

Obj. 4. The Psalm says: "You hate all who do evil."[14] But one cannot at the same time love and hate something. Therefore, God does not love everything.

On the contrary, the Book of Wisdom says: "You love everything that exists, and you hate nothing that you have made."[15]

I answer that God loves everything that exists. For everything that exists, as such, is good, since the very existing of each thing is a certain good, and every perfection of each thing is likewise. Moreover, I have shown before that God's will causes everything,[16] and so a thing needs to have as much existing or as much of any other perfection as God wills. Therefore, God wills some good for everything that exists. And hence, since loving is nothing else but willing good for something, God evidently loves everything that exists.

But he does not love in the same way that we do. For our will does not cause the goodness of things, but their goodness, as the will's object, moves the will. Therefore, our love, whereby we will good for something, does not cause the goodness of that thing, but, conversely, the thing's goodness, whether real or putative, evokes the love whereby we will for the thing both that the good that it possesses, be preserved, and that the good that it does not possess, be added to it. And we act to achieve this. But God's love pours out and creates the goodness in things.

Reply to Obj. 1.   The lover becomes thus transposed out of himself into the beloved inasmuch as he wills good for the beloved, and inasmuch as he acts for that good by his providence, just as he does for himself. And so also does Denis say in his *De divinis nominibus*: "We, moreover, dare to say even this in behalf of truth, that even he, the cause of everything, by the richness of his loving goodness comes to exist outside of himself by his providence for everything that exists."[17]

Reply to Obj. 2.   Although creatures from eternity existed only in God, yet God from eternity knows them in their own natures, because they eternally existed in God, and he loved them for the same reason. And in like manner, we know things that exist in themselves, by their likenesses, which exist in us.

Reply to Obj. 3.   One can only have friendship toward rational creatures, among whom there can be mutual love and life's shared activities, and for whom things may, by good or bad fortune, turn out well or ill, just as there is benevolence in the proper sense toward such creatures. But creatures that lack reason, cannot attain to loving God or sharing the intellectual and blessed life that he enjoys. Thus God, properly speaking, does not love creatures that lack reason, with a love of friendship, but with a love of desire, as it were, inasmuch as he ordains them for rational creatures and even for himself. This is not as if he needs them, but because of his goodness and their benefit to us. For we desire some things both for ourselves and for others.

Reply to Obj. 4.   Nothing prevents one and the same thing from being loved in one respect and hated in another. Moreover, God loves sinners inasmuch as they have a certain nature, for they both exist in such a way, and he made them to exist in such a way. But sinners, inasmuch as they sin, do not exist but fall short of existing, and they do not have this from God. And hence he hates them in this respect.

Third Article

Does God Love Everything Equally?

I proceed in this way to the third article: it seems that God loves everything equally.

Obj. 1. The Book of Wisdom says: "He has equal care of everything."[18] But the providence that God has for things, is from the love wherewith he loves them. Therefore, he loves everything equally.

Obj. 2. God's love is his essence. But God's essence does not admit of degrees. Therefore, neither does his love. Therefore, he does not love certain things more than others.

Obj. 3. God's love extends to created things in the way in which his knowing and willing do. But we do not say that God knows certain things more than others, nor that he wills certain things more than others. Therefore, neither does he love certain things more than others.

On the contrary, Augustine says in his commentary on the Gospel of John: "God loves everything that he made, and of these, he loves rational creatures more, and of these, he loves still more those who are members of his only-begotten Son, and far more does he love his very own only-begotten Son."[19]

I answer that, since loving consists in willing good for something, something can be loved more or less in two ways. In one way, on the part of the very act of the will, which act is more or less intense. And in this way, God does not love certain things more than others, because he loves everything by an act of the will that is one and uncomposed and always disposed in the same way. In the second way, something can be loved more or less on the part of the good itself that one wills for the object of one's love. And in this way, we say that we love more than another the one for whom we will a greater good, although not by a more intense will. And we need in this way to say that God loves certain things more than others. For, since God's love causes the goodness of things, as I have said,[20] nothing would be better than something else if God were not to will a greater good for one thing than for another.

Reply to Obj. 1. The Book of Wisdom says that God has equal care of everything, not because his care dispenses equal goods to everything, but because he directs everything with equal wisdom and goodness.

Reply to Obj. 2. That argument holds concerning the intensity of love on the part of the act of his will, which is his essence. But the good that God wills for creatures, is not the divine essence. And hence nothing prevents that good from being expanded or contracted.

Reply to Obj. 3. Understanding and willing signify only acts, and they do not include in their meaning any objects, by the diversity of which we could say that God knows or wills more or less, as I have said with respect to God's love.[21]

Notes

1. *De divinis nominibus* 4. PG 3:709.
2. 1 Jn. 4:16.
3. Q. 19, A. 1.
4. Cf. Q. 78, A. 4.
5. Aristotle, *De anima* III, 11. 434a16, 21.
6. *Ethics* VII, 14. 1154b24–28.
7. Aristotle, *De anima* I, 1. 403a29–b2.
8. This article, *ad* 1.
9. Q. 3, A. 2, *ad* 2. Q. 19, A. 11.
10. This article, *ad* 1.
11. Q. 6, A. 3.
12. *De divinis nominibus* 4. PG 3:712.
13. *Ethics* VIII, 2. 1155b27–31.
14. Ps. 5:6.
15. Wis. 11:24.
16. Q. 19, A. 4.
17. *De divinis nominibus* 4. PG 3:712.
18. Wis. 6:8.
19. *In Ioannis Evangelium*, tract. 110. PL 35:1924.
20. Q. 20, A. 2.
21. In the body of the article.

ST I
Question 21
On God's Justice and Mercy

[This question is divided into four articles, three of which are included here.]

First Article

Is God Just?

I proceed in this way to the first article: it seems that justice does not exist in God.

Obj. 1. We distinguish justice from moderation.[1] But there is no moderation in God. Therefore, neither does justice exist in God.

Obj. 2. Whoever does everything at the pleasure of his own will, does not act according to justice. But God "does everything according to the counsel of his will," as the Apostle says in the Letter to the Ephesians.[2] Therefore, we ought not to ascribe justice to him.

Obj. 3. An act of justice consists in rendering what is due to another. But God does not owe anything to anyone. Therefore, justice does not belong to God.

Obj. 4. Everything in God is his essence. But such does not belong to justice. For Boethius says in his work *De hebdomatibus* that "the good regards an essence, but the just regards an act."[3] Therefore, justice is not proper to God.

On the contrary, the Psalm says: "The Lord is just, and he has loved justice."[4]

I answer that there are two types of justice. One consists in reciprocal giving and receiving, as, for example, in buying and selling, and other such apportionments[5] or exchanges. And the Philosopher in the *Ethics* calls this justice commutative justice,[6] the justice that governs apportionments or exchanges. And this justice does not belong to God, because, as the Apostle says, "Who has given him anything first, and will there be recompense for such a person?"[7]

181

The other justice consists in distributing goods, and we call such justice distributive justice, the justice whereby a ruler or administrator distributes to each according to his or her merit. Therefore, as the order of a family or any directed group manifests such justice in the one who directs the group, so the order of the universe, which is evidenced both in the things of nature and in freely willed things, shows God's justice. And hence Denis says in his *De divinis nominibus*: "We necessarily see that true justice belongs to God, in that he bestows on everything what is proper to each, according to the merit of everything that exists, and God preserves the nature of each in its own order and power"[8]

Reply to Obj. 1.   Certain moral virtues concern capacities to be acted upon. For example, moderation concerns desire, fortitude concerns fear and foolheartiness, meekness concerns anger. And we can attribute such virtues to God only metaphorically, because there are in God neither capacities to be acted upon, as I have said before,[9] nor sense appetites, in which, as subjects, such powers reside, as the Philosopher says in the *Ethics*.[10] But certain moral virtues concern such actions as giving and expending, as, for example, justice and liberality and magnanimity do. And these do not reside in the part of the soul capable of sense perception but in the will. And hence nothing prevents us from positing such virtues in God, although not with respect to civic actions but with respect to actions appropriate for God. For it is absurd, as the Philosopher says in the *Ethics*,[11] to praise God regarding political virtues.

Reply to Obj. 2.   Since an understood good is the object of the will, God can only will what the plan of his wisdom has in mind. And the plan of his wisdom is indeed, as it were, the law of justice by which his will is right and just. And hence he does justly what he does according to his will, as we too do justly what we do according to law. But we, of course, do things according to the law of superiors, while God legislates for himself.

Reply to Obj. 3.   We owe to every person what belongs to that person. Moreover, we say that what is ordered to a person, belongs to the person; for example, a slave belongs to his master, and not vice versa, since something free exists for its own sake. Therefore, the word "debt" implies a certain contingent or necessary order of something to that to which it is ordered. Moreover, we need to consider two orders in things. One is the order whereby something created is ordered to another created thing; for example, parts are ordered to a whole, and accidents to substances, and each thing to its end. The second is the order whereby every created thing is ordered to God. Therefore, we can also note in two ways what is due in God's action: either as something is owed to God, or as something is owed to a creature.

And in both ways, God renders what is due. For it is owed to God that things fulfill what his wisdom and will have in mind, and what manifests his goodness. And accordingly, God's justice regards what befits him, as he renders to himself what he owes himself. It is also owed to any creature that it have the things ordered to it; for example, it is due to human beings that they have hands, and that other animals serve human beings. And so God also effects justice when he bestows on each thing what is due to it by the plan of its nature and state. But what is due in the latter way, depends on what is due in the former way, since what God's wisdom ordains for each being, is due to it.

And although God in the latter way bestows what is due to things, yet he is not himself a debtor, because he is not ordered to other things, but rather other things are ordered to him. And so we sometimes call God's justice the becomingness of his goodness, and sometimes the reward for merits. And Anselm touches on both ways when he says: "When you punish the wicked, it is just because it befits their merits, but when you spare the wicked, it is just because it befits your goodness."[12]

Reply to Obj. 4. Although justice regards acts, yet this does not exclude justice being God's essence, since what belongs to a thing's essence, can be the source of action. But good does not always regard acts, since we call something good both by what it does, and by what is perfect in its essence. And for this reason, Boethius says in the same place that the good is related to the just as the general is to the particular.

Third Article

Does Mercy Belong to God?

I proceed in this way to the third article: it seems that mercy does not belong to God.

Obj. 1. Mercy is a kind of sorrow, as Damascene says.[13] But God has no sorrow. Therefore, neither is there mercy in him.

Obj. 2. Mercy eases justice. But God cannot overlook what belongs to his justice. For the Second Letter to Timothy says: "Though we are not faithful, he remains faithful; he cannot deny himself."[14] But a gloss on the same text says that he would deny himself if he were to deny what he has said.[15] Therefore, mercy is not a property of God.

On the contrary, the Psalm says: "The Lord is compassionate and merciful."[16]

I answer that we should especially attribute mercy to God, but in its effect, not as the emotion of a capacity to be acted upon. And for evidence of this, we need to consider that we call a person merciful as if that person has a tormented heart,[17] namely, that the distress of another causes the person to be sad, as if the other's distress were the person's own. And such a person consequently acts to dispel the distress of the other, as he would act to dispel his own distress. And this is the effect of mercy. Therefore, it does not belong to God to be saddened at the distress of another, but it especially belongs to God to drive away the distress of another, as we understand by distress any deficiency. But only the perfection of some goodness takes away a deficiency. Moreover, the first source of goodness is God, as I have shown before.[18]

But we need to consider that lavishing perfections on things indeed belongs to God's goodness, his justice, his generosity, and his mercy, but in one or another respect. For imparting perfections, absolutely considered, belongs to goodness, as I have shown.[19] But imparting perfections, inasmuch as God bestows them on things proportionately, belongs to justice, as I have said before.[20] And imparting perfections, inasmuch as he does not bestow them on things because of any profit to himself but only because of his goodness, belongs to his generosity. And imparting perfections, inasmuch as the perfections bestowed by God dispel every deficiency, belongs to his mercy.

Reply to Obj. 1. That objection holds with respect to mercy as to the emotion of a capacity to be acted upon.

Reply to Obj. 2. God acts mercifully, not indeed by acting contrary to his justice but by doing something superior to justice. For example, if a person who owes someone a hundred pieces of silver, should give him two hundred of his own, he nonetheless does nothing contrary to justice but acts generously and mercifully. And the case is similar if a person pardons an offense committed against him. For a person who forgives something, somehow gives something. And hence the Apostle calls forgiveness a giving: "Give forgiveness to one another, as Christ has also given you forgiveness."[21] And it is thus clear that mercy does not take away justice, but mercy is a certain fulness of justice. And hence the Letter of James says that "mercy triumphs over judgment."[22]

Fourth Article

Are There Mercy and Justice in All God's Works?

I proceed in this way to the fourth article: it seems that mercy and justice are not in every work of God.

Obj. 1. We attribute certain works of God, such as justifying the wicked, to his mercy, but we attribute other works of God, such as damning the wicked, to his justice. And hence the Letter of James says: "Judgment without mercy will be done to one who has shown no mercy."[23] Therefore, mercy and justice are not evident in every work of God.

Obj. 2. The Apostle, in the Letter to the Romans, ascribes the conversion of the Jews to justice and truth but the conversion of the Gentiles to mercy.[24] Therefore, we do not find justice and mercy in every work of God.

Obj. 3. Many upright people suffer in this world. But this is unjust. Therefore, we do not find justice and mercy in every work of God.

Obj. 4. Justice consists in rendering what is due, while mercy consists in
alleviating distress, and so both justice and mercy presuppose something in
their actions. Therefore, there is neither justice nor mercy in creation.

On the contrary, the Psalm says: "All the Lord's ways are mercy and
justice."[25]

I answer that we need to find mercy and truth in every work of God, provided we understand mercy to mean the taking away of any kind of deficiency. But we cannot in a proper sense call every deficiency a distress, but only
the deficiency in a rational nature, which can be happy, for distress is contrary to happiness.

Moreover, there is a reason for this necessity. For, since divine justice
renders either what is due to God or what is due to a creature, neither can
be overlooked in any work of God. For God can do nothing that does not
befit his wisdom and goodness, and we have said that something is due to
God in this way.[26] Likewise, he also does with befitting order and proportion everything that he does in created things, and the nature of justice consists in this. And so there needs to be justice in every work of God.

Moreover, the work of God's justice always presupposes the work of his
mercy and is based on it. For creatures are not owed anything except because of something in them that exists or is weighed beforehand. And again,
if creatures are owed something, it will be because of something prior. And
since we cannot regress endlessly, we need to arrive at something that depends only on the goodness of the divine will, which is the ultimate end.
This is as if we should say that it is owed to human beings to have hands because human beings have rational souls, and it is owed to human beings to
have rational souls because human beings are human, and it is owed to
human beings to be human because of God's goodness.

And so mercy is evident in every work of God as to the action's first
source. And the power of God's mercy is preserved in everything that
results, and also works more strongly in everything that results, as primary
causes influence effects more strongly than secondary causes do. And consequently, God, out of the richness of his goodness, dispenses even the things
owed to creatures more abundantly than anything proportional to creatures
demands. For what would suffice to preserve the order of justice, is less than
what God's goodness brings. And God's goodness surpasses every proportion to creatures.

Reply to Obj. 1. We ascribe certain works to his justice, and others to his
mercy, because justice is more strongly evident in some actions, mercy more
strongly in others. And yet his mercy is evident in damning the reprobate;
his mercy indeed does not entirely remit, but it does in some way lessen,
their punishment when he inflicts less punishment on them than they deserve. And his justice is evident in justifying the wicked when he remits

their wrongdoings because of his love, which he nonetheless mercifully pours out. For example, we read of Mary Magdalene in the Gospel of Luke: "Many sins are forgiven her, because she loved much."[27]

Reply to Obj. 2.   Justice and mercy are evident in the conversion of the Jews and the Gentiles. But an aspect of justice is evident in the conversion of the Jews that is not evident in the conversion of the Gentiles, inasmuch as the Jews are saved because of the promises made to their fathers.

Reply to Obj. 3.   Justice and mercy are evident even in the fact that the upright are punished in this world, inasmuch as such afflictions cleanse them of minor faults and lift them from earthly desires to God. Gregory accordingly says: "The evils that press on us in this world, impel us to move toward God."[28]

Reply to Obj. 4.   Although creation presupposes nothing in the universe, yet creation does presuppose something in God's knowledge. And accordingly, the aspect of justice is also preserved in creation, inasmuch as things are brought into existence as befits God's wisdom and goodness. And the aspect of mercy is somehow preserved, inasmuch as things are brought from not existing to existing.

Notes

1. St. Thomas refers here to the virtue of moderation, the characteristic disposition to engage moderately in activities, especially pleasurable activities. For example, moderation in eating, drinking, and sleeping.

2. Eph. 1:11.

3. *De hebdomatibus.* PL 64:1314.

4. Ps 11:7.

5. St. Thomas appears to refer here to the division of the proceeds of business partnerships.

6. *Ethics* V, 4. 1131b26–28.

7. Rom. 11:35.

8. *De divinis nominibus* 8. PG 3:896.

9. Q. 20, A. 1, *ad* 1.

10. *Ethics* III, 10. 1117b23–24.

11. *Ethics* X, 8. 1178b7–23.

12. *Proslogium* 10. PL 158:233.

13. *De fide orthodoxa* II, 14. PG 94:932.

14. 2 Tim. 2:13.

15. Peter Lombard, *In Epistolam 2am ad Timotheum.* PL 192:370.

16. Ps. 111:4.

17. St. Thomas refers to the roots of the Latin word for merciful, "*misericors*": "*miserum cor*" ("tormented heart").

18. Q. 6, A. 4.

19. Q. 6, AA. 1, 4.

20. Q. 21, A. 1.

21. Eph. 4:32.

22. Jas. 2:13.
23. Ibid.
24. Rom. 15:8–9.
25. Ps. 25:10.
26. Q. 21, A. 1, *ad* 3.
27. Lk. 7:47.
28. *Moralia* XXVI, 13. PL 76:360.

ST I
Question 22
On God's Providence

[This question is divided into four articles, all of which are included here.]

First Article

Is Providence Appropriate for God?

I proceed in this way to the first article: it seems that providence is not appropriate for God.

Obj. 1. Providence, according to Cicero,[1] is part of practical wisdom. But since practical wisdom deliberates well, as the Philosopher says in the *Ethics*,[2] it cannot belong to God, who has no uncertainty whence he needs to deliberate. Therefore, providence does not belong to God.

Obj. 2. Everything in God is eternal. But providence is nothing eternal, for it is "about things that exist" that are not eternal, as Damascene says.[3] Therefore, there is no providence in God.

Obj. 3. There is nothing composite in God. But providence seems to be something composite, because it includes will and intellect. Therefore, there is no providence in God.

On the contrary, the Book of Wisdom says: "But you, Father, direct everything by your providence."[4]

I answer that we need to hold that there is providence in God. For God created everything good in the world, as I have shown before.[5] But we find good in things not only as regards their substance but also as regards their order to ends, and especially to their final end, which is God's goodness, as I have considered before.[6] Therefore, God created the good that exists in created things regarding their order. Moreover, since God causes things by his intellect, and so the nature of every one of his effects needs to pre-exist in him, as is clear from what I have said before,[7] the plan of the order of things to their ends needs to pre-exist in his mind. And the plan ordering things to ends is providence in the proper sense. For providence is the chief part of practical wisdom, toward which the other two parts, namely, remembering the past and understanding the present, are ordered, inasmuch as we draw conclusions about providing for the future from remembering the past and understanding the present.

Moreover, as the Philosopher says in the *Ethics*,[8] it belongs to practical wisdom to order other things to ends, either regarding oneself, as, for example, we call human beings wise who rightly order their actions to the goal of their life; or regarding others subject to them, in the case of a family or a local political community or a kingdom, and the Gospel of Matthew so speaks of "the faithful and wise servant whom the master has put in charge of his household."[9] And practical wisdom or providence can in this second way be appropriate for God. (For nothing in God himself can be ordered to an end, since he is the final end.) We thus call the very plan ordering things to ends, God's providence. And hence Boethius says in his *On the Consolation of Philosophy* that "providence is the divine plan itself, established in the highest ruler of everything, which arranges everything."[10] Moreover, we can say that both the plan ordering things to ends and the plan ordering individual parts in the whole are dispositions.

Reply to Obj. 1. According to the Philosopher in the *Ethics*, practical wisdom in the strict sense commands the things of which "sound deliberation" duly deliberates, and "understanding" duly judges.[11] And hence, although it does not belong to God to deliberate, as deliberation consists in an inquiry about things that are doubtful, yet it belongs to God to give commands with respect to ordering things to ends, and he has an exact plan for these things, as the Psalm says: "He has established commands, and they will not pass away."[12] And the nature of practical wisdom and providence accordingly belongs to God.

And yet we can also call the very plan for the things to be executed, counsel in him, not because of any inquiry by him, but because of the certainty of his knowledge, at which certainty those who deliberate, arrive by investigation. And hence the Letter to the Ephesians says: God "does everything at the counsel of his will."[13]

Reply to Obj. 2. Two things belong to the care of providence, namely, planning the order, which we call providence and disposition, and executing the order, which we call governance. And of these, the first is eternal, the second temporal.

Reply to Obj. 3. Providence resides in the intellect but presupposes the willing of an end, for one gives commands about things to be done because of an end only if one wills the end. And so also practical wisdom presupposes the moral virtues, by which the appetites are disposed toward the good, as the *Ethics* says.[14]

And yet if providence were equally to regard God's will and intellect, this would be without detriment to God's simplicity, since his will and intellect are the same, as I have said before.[15]

Second Article

Is Everything Subject to God's Providence?

I proceed in this way to the second article: it seems that some things are not subject to God's providence.

Obj. 1. Nothing foreseen is fortuitous. Therefore, if God has foreseen everything, nothing will be fortuitous, and so there will be no chance or luck. And this is contrary to the general opinion.

Obj. 2. Every wise provider prevents deficiencies and evils from things in his charge as much as he can. But we see that there are many evils in the world. Therefore, either God cannot prevent them and so is not omnipotent, or he is not in charge of everything.

Obj. 3. Events that necessarily come to be, do not require providence or practical wisdom. And hence, according to the Philosopher in the *Ethics*, practical wisdom is right reasoning about contingent things, concerning which there is deliberation and choice.[16] Therefore, since many things in the world necessarily come to be, some things are not subject to God's providence.

Obj. 4. Everything left to itself is not subject to the providence of one who directs. But God leaves human beings to themselves, as the Book of Sirach says: "God constituted human beings from the beginning, and he left them in the hands of their own counsel."[17] And he especially did so in the case of the wicked, as the Psalm says: "He left them to the desires of their hearts."[18] Therefore, some things are not subject to divine providence.

Obj. 5. The Apostle says in the First Letter to the Corinthians that "God does not concern himself about oxen,"[19] and, by the same reasoning, he is not concerned about other creatures that lack reason. Therefore, some things are not subject to divine providence.

On the contrary, the Book of Wisdom says of God's wisdom that "it reaches mightily from one end of the world to the other, and it orders everything agreeably."[20]

I answer that certain thinkers, such as Democritus and the Epicureans, who held that the world was made by chance, entirely rejected providence. And certain others held that only things that cannot pass away, are subject to providence, and that things that can pass away, are subject to providence regarding their species but not individually, for such things cannot pass away as species. And the Book of Job says out of their mouth: "The clouds are his hiding-place, and he walks around the poles of the heavens, and he does not consider our affairs."[21] Rabbi Moses, however, excepted human beings from the generality of things that can pass away, because of the excellence of the intellect that human beings share, but he followed the opinion of the others regarding nonhuman individual things that can pass away.[22]

But we need to say that everything is subject to God's providence, both in general and in particular. And this is made clear as follows. For, since every efficient cause acts for an end, the ordering of effects to ends reaches as far as the causality of the primary efficient cause reaches. For something unrelated to an end may come to be in what an efficient cause produces because some other cause produces that effect, which is not what the primary cause strives for. But the causality of God, who is the first efficient cause, reaches to all beings, not only with respect to their specific sources but also with respect to their individual sources, not only to things that cannot pass away, but also to things that can. And hence God needs to order to its end everything that exists in whatever way, as the Apostle says in the Letter to the Romans: "God has ordered everything that exists."[23] Therefore, since God's providence is nothing other than the plan ordering things to ends, as I have said,[24] everything needs to be subject to his providence as much as it shares existing.

I have also in like manner shown before that God knows everything, both what is universal and what is particular.[25] And since his knowledge is ordered to things as the knowledge of a craft is ordered to the products of the craft, as I have said before,[26] everything needs to be subject to his order, just as every product of a craft is subject to the order of the craft.

Reply to Obj. 1. There is a difference between a universal cause and a particular cause. For something can depart from the order of particular causes but not from the order of universal causes. For something is taken away from the order of one particular cause only because another particular cause prevents that order; for example, the action of water prevents wood from burning. And hence, since all particular causes are included under a universal cause, no effect can escape the order of a universal cause. Therefore, we say that an effect is by chance or luck with respect to a particular cause, inasmuch as the effect escapes the order of that cause, but we say that the effect is foreseen with respect to the universal cause, from whose order the effect cannot be withdrawn. For example, the meeting of two slaves, although by chance on their part, is nonetheless foreseen by their master, who knowingly sends them to one place in such a way that one slave does not know about the other.

Reply to Obj. 2. There is a difference between those who have charge of particular matters, and one who has charge of overall provision. This is the case because particular providers prevent as much deficiency from matters subject to their charge as they can, but one in charge of general provision allows deficiencies to occur in particular things in order that the good of the whole not be obstructed. And hence we say that passing away and deficiencies in things of nature are contrary to a particular nature. But passing away and deficiencies in things of nature are nonetheless part of the aim of nature as a whole, inasmuch as the deficiency of one thing yields to the good of another or to the good of the whole universe, for the passing away of one thing is the coming-to-be of another, and this preserves the species. Therefore, since God universally provides for the whole of being, it belongs to his providence to allow certain deficiencies in particular things in order not to obstruct the complete good of the universe. For, if every evil were to be prevented, the universe would lack many goods; for example, lions would not survive if they were not to kill animals, and there would be no patience of martyrs if there were no persecution by tyrants. And hence Augustine says in his *Enchiridion*: "Almighty God would in no way allow any evil to exist in his works unless he were also so omnipotent and good as to act well even in the case of evil."[27]

Moreover, the two arguments that we have just answered, seem to have motivated those who withdrew from God's providence things that can pass away, in which we find things of chance and evils.

Reply to Obj. 3. Human beings do not construct nature, but they employ the things of nature for their needs in acts of skill and virtue. And hence human providence does not extend to necessary things, which come to be by nature. And yet the providence of God, who is the author of nature, extends to these.

And the argument of this objection seems to have motivated those who took the course of natural things away from God's providence and ascribed the course of natural things to the necessity of matter, as Democritus and other ancient fathers did.

Reply to Obj. 4. The saying that God left human beings to themselves, does not remove human beings from his providence. But it shows that human beings do not have a pre-established power of action that is limited to only one thing, like the things of nature, which are only acted upon, as if directed by something else to their ends. And things of nature do not move themselves to act, as if directing themselves to their end, as rational creatures do by their power of free choice, whereby they deliberate and choose. And hence the text of Sirach says significantly: "in the hands of their own counsel." But since we trace the very acts of free choice back to God as their cause, deeds done by free choice need to be subject to his providence, for the providence of human beings is included under the providence of God, as particular causes are included under a universal cause.

But God provides for the just in a certain more excellent way than he does for the wicked, inasmuch as he does not allow anything to happen that would definitively prevent the salvation of the just. For "everything works unto good for those who love God," as the Letter to the Romans says.[28] On the other hand, we say that he abandons the wicked, because he does not draw them back from the evil of wrongdoing. He does not do this, however, in such a way that he entirely excludes them from his providence; otherwise, they would fall into nothingness if his providence were not to preserve them.

And the argument of this objection seems to have persuaded Cicero, who withdrew from God's providence human affairs, about which we deliberate.[29]

Reply to Obj. 5. Because rational creatures are masters of their actions by their power of free choice, as I have said,[30] such creatures are subject to divine providence in a certain special way, namely, as things are imputed to them for blame or merit, and things are rendered them as punishment or reward. And it is with respect to this that the Apostle removes oxen from God's care. But he does not do so in such a way that individual creatures lacking reason do not belong to his providence, as the Rabbi Moses thought.[31]

Third Article

Does God Directly Provide for Everything?

I proceed in this way to the third article: it seems that God does not directly provide for everything.

Obj. 1. We need to ascribe to God everything that belongs to rank. But it belongs to the rank of a king that he have ministers as intermediaries to provide for his subjects. Therefore, much less does God directly provide for everything.

Obj. 2. It belongs to providence to order things to their ends. But the end of everything is its perfection and good. Moreover, it belongs to every cause to bring its effect to good. Therefore, every efficient cause produces the effect of providence. Therefore, if God directly provides for everything, all secondary causes are taken away.

Obj. 3. Augustine says in his *Enchiridion* that "it is better not to know certain things than to know them,"[32] for example, contemptible things. And the Philosopher says the same thing in the *Metaphysics*.[33] But we should ascribe to God what is better. Therefore, God does not directly have providence regarding certain contemptible and evil things.

On the contrary, the Book of Job says: "Whom else did he set up over the earth? Or whom did he place over the world that he made?"[34] And Gregory comments on this passage: "He by himself rules the world he by himself made."[35]

I answer that two things belong to providence, namely, the plan ordering foreseen things to ends, and the execution of this order, which we call governance. With respect to the first of these, therefore, God directly provides for everything. This is because he has the plan of everything, even the least, in his intellect, and he gave to all the causes he appointed for particular effects, the power to produce those effects. And hence he needs to have considered the order of those effects in his plan beforehand.

With respect to the second, the execution of the order, there are some intermediaries of God's providence. This is because he governs lower things by means of higher things, not because of any deficiency of his own power, but because of the richness of his goodness, so that he communicates the excellence of causal power to creatures as well.

And we accordingly exclude the opinion of Plato,[36] who posited three kinds of providence, as Gregory of Nyssa relates.[37] And the first kind of providence belongs to the supreme deity, who provides first and foremost for spiritual things and so for the entire world with respect to genera, species, and universal causes. And the second kind of providence is one whereby there is provision for individuals belonging to things that can come to be and pass away, and he ascribed this providence to the gods who go around the heavens, i.e., the separate substances that move heavenly bodies in a circular motion. And the third kind of providence belongs to human affairs, and he attributed this providence to supernatural beings, whom the Platonists situated between us and the gods, as Augustine relates in *The City of God.*[38]

Reply to Obj. 1.   It belongs to a king's rank to have ministers who carry out his providence. But it results from his own deficiency that he have no plan about what his ministers are to do. For the more all practical knowledge considers the particulars in which an action consists, the more perfect such knowledge is.

Reply to Obj. 2.   The fact that God directly makes provision for everything, does not exclude secondary causes, which carry out this order, as is clear from what I have said before.[39]

Reply to Obj. 3.   It is better for us not to know evil and contemptible things, inasmuch as these prevent us from considering better things (since we cannot at the same time understand many things), and inasmuch as knowledge of evil things sometimes turns our will to evil. But this does not hold in the case of God, who sees everything at the same time at one glance, and whose will cannot be inclined to evil.

Fourth Article

Does Providence Impose Necessity on Foreseen Things?

I proceed in this way to the fourth article: it seems that God's providence imposes necessity on foreseen things.

Obj. 1.   Every effect that has a present or past intrinsic cause, from which the effect necessarily results, necessarily comes to be, as the Philosopher proves in the *Metaphysics.*[40] But God's providence, since it is eternal, pre-exists, and effects necessarily result from it, for his providence cannot be frustrated. Therefore, God's providence imposes necessity on foreseen things.

Obj. 2.   Every provider makes his work as secure as possible, lest it be wanting. But God is supremely powerful. Therefore, he gives the security of necessity to the things he has foreseen.

Obj. 3. Boethius says in his *On the Consolation of Philosophy* that fate, "springing from the sources of immutable providence, unites the acts and fortunes of human beings by an indissoluble combination of causes."[41] Therefore, it seems that providence imposes necessity on foreseen things.

On the contrary, Denis says in his *De divinis nominibus* that "it does not belong to providence to destroy nature."[42] But it belongs to the nature of certain things that they be contingent. Therefore, God's providence does not impose a necessity on things that excludes contingency.

I answer that God's providence imposes necessity on certain things but not on everything, as certain thinkers believed. For it belongs to providence to order things to ends. Moreover, next after God's goodness, which is an end distinct from things, the chief end, one that exists in things themselves, is the perfection of the universe, and that perfection indeed would not exist if we were not to find in the world every grade of existing. And hence it belongs to God's providence to produce every grade of beings. And so God's providence has prepared necessary causes for certain effects, so that the latter necessarily come to be. But it has prepared contingent causes for certain effects, so that the latter contingently come to be, according to the conditions of proximate causes.

Reply to Obj. 1. The effect of divine providence is not only that things come to be in any way, but also that they either contingently or necessarily come to be. And so what divine providence arranges inescapably and necessarily to come to be, inescapably and necessarily comes to be, and what divine providence plans contingently to come to be, contingently comes to be.

Reply to Obj. 2. The invariable and sure order of God's providence consists in the fact that everything that he provides for, comes to be in the way he provides for it, whether that way be necessary or contingent.

Reply to Obj. 3. The indissolubility and immutability that Boethius touches upon, belong to the certainty of providence, which does not lack its effects or the ways of coming-to-be that it provides for, but indissolubility and immutability do not belong to the effects' necessity. And we need to reflect that the necessary and the contingent in their proper senses result from being as such. And hence the modes of contingency and necessity fall within the foresight of God, who universally provides for the whole of being, but not within the foresight of those who provide for some particular things.

Notes

1. *De inventione* II (near the end).
2. *Ethics* VI, 5. 1140a25–31.

3. *De fide orthodoxa* II, 29. PG 94:964.
4. Wis. 15:2.
5. Q. 6, A. 4.
6. Q. 21, A. 4.
7. Q. 15, A. 2. Q. 19, A. 4.
8. *Ethics* VI, 5. 1140a28–31.
9. Mt. 24:45.
10. *On the Consolation of Philosophy* IV, 6. PL 63:814.
11. *Ethics* VI, 9. 1142b28–34.
12. Ps. 148:6.
13. Eph. 1:11.
14. Aristotle, *Ethics* VI, 13. 1144b25–32.
15. Q. 19, A. 1.
16. *Ethics* VI, 5. 1140a25–b4.
17. Sir. 15:14.
18. Ps. 81:12.
19. 1 Cor. 9:9.
20. Wis. 8:1.
21. Job 22:14.
22. Moses Maimonides, *Guide of the Perplexed*, part 3, chap. 17.
23. Rom. 13:1.
24. Q. 22, A. 1.
25. Q. 14, A. 11.
26. Q. 14, A. 8.
27. *Enchiridion* 11. PL 40:236.
28. Rom. 8:28.
29. *De divinatione* II.
30. In the preceding reply and Q. 19, A. 10.
31. See the body of the article and n. 22, *supra*.
32. *Enchiridion* 17. PL 40:239.
33. *Metaphysics* XI, 9. 1074b29–34.
34. Job 34:13.
35. *Moralia* XXIV, 20. PL 76:314.
36. The Neoplatonists evolved this threefold providence from Plato's theory of intermediate powers. Cf. Plato, *Timaeus* 6, 13, 14. 29E, 41A–42E.
37. See Nemesius, *De natura hominis* 44. PG 40:793–96. St. Thomas erroneously attributed this work to Gregory of Nyssa.
38. *The City of God* IX, 1, 2. PL 41:255–57.
39. In the body of the article.
40. *Metaphysics* V, 3. 1037a29–b11.
41. *On the Consolation of Philosophy* IV, 6. PL 63:817.
42. *De divinis nominibus* 4. PG 3:733.

ST I
Question 23
On Predestination

[This question is divided into eight articles, the first seven of which are included here.]

First Article

Does God Predestine Human Beings?

I proceed in this way to the first article: it seems that God does not predestine human beings.

Obj. 1. Damascene says in his *De fide orthodoxa*: "We should recognize that God foreknows everything, but he does not predestine everything. For he foreknows what is in us, but he does not predetermine such."[1] But human merits and demerits exist in us, inasmuch as we are masters of our acts by our power of free choice. Therefore, God does not predestine what belongs to merit or demerit. And so the predestination of human beings is eliminated.

Obj. 2. God's providence orders all creatures to their ends, as I have said before.[2] But we do not say that God predestines creatures other than human beings. Therefore, neither should we say that God predestines human beings.

Obj. 3. Angels are capable of happiness, just as human beings are. But it does not belong to angels to be predestined, as it seems, since they have never been unhappy, while predestination is "a plan of compassion," as Augustine says.[3] Therefore, God does not predestine human beings.

Obj. 4. The Holy Spirit reveals to holy men the benefits that God confers on human beings, according to the saying of the Apostle in the First Letter to the Corinthians: "And we have not received the spirit of this world but the Spirit that is from God, that we may know what God has bestowed on us."[4] Therefore, if God were to predestine human beings, since predestination is a benefit from God, the predestined would know his predestination of them. And this is clearly false.

197

On the contrary, the Letter to the Romans says: "Those whom he pre-destined, he also called."[5]

I answer that it is appropriate that God predestine human beings. For everything is subject to divine providence, as I have shown before.[6] More-over, it belongs to God's providence to order things to ends, as I have said.[7] Moreover, there are two ends to which God orders created things. There is one end that surpasses the proportion and ability of created nature, and this end is eternal life, which consists in the vision of God, and such a vision is above the nature of every creature, as I have maintained before.[8] And the other end is proportioned to a created nature, namely, the end that a created nature can reach by the power of its own nature.

But another needs to convey something to a destination that the latter cannot reach by the power of its own nature; for example, an archer conveys an arrow to its target. And hence, properly speaking, rational creatures, creatures capable of eternal life, are brought to that life as if conveyed by God. And the plan for this transmission indeed pre-exists in God, just as the plan ordering everything to ends exists in him, and we have said that this plan is providence.[9] Moreover, the plan of something to be made that exists in the mind of the maker, is a certain pre-existence of the thing in the maker. And hence we call God's plan for the aforementioned conveyance of rational creatures to their end of eternal life, predestination, for to destine is to send forth. And so predestination, as regards its objects, is one part of providence.

Reply to Obj. 1. Damascene calls predetermination an imposition of necessity, such as exists in the case of things of nature, which are predeter-mined to one thing. And this is clear from what he adds: "For he does not will evil or compel virtue."[10] And so he does not exclude predestination.

Reply to Obj. 2. Creatures that lack reason, are incapable of the end that surpasses the ability of human nature. And hence we do not say in a proper sense that God has predestined them, although we sometimes inaccurately use the term "predestination" with respect to every other end.

Reply to Obj. 3. Being predestined is just as appropriate for angels as it is for human beings, although angels have never been unhappy. For motion does not get its nature from its point of origin but from its destination, as, for example, it does not at all matter, with respect to the nature of making something white, whether the object made white was hitherto black or yel-low or red. And it likewise does not at all matter with respect to the nature of predestination whether or not one is predestined to eternal life from a condition of distress, although we can say that every conferring of a good above what is due to the one on whom the good is conferred, belongs to mercy, as I have said before.[11]

Reply to Obj. 4. Even if the predestination of some is by a special privilege revealed to them, it is nonetheless unfitting that it be revealed to all, be-cause then those not predestined would despair, and security would beget negligence in those predestined.

Second Article

Does Predestination Put Anything into the Predestined?

I proceed in this way to the second article: it seems that predestination puts something in the predestined.

Obj. 1. Every action of itself causes a capacity to be acted upon. Therefore, if predestination is action in God, predestination needs to be a capacity to be acted upon in the predestined.

Obj. 2. Origen comments on the text of the Letter to the Romans, "One who is predestined,"[12] etc.: "Predestination belongs to one who does not exist, but destination to one who exists."[13] But Augustine says in his work *De praedestinatione sanctorum*: "What is predestination except the destination of someone"?[14] Therefore, predestination belongs only to somone who exists. And so predestination puts something into the one predestined.

Obj. 3. Preparation is something in the thing prepared. But predestination is "the preparation of God's benefits," as Augustine says in his work *De praedestinatione sanctorum*.[15] Therefore, predestination is something in the predestined.

Obj. 4. We do not posit the temporal in the definition of the eternal. But we posit grace, which is something temporal, in the definition of predestination, for predestination is said to be "the preparation of grace in the present life and of glory in the future life."[16] Therefore, predestination is not something eternal. And so it needs not to exist in God but in the predestined, for everything in God is eternal.

On the contrary, Augustine says that predestination is "the foreknowledge of God's benefits."[17] But foreknowledge does not exist in the things foreknown but in the one who foreknows. Therefore, neither does predestination exist in the predestined, but it exists in the one who predestines.

I answer that predestination is not something in the predestined but exists only in the one who predestines. For I have said that predestination is one part of providence.[18] Moreover, providence does not exist in the things foreseen, but a certain plan exists in the intellect of the provider, as I have said before.[19] But the execution of providence, which we call governance, indeed exists in a passive way in the things governed as well as in an active way in the one who governs. And hence predestination is evidently a certain plan for ordering some persons to eternal salvation, and this plan exists in God's mind. The execution of this order, however, indeed exists in a passive way in the predestined as well as in an active way in God. Moreover, the execution of predestination is a "calling" and "magnification," as the Apostle says in the Letter to the Romans: "Those whom he predestined, he also called, and those whom he called, he also magnified."[20]

Reply to Obj. 1. Actions that pass into external matter, intrinsically cause capacities to be acted upon, as, for example, the actions of heating and cutting do, but actions that remain in their active cause, do not, as, for example, the actions of understanding and willing do not, as I have said before.[21] And predestination is an action of the latter sort. And hence predestination does not put anything in the predestined. But the execution of predestination, which passes into external things, puts effects in the predestined.

Reply to Obj. 2. We sometimes understand destination to denote the actual sending of someone to a destination, and destination in this way belongs only to what exists. We understand destination in another way to denote a sending that one mentally conceives, as we say that we destine what we firmly intend in our minds. And the Second Book of Maccabees says in the latter way that Eleazar "determined not to allow unlawful things because he loved life."[22] And so destination can belong to what does not exist. Nonetheless, by reason of the antecedent cause that predestination implies, predestination can belong to what does not exist, in whatever sort of way we may understand destination.

Reply to Obj. 3. There are two kinds of preparation. One kind of preparation belongs to the thing acted upon, in order that it be acted upon, and this kind of preparation exists in the thing prepared. The second kind of preparation belongs to the efficient cause, in order that it act, and this kind of preparation exists in the efficient cause. And the latter kind of preparation is predestination. For example, we say that an efficient cause by its intellect prepares itself to act, inasmuch as it preconceives the plan of the work to be made. And so God from eternity prepared salvation by predestining when he conceived his plan for ordering some persons to salvation.

Reply to Obj. 4. We do not posit grace in the definition of predestination as if grace were an entity belonging to the essence of predestination, but inasmuch as predestination implies a relation to grace, as a relation of cause to effect and of act to object. And hence it does not follow that predestination is anything temporal.

Third Article

Does God Condemn Any Human Being?

I proceed in this way to the third article: it seems that God condemns no human being.

Obj. 1. No one condemns one whom he loves. But God loves every human being, as the Book of Wisdom says: "You love everything that exists, and you hate nothing that you have made."[23] Therefore, God does not condemn any human being.

Obj. 2. If God condemns any human being, condemnation would need to be related to the condemned in the same way that predestination is related to the predestined. But predestination causes the salvation of the predestined. Therefore, condemnation will cause the destruction of the condemned. But this is false, for the Book of Hosea says: "Your destruction, O Israel, is from yourself; your help is only from me."[24] Therefore, God does not condemn anyone.

Obj. 3. We ought not to impute to anyone what such a one cannot avoid. But if God condemns anyone, such a one cannot escape being destroyed, for the Book of Ecclesiastes says: "Consider the works of God, that no one can improve one whom God has looked away from."[25] Therefore, we should not impute to human beings that they perish. But this conclusion is false. Therefore, God does not condemn anyone.

On the contrary, the Book of Malachi says: "I loved Jacob, but I hated Esau."[26]

I answer that God condemns certain persons. For I have said before that predestination is part of providence.[27] Moreover, it belongs to providence to allow deficiencies in things subject to providence, as I have said before.[28] And hence, since divine providence orders human beings to eternal life, it also belongs to God's providence to allow some human beings to fall short of that end. And we call this to condemn.

Thus, as predestination is a part of providence with respect to those whom God orders to eternal life, so condemnation is a part of providence with respect to those who fall away from this end. And hence condemnation not only denotes foreknowledge but adds something conceptually, just as providence does, as I have said before.[29] For, as predestination includes the will to confer grace and glory, so condemnation includes the will to allow someone to fall into wrongdoing and to cause the punishment of damnation for wrongdoing.

Reply to Obj. 1. God loves every human being and also every creature, inasmuch as he wills some good for all of them but he does not will every good for everything. Therefore, inasmuch as God does not will for some human beings the good that is eternal life, we say that he hates or condemns them.

Reply to Obj. 2. In causing, condemnation is disposed in a different way than predestination is. For predestination causes both what the predestined hope for in the future life, namely, glory, and what they receive in the present life, namely, grace. But condemnation does not cause what exists in the present life, namely, wrongdoing, although condemnation causes abandonment by God. Condemnation nonetheless causes what is rendered the condemned in the future life, namely, eternal punishment, but wrongdoing results from the free choice of those condemned and abandoned by grace. And the saying of the prophet, namely, "Your destruction, O Israel, is from yourself," is accordingly true.

Reply to Obj. 3. God's condemnation does not take anything away from the power of the condemned. And hence, when we say that the condemned cannot receive grace, we should not understand this as an absolute impossibility but as a conditional impossibility, just as I have previously said that the predestined are necessarily saved by a hypothetical necessity that does

not take away their freedom of choice.[30] And hence, although one condemned by God cannot obtain grace, yet it happens by such a person's
free choice that the person fall into this or that particular sin. And so also
we deservedly impute sin as wrongdoing to such a one.

Fourth Article

Does God Choose the Predestined?

I proceed in this way to the fourth article: it seems that God does not choose
the predestined.

Obj. 1. Denis says in his *De divinis nominibus* that, as the corporeal sun
sheds light on all material substances without choosing some, so also does
God pour out his goodness.[31] But God especially communicates his goodness to some by their sharing in grace and glory. Therefore, God communicates grace and glory without choosing the recipients. And this belongs to
predestination.

Obj. 2. Choice concerns things that exist. But there is also predestination
from eternity of things that do not exist. Therefore, God predestines some
without choice.

Obj. 3. Choice implies a certain discrimination. But God "wills that every
human being be saved," as the First Letter to Timothy says.[32] Therefore,
predestination, which pre-ordains human beings for salvation, exists apart
from choice.

On the contrary, the Letter to the Ephesians says: "He chose us in him
[Christ] before the foundation of the world."[33]

I answer that predestination conceptually presupposes choice, and choice
presupposes love. And the reason for this is because predestination is part
of providence, as I have said.[34] Moreover, providence, as well as practical
wisdom, is a plan that exists in the intellect, prescribing the ordering of some
things to an end, as I have said before.[35] But nothing is prescribed to be
ordered to an end except by a pre-existing willing of the end. And hence the
predestination of some for eternal salvation conceptually presupposes that
God wills their salvation. And choice and love belong to this willing. Love,
indeed, inasmuch as he wills the good of eternal salvation for the predestined, for to love is to will good for someone, as I have said before.[36] And
choice belongs to this willing inasmuch as he wills this good for some over
others, since he condemns some, as I have said before.[37]

Choice and love, however, are ordered in us and in God in different ways,
because our will does not cause something good by loving, but a pre-existing
good stirs us to love. And thus we choose the person we love, and so choice
precedes love in our case. But it is the converse in the case of God. For his
will, whereby he wills good for someone by loving, causes such a one rather
than others to have that good. And so it is clear that, conceptually, choice

presupposes love, and predestination presupposes choice. And hence God has chosen and loved those whom he predestined.

Reply to Obj. 1. If we were to consider the communication of God's goodness in general, he communicates his goodness without choosing, namely, inasmuch as there is nothing that does not share something of his goodness, as I have said before.[38] But if we were to consider the communication of this or that particular good, he does not bestow goods without choice, because he gives certain goods to some that he does not give to others. And so we attend to choice in his conferring grace and glory.

Reply to Obj. 2. When a good that pre-exists in things, stirs the will of a chooser to choose, there necessarily is a choice about things that exist, as happens in the case of our choosing. But it is otherwise in the case of God, as I have said.[39] And so, as Augustine says: "God chooses those who do not exist, and yet he who chooses, does not err."[40]

Reply to Obj. 3. As I have said before, God wills "antecedently" that all human beings be saved, and this is not to will absolutely but to will conditionally. But God does not will "consequently" that all human beings be saved, which is to will absolutely.[41]

Fifth Article

Does God's Foreknowledge of Merits Cause Predestination?

I proceed in this way to the fifth article: it seems that God's foreknowledge of merits causes predestination.

Obj. 1. The Apostle says in the Letter to the Romans: "Those whom he foreknew, he also predestined."[42] And Ambrose comments on Rom. 9:15, "I shall have mercy on the one on whom I shall have mercy," etc.: "I shall bestow mercy on the one who I foreknow will turn back to me wholeheartedly."[43] Therefore, it seems that God's foreknowledge of merits causes predestination.

Obj. 2. God's predestination includes his will, and his will cannot be without a reason, since predestination is "a decision to have mercy," as Augustine says.[44] But the only reason for predestination is foreknowledge of merits. Therefore, God's foreknowledge of merits is the cause or reason of predestination.

Obj. 3. "There is no unfairness in God," as the Letter to the Romans says.[45] Moreover, it seems unfair to give unequal benefits to those who are equal. But all human beings are equal as regards both their nature and original sin, while we note inequality in human beings as regards the merits or demerits of their own acts. Therefore, God prepares unequal rewards for human beings by predestining some and condemning others only because he foreknows their diverse merits.

On the contrary, the Apostle says in the Letter to Titus: "He did not cause us to be saved by the just actions that we perform, but by his mercy."[46] But as God caused us to be saved, so also has he predestined us to be saved. Therefore, his foreknowledge of merits is not the cause or reason of predestination.

I answer that, since predestination includes willing, as I have said before,[47] we need to seek the reason for predestination in the same way that we seek the reason for God's willing. Moreover, I have said before that we cannot ascribe a cause of God's willing as regards the act of willing, but we can ascribe a reason as regards the things willed, namely, inasmuch as God wills one thing to exist because of something else.[48] Therefore, no one has been of so unsound a mind as to say that merits cause God's predestination as regards the act of predestining. But this is transformed to the question: does predestination have any cause as regards the effects of predestination? And this is to ask whether or not God pre-ordained that he would bestow the effect of predestination on someone because of some merits of that person.

There have thus been certain thinkers who said that God pre-ordained the effect of predestination for someone because of that person's pre-existing merits in another life. And this was the position of Origen, who held that human souls were created from the beginning, and that, according to their different works, different conditions were allotted the souls when united to bodies in this world.[49] But the Apostle excludes this opinion, saying in the Letter to the Romans: "When they [Esau and Jacob] were not yet born nor had done anything good or bad, . . . not because of their works but because of him who calls them, the Lord said to her [Rebecca] that the elder will serve the younger."[50]

And then there were others who said that pre-existing merits in this life are the reason and cause of the effect of predestination. For example, the Pelagians held we initiate good actions, but that God completes them. And so the effect of predestination thereby happens to be given to one and not to another, because one person gives himself a start toward predestination by preparing himself, and another person does not do so. But this is contrary to what the Apostle says in the Second Letter to the Corinthians, that "we are not sufficient to think that anything is from ourselves, as if we caused it."[51] And we can find no source of action prior to a design. And hence we cannot say that there exists in us any beginning that is the reason for the effect of predestination.

And then there were others who said that merits resulting from the effect of predestination are the reason for predestination. Thus we are to understand that God so bestows grace on someone and has pre-ordained that he will give it to that person, because he foreknew that the person will make use of grace. This is as if a king should give a horse to a soldier who he knows will make good use of it. But these thinkers seem to have distinguished between what results from grace, and what results from free choice, as if the same thing could not be the product of both. It is nonetheless evident that what belongs to grace, is the effect of predestination, and we cannot posit this as the reason for predestination, since it is included in predestination. Therefore, if anything else on our part is the reason for predestination, this will be something beyond the effect of predestination. Moreover, what results from grace, and what results from free choice, are not separate, just as what results from a secondary cause, and what results from a primary cause, are not separate. For God's providence produces effects by the actions of secondary causes, as I have said before.[52] And so also what results from free choice, results from predestination.

Therefore, we need to say that we can consider the effect of predestination in two ways. In one way, in particular. And so nothing prevents one effect of predestination from being the cause and reason of another effect, a subsequent effect indeed being the cause of a prior effect by way of a final cause, but a prior effect being the cause of a subsequent effect by way of a meritorious cause, which we trace back to the disposition of the matter. This is as if we should say that God pre-ordained that he will give glory to someone because of that person's merits, and that he pre-ordained that he will give grace to someone in order that that person merit glory.

In the second way, we can consider the effect of predestination in general. And the entire effect of predestination in general then cannot have any cause on our part. This is so because everything in human beings that orders them to salvation, is all included in the effect of predestination, even the very preparation for grace. For this happens only by God's assistance, as the Book of Lamentations says: "Direct us to you, O Lord, and we shall be so directed."[53] Nonetheless, predestination in this way has, on the part of its effect, God's goodness for its reason, and the whole effect of predestination is ordered to his goodness as its end, and it proceeds from his goodness as the first source of its movement.

Reply to Obj. 1. God's foreknowlege of the use of grace is only by way of a final cause the reason why he confers grace, as I have said.[54]

Reply to Obj. 2. Predestination in general has God's very goodness as its reason as regards effects. But in particular, one effect of predestination is the reason for another effect, as I have said.[55]

Reply to Obj. 3. We can understand from his very goodness the reason why God predestines some and condemns others. For we thus say that God made everything because of his goodness, that his goodness be manifested in things. Moreover, God's goodness, which is in itself one and uncomposed, needs to be manifested in things in many ways, because created things cannot attain his simplicity. And hence different grades of things are required to fill up the universe, and certain creatures have a high rank, and certain others a low rank, in the universe. And to preserve the multiplicity of grades in things, God allows some evils to occur, lest many good things be prevented, as I have said before.[56]

Let us then consider the whole human race as the entire universe of things. God willed to manifest his goodness in human beings thus: as to some, those he predestines, by way of mercy, by sparing them; as to others, those he condemns, by way of justice, by punishing them. And this is the reason why God chooses some and condemns others. And the Apostle assigns this cause in the Letter to the Romans, saying: "God, willing to show his anger," that is, just punishment, "and to make his power known, with much patience maintained," that is, allowed, "vessels of wrath fit for destruction, that he might show the riches of his glory in the vessels of mercy that he has prepared for glory."[57] And the Second Letter to Timothy says: "Moreover, there are in a large household not only vessels of gold and silver but also vessels of wood and clay, some indeed for noble purposes, others for ignoble purposes."[58]

But why he chose some and condemned others, has no reason except God's willing it so. And hence Augustine comments on the Gospel of John: "Do not wish to judge why he draws this individual and does not draw that individual, if you do not wish to err."[59] So also, in the case of things of nature, since all of prime matter is intrinsically uniform, we can ascribe a reason why God from the beginning established one part of prime matter under the form of fire and another part under the form of earth, namely, so that there be a diversity of species in the things of nature. But why this particular part of matter is under this particular form, and that particular part of matter under another form, depends on God's absolute will. For example, it depends on the absolute will of a craftsman that this particular stone is in this particular part of a wall, and that that particular stone is in another part of the wall, although the nature of the craft requires that some stones be in this part of the wall, and that other stones be in that part of the wall.

Nonetheless, neither is there consequently unfairness in God if he prepares unequal benefits for things that are not equal. For it would be contrary to the nature of justice if God were to render the effect of predestination by reason of a debt and not as a favor. For in things bestowed as a favor, one can at his pleasure give more or less to whom he wishes, without detriment to justice, provided he does not take away from anyone what is due to him or her. And this is what the head of a household says in the Gospel of Matthew: "Take what is yours, and go. Or am I not free to do as I wish"?[60]

Sixth Article

Is Predestination Certain?

I proceed in this way to the sixth article: it seems that predestination is not certain.

Obj. 1. Augustine comments on Revelation 3:11, "Hold on to what you possess, lest another take your crown": "One person will not receive the crown unless another has lost it."[61] Therefore, one can both gain and lose the crown, that is, the effect of predestination. Therefore, predestination is not certain.

Obj. 2. Given that something is possible, no logical consequence is impossible. But someone predestined, for example, Peter, can sin and then be killed. Moreover, if this be granted, the effect of predestination is consequently thwarted. Therefore, this result is possible. Therefore, predestination is not certain.

Obj. 3. God can do whatever he could have done. But he could have not predestined one whom he predestined. Therefore, he can now not predestine such a one. Therefore, predestination is not certain.

On the contrary, Augustine comments on Rom. 8:29, "Those whom he foreknew, he also predestined," etc.: "Predestination is the foreknowledge and preparation of God's benefits, whereby all the redeemed are most surely redeemed."[62]

I answer that predestination most surely and unerringly achieves its effect, and yet it imposes no necessity, namely, that its effect should come to be by necessity. For I have said before that predestination is part of providence.[63] But not everything subject to providence is necessary; rather, certain things come about contingently, due to the circumstances of proximate causes, which divine providence orders to such effects. And yet the order of providence is unerring, as I have shown before.[64] Thus the order of predestination is also certain, and yet predestination does not take away freedom of choice, whereby the effect of predestination contingently comes about.

With respect to the foregoing, we need also to consider what I have said before about God's knowing and willing, which do not take contingency away from things, however most certain and unerring those things are.[65]

Reply to Obj. 1. We say in two ways that the crown belongs to someone. In one way, by God's predestination, and so no one loses his crown. In the second way, by the merit of grace, for what we merit, is ours in some way. And so one can lose his crown by a subsequent mortal sin. But another person receives that lost crown inasmuch as the second person takes the place of the first. For God does not allow some to fall without raising up others, as the Book of Job says: "He shall destroy countless numbers of persons and cause others to take their place."[66] Thus, for example, he has substituted human beings in place of the fallen angels, and Gentiles in place of Jews. And also with respect to the crown of the one who falls, the one substituted in the state of grace receives this benefit, that he will in eternal life rejoice in the good that the other has done, and everyone will in that life rejoice in the good done both by himself and others.

Reply to Obj. 2. Although one predestined, absolutely considered, can die in mortal sin, yet this cannot be the case if we hold, as we do indeed hold, that such a one is predestined. And hence it does not follow that predestination can fail.

Reply to Obj. 3. Predestination includes God's will. Consequently, as I

have said before that God's willing a created thing is hypothetically necessary, on account of the immutability of his will, but not absolutely,[67] so we
need to say the same thing here about predestination. And hence we should
not say that God is able not to predestine one whom he has predestined,
understanding the matter in a composite sense, although considering the
matter absolutely, God can predestine or not predestine. But the latter does
not take away the certainty of predestination.

Seventh Article

Is the Number of the Predestined Fixed?

I proceed in this way to the seventh article: it seems that the number of the
predestined is not fixed.

Obj. 1. A number that can be added to, is not fixed. But there can be an
addition to the number of predestined, as it seems, for the Book of Deuteronomy says: "May the Lord our God add many thousands to this
number."[68] And a gloss adds: "that is, the number fixed by God, who knows
who belong to him."[69] Therefore, the number of the predestined is not
fixed.

Obj. 2. We cannot assign a reason why God pre-ordains to salvation this
number of human beings rather than that number. But God disposes
nothing without reason. Therefore, God has not pre-ordained a fixed number of human beings to be saved.

Obj. 3. God's action is more perfect than the action of nature. But we find
good in the works of nature for the most part, while we find deficiency and
evil in rather few cases. Therefore, if God were to fix the number of those to
be saved, more would be saved than condemned. But the Gospel of Matthew indicates the contrary, saying: "Wide and large is the way that leads to
destruction, and there are many who enter by that way; narrow is the gate,
and small the way, that leads to life, and there are few who find it."[70] Therefore, God has not pre-ordained the number of those to be saved.

On the contrary, Augustine says in his *De correptione et gratia*: "The number of the predestined is fixed, which number can neither be increased nor
lessened."[71]

I answer that the number of predestined is fixed. But certain thinkers have
said that the number is formally but not materially fixed, as if, for example,
we were to say that it is certain that 100 or 1,000 human beings should be
saved, but not that these or those particular individuals should be. But this
takes away the certainty of predestination, about which we have already
spoken.[72] And so we need to say that the number of predestined is fixed not
only formally but also materially.

But we should note that we say that God is certain of the number of the predestined, not only by reason of his knowledge, namely, because he knows how many are to be saved (for God is in this way certain of the number of drops of water and the number of the sands of the sea), but by reason of a choice and determination by him.

And for evidence of this, we need to recognize that every efficient cause strives to make something limited, as is clear from what I have previously said about the unlimited.[73] Moreover, whoever intends a fixed character in an effect, calculates a particular number in the case of its essential parts, which are intrinsically required for the perfection of the whole. For he does not as such select a particular number in the case of things that are required only because of something else and not chiefly; rather, he obtains such things in the number necessary for something else. For example, a builder calculates the fixed size of a house as well as the fixed number of rooms that he wishes to construct in the house, and the fixed dimensions of the walls or roof; on the other hand, he does not choose a fixed number of stones but obtains as many as suffice to satisfy such measurements of the walls.

We thus need to consider the foregoing in the case of God with respect to the whole universe, which is his effect. For he has pre-ordained in what measure the whole universe ought to exist, and what number would be appropriate for the essential parts of the universe, namely, parts that are somehow naturally ordered to last indefinitely, namely, how many spheres, how many stars, how many elements, how many species of things. But individual things that can pass away, are not ordered to the good of the universe chiefly, as it were, but secondarily, as it were, inasmuch as the good of species is preserved in them. And hence, although God knows the number of all the individual things, God nonetheless did not intrinsically pre-ordain the number of oxen or gnats or other such things; rather, God's providence produced as many such individuals as suffice to preserve the species.

Moreover, of all creatures, rational creatures, which, as such, cannot pass away, are more importantly ordered to the good of the universe, and most particularly are those that gain beatitude, those that more directly attain their final end. And hence God is certain of the number of the predestined not only by way of his knowledge but also by way of his original pre-ordination. But it is not entirely so in the case of the number of the condemned, whom God seems to have pre-ordained for the good of the chosen, for whom all things work together for good.

Moreover, concerning the total number of predestined human beings, certain thinkers say that as many human beings will be saved as angels fell. But certain others say that as many human beings will be saved as the angels who remained faithful. Still others say that as many human beings will be saved as the angels who fell, and, in addition, as many as the angels who were created. But we prefer to say that "to God alone is known the number of the chosen destined for everlasting happiness."[74]

Reply to Obj. 1. We need to understand those words of Deuteronomy to be about those whom God has marked out beforehand with respect to present righteousness. For the number of these both increases and decreases, but not the number of the predestined.

Reply to Obj. 2. We need to understand the reason for the quantity of a part by the proportion of the part to the whole. For God thus has a reason why he made so many stars or so many species, and why he predestined so many human beings, from the proportion of the universe's chief parts to its good.

Reply to Obj. 3. The good proportioned to the general state of nature comes to be for the most part, and things are wanting of this good in rather few cases. But we find in rather few cases goods that surpass the general state of nature, and we find in most cases deficiencies of such goods. For example, there are evidently rather many human beings who have sufficient knowledge to guide their life, while there are rather few who lack such knowledge, those whom we call stupid and foolish. But there are very few, in comparison with the others, who attain to possession of a deep knowledge of intelligible things. Therefore, since eternal happiness, which consists in the vision of God, surpasses the general state of nature, and especially as the corruption of original sin deprives nature of grace, there are rather few who are saved. And God's mercy is most especially evident in the fact that he raises up some to that salvation, from which very many fall short through the general course and inclination of nature.

Notes

1. *De fide orthodoxa* II, 30. PG 94:969–72.
2. Q. 22, AA. 1, 2.
3. *De diversis quaestionibus ad Simplicium* II, 2. PL 40:140.
4. 1 Cor. 2:12.
5. Rom. 8:30.
6. Q. 22, A. 2.
7. Q. 22, A. 1.
8. Q. 12, A. 4.
9. Q. 22, A. 1.
10. See n. 1, *supra.*
11. Q. 21, A. 3, *ad* 2, and A. 4.
12. Rom. 1:4.
13. *In Epistolam ad Romanos.* PG 14:849.
14. Cf. *De dono perseverantiae* 14. PL 45:1013–14.
15. *De dono perseverantiae* 14. PL 45:1014.
16. Peter Lombard, *Sentences* I, dist. 40, 2.
17. See n. 15, *supra.*
18. Q. 23, A. 1.
19. Q. 22, A. 1.
20. Rom. 8:30.
21. Q. 14, A. 2. Q. 18, A. 3, *ad* 1.
22. 2 Mac. 6:20.

23. Wis . 11:24.
24. Hos. 13:9.
25. Eccl. 7:14.
26. Mal. 1:2–3.
27. Q. 23, A. 1.
28. Q. 22, A. 2, *ad* 2.
29. Q. 22, A. 1, *ad* 3.
30. Q. 19, A. 8, *ad* 1.
31. *De divinis nominibus* 4. PG 3:693.
32. 1 Tim. 2:4.
33. Eph. 1:4.
34. Q. 23, A. 1.
35. Q. 22, A. 1.
36. Q. 20, AA. 2, 3.
37. Q. 23, A. 3.
38. Q. 6, A. 4.
39. In the body of the article and Q. 20, A. 2.
40. *Sermo ad populum* 26, 4. PL 38:173.
41. See Q. 19, A. 6, *ad* 1.
42. Rom. 8:29.
43. *In Epistolam ad Romanos*. PL 17:142.
44. *De diversis quaestionibus ad Simplicium* I, 2. PL 40:140.
45. Rom. 9:14.
46. Tit. 3:5.
47. Q. 23, AA. 3, 4.
48. Q. 19, A. 5.
49. *Peri Archon* II, 9. PG 11:230.
50. Rom. 9:11–13.
51. 2 Cor. 3:5.
52. Q. 22, A. 3.
53. Lam. 5:21.
54. In the body of the article.
55. Ibid.
56. Q. 2, A. 3, *ad* 1. Q. 22, A. 2.
57. Rom. 9: 22–23.
58. 2 Tim. 2:20.
59. *In Ioannis Evangelium*, tract. 26. PL 35:1607.
60. Mt. 20:14–15.
61. *De correptione et gratia* 13. PL 44:940.
62. *Glossa ordinaria*, on v. 30. PL 114:498. Cf. *De dono perseverantiae* 14. PL 45:1014.
63. Q. 23, A. 1.
64. Q. 22, A. 4.
65. Q. 14, A. 13; Q. 19, A. 8.
66. Job 34: 24.
67. Q. 19, A. 3.
68. Dt. 1:11.
69. *Glossa ordinaria*. PL 113:450.
70. Mt. 7:13–14.
71. *De correptione et gratia* 13. PL 44:940.
72. Q. 23, A. 6.
73. Q. 7, A. 4.
74. From the Secret (Prayer over the Gifts) of the pre–Vatican II Mass for the Living and the Dead.

ST I
Question 25
On God's Power

[This question is divided into six articles, four of which are included here.]

First Article

Does God Have Power?

I proceed in this way to the first article: it seems that God has no power.
Obj. 1. As prime matter is related to potentiality,[1] so is God, who is the prime efficient cause, related to actuality. But prime matter, absolutely considered, is devoid of all actuality. Therefore, the first efficient cause is devoid of potentiality.
Obj. 2. Better than any power is its act, as the Philosopher says in the *Metaphysics*.[2] For form is better than matter, and action better than a power to act, since form is the goal of matter, and action the goal of a power to act. But nothing is better than what exists in God, since everything in God is God, as I have shown before.[3] Therefore, God has no power.
Obj. 3. Power is the source of action. But God's action is his essence, since nothing is accidental in him. Therefore, the nature of power is inappropriate for God.
Obj. 4. I have shown before that God's knowing and willing cause things to exist.[4] But cause is the same as source. Therefore, we should not ascribe power to God but only knowing and willing.

On the contrary, the Psalm says: "You are powerful, O Lord, and your truth surrounds you."[5]

I answer that there are two kinds of power, namely, passive power, which in no way exists in God, and active power, which we need to posit in God in the highest degree. For everything is manifestly the efficient source of something else insofar as the former is actual and perfect, while everything is acted upon insofar as it is lacking something and imperfect. Moreover, I have shown before that God is pure actuality and both absolutely and entirely perfect,[6] nor does he have any imperfection. And hence it is most proper for him to be an active source and not to be acted upon in any way. Moreover, the nature of active source belongs to active power. For active power is the source of acting on another, while passive power is the source of being acted upon by another, as the Philosopher says in the *Metaphysics*.[7] We conclude, therefore, that active power most of all exists in God.

Reply to Obj. 1. We do not contradistinguish active potentiality from actuality; rather, we base active potentiality on actuality, for everything acts insofar as it is actual. But we do distinguish passive potentiality from actuality, for everything is acted upon insofar as it is potential. And hence we exclude passive potentiality but not active potentiality from God.

Reply to Obj. 2. Whenever an act is distinct from a power, the act is necessarily more excellent than the power. But God's action is not distinct from his power; rather, both are his essence, because his existing is not distinct from his essence. And hence nothing needs to be more excellent than his power.

Reply to Obj. 3. Power in created things is not only the source of action but also the source of effects. Thus the nature of power is preserved in God with respect to power being the source of effects but not with respect to power being the source of action, which is the divine essence. But we might, according to our way of understanding, perchance consider God's power as the source of action, inasmuch as we can understand his essence, which in a noncomposite way possesses beforehand every perfection that exists in created things, both under the aspect of action and under the aspect of power; just so do we understand God's essence both under the aspect of an individually existing subject possessing a nature and under the aspect of a nature.

Reply to Obj. 4. We do not posit power in God as something really distinct from his knowing and willing but only as something conceptually distinct from them, namely, inasmuch as power implies the aspect of a source carrying out what the will commands, and that at which knowledge aims. And these three belong identically to God.

Or the very knowing and willing of God, as the source of effects, have the aspect of power. And hence the consideration of knowing and willing in the case of God precedes consideration of power, as causes precede their actions and effects.

Third Article

Is God All-Powerful?

I proceed in this way to the third article: it seems that God is not all-powerful.

Obj. 1. Being moved and being acted upon belong to everything. But God cannot be moved or acted upon, for he is unmovable, as I have said before.[8] Therefore, he is not all-potential.

Obj. 2. Sinning consists in doing something. But God cannot sin or "deny himself," as the Second Letter to Timothy says.[9] Therefore, God is not all-powerful.

Obj. 3. It is said of God that "he shows his omnipotence most of all by forebearance and compassion."[10] Therefore, the greatest thing that God's power can do, is to forebear and have mercy. But there is something far greater than to forebear and have mercy, as, for example, to create another world, or some such thing. Therefore, God is not all-powerful.

Obj. 4. A gloss on Cor. 1:20, "God has made foolish the wisdom of this world," says: "God made the wisdom of this world foolish by showing to be possible what that wisdom judged to be impossible."[11] And hence it seems that we are not to judge something possible or impossible by inferior causes, as the wisdom of this world judges, but by God's power. Therefore, if God is all-powerful, everything is possible. Therefore, nothing is impossible. But if we take away the impossible, we take away the necessary, for what necessarily exists, cannot not exist. Therefore, nothing in the world will be necessary if God is all-powerful. But this conclusion is impossible. Therefore, God is not all-powerful.

On the contrary, the Gospel of Luke says: "Nothing declared will be impossible with God."[12]

I answer that everyone commonly professes that God is all-powerful. But it seems difficult to assign the reason for his omnipotence. For, when we say that God can do everything, there is uncertainty about what is included in "everything." But if one should consider the matter rightly, since we speak of power in relation to things that are possible, we understand more correctly by the proposition "God can do everything" only that he can do everything that is possible, and we call him all-powerful for that reason.

Moreover, according to the Philosopher in the *Metaphysics*,[13] we can say in two ways that something is possible. In one way, with respect to some power; for example, we call "possible for a human being" what is subject to human power. But we cannot say that we call God all-powerful because he can do everything that created nature can do, because his power extends to more things. And if we should say that God is all-powerful because he can do everything that his power can do, there will be circular reasoning in showing his omnipotence, for the statement will only assert that God is all-powerful because he can do everything that he can do.

We conclude, therefore, that we call God all-powerful because he can do everything that is absolutely possible, and this is the second way of saying that something is possible. Moreover, we say that something is absolutely possible or impossible by the relationship of terms of a proposition; something is indeed possible if a predicate is compatible with a subject, as in the proposition "Socrates is sitting", but something is absolutely impossible if a predicate is incompatible with a subject, as in the proposition, "Human beings are donkeys".

But we need to consider that, since every efficient cause produces an effect like itself, something possible corresponds to every active power as the power's proper object by reason of the act on which the active power is based; for example, the power to heat is related to a capacity to be heated, as the power's proper object. But divine existing, on which the nature of God's power is based, is unlimited existing, not existing limited to a particular type of being but possessing in itself beforehand the perfection of all existing. And hence everything that can have the nature of being, is included in the class of things absolutely possible, and we call God all-powerful with respect to these.

Moreover, only nonbeing is contrary to the nature of being. What as such implies existing and nonexisting at the same time, is thus contrary to the nature of something absolutely possible, something subject to God's omnipotence. For something contradictory is not subject to his omnipotence, not because of any deficiency of his power, but because it cannot have the nature of something that can be made or can exist. Therefore, everything that implies no contradiction, is included in that class of possible things with respect to which we call God all-powerful. But things that imply a contradiction, are not included in God's power, because they cannot have the nature of being possible. And hence we more appropriately say that they cannot be made, than that God cannot make them.

Nor is this contrary to what the angel says: "Nothing declared will be impossible with God."[14] For what implies a contradiction, cannot be "declared," since no intellect can conceive it.

Reply to Obj. 1. We say that God is all-potential by active potentiality, not by passive potentiality, as I have said.[15] And hence his inability to be moved or acted upon is not contrary to his being all-potential.

Reply to Obj. 2. To sin is to fall short of perfect action, and hence to be able to sin is to be able to fail in action, and this is contrary to God's omnipotence. And consequently, God, who is all-powerful, cannot sin. And yet the Philosopher says in the *Topics* that "God, even intentionally, can do evil."[16] But we understand the statement of the Philosopher as a conditional proposition whose antecedent cannot be true, as if, for instance, we were to say that God can do evil "if he were to will to do so," for nothing prevents a conditional proposition from being true if its antecedent and consequent cannot be true. For example, if one should say, "If human beings are donkeys, they have four feet." Or else we understand that God can do certain things that now seem to be evil, but that would be good if God were to do them. Or else he speaks according to the general opinion of the pagans, who said that human beings were transformed into gods like Jupiter or Mercury.

Reply to Obj. 3. God shows his omnipotence most of all in forebearance and compassion, because, by freely forgiving sins, he shows that he possesses supreme power. For it does not belong to one who is bound by the law of a superior, to forgive sins freely.

Or God shows his omnipotence most of all in forebearance and compassion because he thereby brings human beings to share in an unlimited good, and this is the greatest effect of his power.

Or God shows his omnipotence most of all in forebearance and compassion because, as I have said before,[17] the effect of his mercy is the foundation of all his works. For God owes nothing to anyone except because of what he has gratuitously bestowed on that person. Moreover, God especially manifests his omnipotence in the fact that the first institution of everything good belongs to that omnipotence.

Reply to Obj. 4. We do not call something absolutely possible by reason of superior or inferior causes but by reason of its very self. But what we call possible by a particular power, we call possible by a proximate cause. And hence we call things whose nature it is to be directly produced by God alone, such as creating, justifying, and the like, possible by a higher cause. On the other hand, we call things whose nature it is to be produced by inferior causes, possible by such causes. For an effect has contingency or necessity according to the condition of a proximate cause, as I have said before.[18] Moreover, we reckon the wisdom of the world foolish because that wisdom judges things impossible for nature to be also impossible for God. And so God's omnipotence clearly does not take away impossibility and necessity from things.

Fifth Article

Can God Make Things That He Does Not Make?

I proceed in this way to the fifth article: it seems that God can only make the things he makes.

Obj. 1. God cannot make what he did not foreknow and pre-ordain that he will make. But God foreknew and pre-ordained that he will make only the things he makes. Therefore, God can make only the things he makes.

Obj. 2. God can only do what he ought to do, and what is right for him to do. But God ought not to make what he does not make, nor is it right that he should make what he does not make. Therefore, God can only make the things he makes.

Obj. 3. God can only make what is good and befits the things he has made. But it is not good or fitting that the things he has made, exist otherwise than they do. Therefore, God can only make the things he makes.

On the contrary, the Gospel of Matthew says: "Can I not ask my Father, and he will immediately hand over to me more than twelve legions of angels"?[19] But Christ did not ask for them, nor did his Father produce them to resist the Jews. Therefore, God can do other than what he does.

I answer that certain thinkers have erred in this matter in two ways. For some have held that God acts by a necessity from nature, as it were, in such a way that, as actions by things of nature can produce only what comes to be (as, e.g., the seed of human beings begets human beings, and olive seeds generate olive trees), so God's actions could not produce things, or an order of things, other than in the way things now exist. But I have shown before that God does not act as if by a necessity from nature, but that his will causes everything, and that his will is not determined by nature and necessity to the things he created.[20] And hence in no way does the present course of things come necessarily from God in such a way that other things could not have come about.

Others, however, have said that God's power is limited to the present course of things because of the order of his wisdom and justice, without which he does nothing. But since God's power, which is his essence, is nothing other than his wisdom, we can indeed appropriately say that he has no power that does not consist in the order of his wisdom, for his wisdom includes the total capacity of his power. And yet the order that God's wisdom implants in things, in which order the aspect of justice consists, as I have said before,[21] is not to be equated to his wisdom in such a way that his wisdom is limited to the present order. For a wise person takes from the end the whole plan of the order that he imposes on the things he has made. Thus, when an end is proportioned to things made for the sake of that end, the wisdom of the maker is limited to a fixed order. But God's wisdom is an end that surpasses created things beyond any proportion. And hence God's wisdom is not limited to a fixed order of things in such a way that no other course of things could flow from his wisdom. And hence we need to say without qualification that God can make other things than those he makes.

Reply to Obj. 1.   In ourselves, in whom power and essence are distinct from will and intellect, and likewise intellect distinct from wisdom, and will from justice, there can be something in our power that cannot exist in a righteous will or a wise intellect. But in the case of God, power and essence and will and intellect and wisdom and justice are identical. And hence there can be nothing in God's power that cannot exist in his righteous will and wise intellect.

Nonetheless, because God's will is not determined necessarily to these or those particular things, except perhaps hypothetically, as I have said before,[22] and his wisdom and justice are not limited to the present order, as I have said before,[23] nothing prevents something from being in his power that he does not will, and that is not included in the order that he established for things. And because we understand power as executing, but will as commanding, and intellect and wisdom as directing, we say that God can do by his absolute power what we attribute to power absolutely considered, and such is everything in which the aspect of being can be preserved, as I have said before.[24] But we say that God can do with regard to his appointed power what we attribute to his power as it executes the command of his righteous will. Accordingly, therefore, we need to say that God can, with respect to his absolute power, make things other than those he foreknew and pre-ordained that he will make, but it cannot be the case that he should make anything that he has not foreknown and pre-ordained that he will make. This is because his very making is subject to his foreknowledge and pre-ordination, but his very power, which belongs to his nature, is not so subject. For God makes something thus because he wills it, but he is able to make something in such a way, not because he wills it, but because he is such in his nature.

Reply to Obj. 2.   God does not owe anything to anybody but himself. And hence, when we say that God can only do what he ought to do, we signify nothing other than that God can only do what is proper and right for him to do. But we can understand the expression "proper and right" in two ways. In one way, such that we understand the expression "proper and right" to be first connected to the word "is," so that the expression is restricted to denoting present things. And the expression in this way is related to power. And the expression is thus false, for its meaning is: God can do only what is in the present order proper and right. But if the expression is first connected to the word "can," which has the force of enlarging the application, and later to the word "is," the expression will signify the present in a certain confused way. And the expression will be true, having this meaning: God can do only what would be proper and right if he were to do it.

Reply to Obj. 3.   Things that exist now, determine the present course of things, but God's wisdom and power are not limited to this course. And hence, although no other way would be good and appropriate for the things that now exist, yet God could make other things and put a different order in them.

Article Six

Can God Make Better the Things He Makes?

I proceed in this way to the sixth article: it seems that God cannot make better the things he makes.

Obj. 1.   Whatever God makes, he makes most powerfully and most wisely. But the more powerfully and the more wisely something is made, the better it is made. Therefore, God cannot make anything better than he makes it.

Obj. 2.   Augustine in his *Contra Maximinum* argues as follows: "God was envious if he could but would not beget a Son equal to himself."[25] By the same reasoning, if God could but would not make things better than he has made them, he was envious. But envy is completely eliminated from God. Therefore, God made everything the best. Therefore, God cannot make anything better than he made it.

Obj. 3. What is most—and very—good, cannot be made better, since nothing is greater than the greatest. But, as Augustine says in his *Enchiridion*, "Each thing made by God is good, and all things collectively are very good, since the wonderful beauty of the universe consists of them all."[26] Therefore, God cannot make the good of the universe better.

Obj. 4. Christ as human is perfect in grace and truth, and he possesses the Spirit beyond measure, and so he cannot be better. We also call created happiness the greatest good, and so it cannot be greater. And the Blessed Virgin Mary has been raised above all the choirs of angels, and so she cannot be better. Therefore, God cannot make better anything he made.

On the contrary, the Letter to the Ephesians says that God "is able to do everything more abundantly than we ask or understand."[27]

I answer that things have two kinds of goodness. One, indeed, that belongs to a thing's essence; for example, being rational belongs to the essence of a human being. And with respect to this good, God cannot make anything better than it itself is, although he can make something else better than it. Similarly, neither can he make a foursome greater, because, were it to be greater, it would then not be a foursome but a different number of things. For adding essential differences in the case of definitions is like adding units in the case of numbers, as the *Metaphysics* says.[28]

The second kind of goodness is one over and above a thing's essence; for example, being virtuous or wise is the good of human beings. And as regards this kind of good, God can make better the things he made. Moreover, absolutely speaking, he can make something else better than anything he has made.

Reply to Obj. 1. The statement that God can make something better than he makes it, is true if the word "better' be taken substantively, for he can make something else that would be better than anything he does make. And he can make the identical thing better in one way rather than another, as I have said.[29] But if the word "better" be taken as an adverb and to refer to the way in which God makes things, then he cannot make anything better than the way in which he does make it, since he cannot make by greater wisdom or goodness. And if the word "better" be taken to refer to the mode of the things made, then he can make better, since he can bestow on the things he made, a better way of existing regarding their accidental characteristics but not regarding their essence.

Reply to Obj. 2. It belongs to the nature of a son that he be his father's equal when he has reached maturity. But it does not belong to the nature of any creature that it be better than God made it. And hence the reasoning is different.

Reply to Obj. 3.   The universe, presupposing the things God made, cannot be better, since God assigned the most becoming order to them, and the good of the universe consists in such order. And if one of them were to be better, the harmony of that order would be destroyed. Similarly, the melodious harmony of the zither would be destroyed if one string were to be plucked more than it ought to be. Nonetheless, God could make other things or add other things to the things he made, and so such a universe would be better.

Reply to Obj. 4.   The humanity of Christ, because it is united to God, and created happiness, because it consists in the enjoyment of God, and the Blessed Virgin, because she is the mother of God, have a certain infinite worth from the infinite good that is God. And in this regard, nothing can be made better than these, just as nothing can be better than God.

Notes

1. As the answer indicates, the objection confuses passive potentiality with active potentiality (power). See Glossary, s.v. "potentiality" and "power."

2. *Metaphysics* VIII, 9. 1051a4–15.

3. Q. 3, A. 3.

4. Q. 14, A. 8. Q. 19, A. 4.

5. Ps. 89:8.

6. Q. 3, A. 1. Q. 4, AA. 1, 2.

7. *Metaphysics* IV, 12. 1019a15–20.

8. Q. 2, A. 3. Q. 9, A. 1.

9. 2 Tim. 2:13.

10. Collect (Opening Prayer) of the pre-Vatican II Mass for the Tenth Sunday after Pentecost.

11. Ambrose, *In Epistolam 1am ad Corinthios*. PL 17:189.

12. Lk. 1:37.

13. *Metaphysics* IV, 12. 1019a33–34.

14. Lk. 1:37.

15. In the body of the article.

16. *Topics* IV, 5. 126a34–35.

17. Q. 21, A. 4.

18. Q. 14, A. 13, *ad* 1.

19. Mt. 26:53.

20. Q. 19, AA. 3, 4.

21. Q. 21, A. 4.

22. Q. 19, A. 3.

23. In the body of the article.

24. Q. 25, A. 3.

25. *Contra Maximinum* II, 8. PL 42:762.

26. *Enchiridion* 10. PL 40:236.

27. Eph. 3:20.

28. Aristotle, *Metaphysics* VII, 3. 1043b36–1044a2.

29. In the body of the article.

Part 2
Creation

ST I

Question 44

On the Procession of Creatures from God and on the First Cause of All Beings

[This question is divided into four articles, all of which are included here.]

First Article

Does Every Being Need to Be Created by God?[1]

I proceed in this way to the first article: it seems that not every being needs to be created by God.

Obj. 1. Nothing prevents things from existing without some things that do not belong to their nature, as, for example, a human being can exist without whiteness. But the relationship of effect to cause does not seem to be an essential property of beings, since we can understand some beings apart from that relationship. Therefore, nothing prevents there being some beings that God does not create.

Obj. 2. Something needs an efficient cause in order to exist. Therefore, what cannot not exist, does not need an efficient cause. But a necessary being cannot not exist, since what exists necessarily, cannot not exist. Therefore, since there are many necessary things in the world, it seems that some beings are not from God.

Obj. 3. In the case of everything that has a cause, we can demonstrate by means of that cause. But we do not demonstrate by efficient causes in the case of mathematical objects, as the Philosopher makes clear in the *Metaphysics*.[2] Therefore, not every being is from God as its efficient cause.

On the contrary, the Letter to the Romans says: "Everything exists from him and by him and in him."[3]

I answer that we need to say that everything that exists in any way, is from God. For whatever perfection we find to exist in things by sharing, needs to be caused in them by something to which the perfection belongs essentially; for example, iron is heated by fire. Moreover, I have shown before, when I treated of God's simplicity, that God is intrinsically subsisting existence itself.[4] And I have also shown that there can be only one subsistent existence,[5] just as, if there existed a subsistent whiteness, there would be only one such, since whiteness is multiplied by its recipients. We conclude, therefore, that everything other than God is not its existence but shares in existing. Therefore, one first being, which exists most perfectly, needs to cause all the things that various sharings in existence make different, so that those things exist more perfectly or less perfectly.

And so also Plato said that we need to posit oneness before every multiplicity.[6] And Aristotle says in the *Metaphysics* that what is being and truth in the highest degree, causes every being and every truth,[7] just as what is hottest, causes all heat.

Reply to Obj. 1. Although relationship to a cause is not part of the definition of a caused being, yet the relationship results from what belongs to the nature of such a being. For, by the fact that something is a being by sharing existence, it is consequently caused by another. And hence such a being cannot exist without being caused, just as a human being cannot be human without the capacity for laughter. But we discover an uncaused being because it does not belong to the nature of being, in an unqualified sense, to be caused.

Reply to Obj. 2. The reasoning of this objection has persuaded certain thinkers to hold that the necessary has no cause, as the *Physics* says.[8] But this seems to be evidently false in the case of demonstrative sciences, in which necessary principles cause necessary conclusions. And thus Aristotle says in the *Metaphysics* that certain necessary things have a cause of their necessity.[9] Therefore, an efficient cause is required, not only because an effect can not-exist, but because an effect would not exist if a cause were not to exist. For the latter conditional proposition is true whether its antecedent and consequent are possible or impossible.

Reply to Obj. 3. We understand mathematical objects as conceptually abstract even though they are not abstract in reality. Moreover, it belongs to everything, insofar as it has existence, to have an efficient cause. Therefore, although mathematical objects do have an efficient cause, yet they do not fall within the consideration of a mathematician by the relationship that they have to their efficient cause. And so we do not demonstrate things in mathematical sciences by efficient causes.

Second Article

Does God Create Prime Matter?

I proceed in this way to the second article: it seems that God does not create prime matter.

Obj. 1. Everything produced is composed of a subject and something else, as the *Physics* says.[10] But prime matter has no subject. Therefore, God does not make prime matter.

Obj. 2. Action and being acted upon are mutually exclusive. But as the first active source is God, so the first passive source is matter. Therefore, God and prime matter are two mutually exclusive sources, neither one of which comes from the other.

Obj. 3. Every efficient cause produces something like itself, and so, since every efficient cause acts inasmuch as it is actual, everything produced is consequently somehow actual. But prime matter as such is only potential. Therefore, it is contrary to the nature of prime matter to be produced.

On the contrary, Augustine says in the *Confessions*: "You, O Lord, have made two things, one almost yourself," namely, angels, "the other almost nothing," namely, prime matter.[11]

I answer that ancient philosophers penetrated knowledge of the truth little by little and step by step, as it were. For they were initially rather untutored and thought that the only beings were sensible material substances. And those of them who held that there is change in material substances, considered change only with respect to certain accidents, such as thinness and thickness, aggregation and separation. And supposing the very substance of material things to be uncreated, they ascribed certain causes of those kinds of accidental changes, such causes as friendship, contention, understanding, or the like.

And advancing further, they intellectually distinguished substantial form from matter, which they held to be uncreated, and recognized that change occurs in material substances with respect to their essential forms. And they posited certain universal causes of those changes, such causes as elliptical orbits (Aristotle)[12] or ideas (Plato).[13]

But we need to consider that form restricts matter to a fixed species, just as an accident added to the substance of a species restricts a substance to a fixed way of existing, as, for example, "white" restricts "human being."

Each of these opinions thus considered being in a certain particular aspect, either as this particular being or as such a kind of being. And so they ascribed particular efficient causes to things.

And some were further encouraged to consider being as such, and they considered the causes of things, not only insofar as things are individual or of such a kind, but as they are beings. Thus, what causes things as beings, necessarily causes things, not only as they are such by their accidental forms, nor as they are these particular things by their substantial forms, but also with respect to everything that belongs to their existing in any way. And so we need to hold that the universal cause of beings also creates prime matter.

Reply to Obj. 1. The Philosopher is speaking in the cited text about particular coming-to-be, that is, coming-to-be from one form to another, whether the form be accidental or substantial. But we are now speaking of things with respect to their coming from the universal source of existing.

And we indeed do not exclude matter from the latter emanation, although we do exclude matter from the former way of being produced.

Reply to Obj. 2.   Being acted upon is the effect of action. And hence it is reasonable that the first passive source be the effect of the first active source, since something perfect causes everything imperfect. For the first source needs to be the most perfect, as Aristotle says in the *Metaphysics*.[14]

Reply to Obj. 3.   The argument of this objection does not show that matter is not created, but that it is not created apart from form. For, although everything created is actual, yet nothing created is pure actuality. And hence even what is disposed regarding potentiality, needs to be created if everything that belongs to its existing, is created.

Third Article

Is the Exemplary Cause Anything besides God?

I proceed in this way to the third article: it seems that the exemplary cause is something besides God.

Obj. 1.   A copy is like its model. But creatures are far from being like God. Therefore, God is not their exemplary cause.

Obj. 2.   We trace everything that exists by sharing existence, back to something that exists as such, as we trace something on fire back to fire, as I have already said.[15] But every sensible thing exists only by participating in some species, and this is evident because we do not find in sensible things only what belongs to the nature of a species, but sources of individuation are added to sources of the species. Therefore, we need to hold that species themselves exist as such, for example, human being as such and horse as such and the like. And we call these forms exemplars. Therefore, certain exemplary causes exist outside God.

Obj. 3.   Sciences and definitions have forms themselves for their objects, not as such forms exist in individual things, because neither sciences nor definitions treat of individual things. Therefore, there are certain beings or forms that do not exist in individual things. And we call such forms exemplars. Therefore, we reach the same conclusion as we did above.

Obj. 4.   The same point is evident in the words of Denis in his *De divinis nominibus*, that "existing itself as such is prior to life existing as such and to wisdom existing as such."[16]

On the contrary, exemplars are the same as the ideas. But the ideas are "the original forms included in God's understanding," as Augustine says in his work *Octoginta trium quaestionum*.[17] Therefore, the exemplars of things do not exist outside God.

I answer that God is the first exemplary cause of all things. And for evidence of this, we need to consider that an exemplar is necessary to produce something, so that the effect attains a definite form. For example, a craftsman produces a definite form in matter because of a model that he envisions, whether the model be something that the craftsman beholds outside himself, or the model be something that the craftsman conceives internally in his mind. Moreover, things that by nature come to be, evidently attain definite forms. And we need to trace the determination of forms back to God's wisdom as their first source, and his wisdom planned the order of the universe, which consists in different things. And so we need to say that there exist in God's wisdom the essences of all things, and I have previously called these essences "ideas," that is, exemplary forms that exist in the divine mind.[18] And although these ideas are indeed multiple with respect to things, yet they are in reality nothing other than God's essence, inasmuch as different things can share his likeness in different ways. Thus God himself is the first exemplar of everything.

We can also call certain created things exemplars of other created things insofar as some are like others, either by reason of the same species or by reason of the similarity of an imitation.

Reply to Obj. 1.   Although creatures do not attain to being like God by their nature, by likeness of species, as human offspring attain to being like their human progenitors, yet creatures attain a likeness to him by representing the nature that he understands, as a house existing in matter is like the house existing in the mind of its builder.

Reply to Obj. 2.   It belongs to the nature of human beings to exist in matter, and so we cannot find a human being existing apart from matter. Therefore, although particular human beings exist by sharing in the species, yet we cannot trace them back to something that as such exists in the same species, but we can to a higher species, such as separate substances.[19] And the argument is the same in the case of other sensible things.

Reply to Obj. 3.   Although all sciences and definitions have only beings for their objects, things nonetheless do not need to exist in the same way that the intellect understands them. For we abstract universal forms from individual conditions by the power of our active intellect, but universal things do not need to subsist outside individual things as exemplars of the individuals.

Reply to Obj. 4.   As Denis says in his *De divinis nominibus*, "life as such" and "wisdom as such" sometimes denote God himself, sometimes the powers bestowed on things themselves,[20] but do not denote any subsistent entities, as the ancient thinkers held.

Fourth Article

Is God the Final Cause of All Things?

I proceed in this way to the fourth article: it seems that God is not the final cause of all things.

Obj. 1.   Acting for the sake of an end seems to belong to something that needs to attain an end. But God needs nothing. Therefore, it does not belong to him to act for the sake of an end.

Obj. 2. The end of the action by which something comes to be, and the form of what has come to be, and the efficient cause of what comes to be, cannot be numerically identical, as the *Physics* says,²¹ because the end of the action whereby something comes to be, is the form of what has come to be. But God is the first efficient cause of all things. Therefore, he is not the final cause of all things.

Obj. 3. Everything desires its end. But some things do not desire God, since some things do not even know him. Therefore, God is not the end of all things.

Obj. 4. Final causes are the first of causes. Therefore, if God be the efficient cause and the final cause, there consequently exists in him something antecedent and something subsequent. But this is impossible.

On the contrary, the Book of Proverbs says: "God made everything because of himself."²²

I answer that every efficient cause acts for the sake of an end; otherwise, the action of an efficient cause would not produce this particular effect rather than that one except by chance. Moreover, the end of the thing that acts, and the end of the thing that is acted upon, as such, are the same, although in respectively different ways, since what the efficient cause strives to imprint, and what the thing acted upon strives to receive, are one and the same thing. And there are certain things that at the same time act and are acted upon, and these are imperfect efficient causes, for whom it is appropriate that they even in acting strive to acquire something. But it is not appropriate for the first efficient cause, which is only active, to act to acquire some end; rather, he strives to communicate his perfection, which is his goodness. And every creature strives to gain its own perfection, which is a likeness of God's perfection and goodness. Thus God's goodness is the end of all things.

Reply to Obj. 1. Acting out of need belongs only to an imperfect efficient cause, which nature constitutes to act and to be acted upon. But such acting does not belong to God. And so he alone is perfectly generous, since he does not act for his own benefit but only because of his goodness.

Reply to Obj. 2. The form of what came to be, is the end of the action whereby the thing comes to be, only inasmuch as that form is the likeness of the form of the efficient cause of what comes to be, and the efficient cause strives to communicate its likeness. Otherwise, the form of what came to be, would be more excellent than the efficient cause of what comes to be, since an end is more excellent than the means to an end.

Reply to Obj. 3. Everything desires God as its end when it desires any good, whether by intellectual appetite or sense appetite or natural appetite (and the latter appetite exists apart from knowledge), because nothing has the nature of good and desirable except insofar as it shares in likeness to God.

Reply to Obj. 4.   Since God is the efficient, exemplary, and final cause of all things, and prime matter is from him, the first source of all things is consequently only one thing in reality. Nonetheless, nothing prevents us from considering many things in him conceptually, and some of these things fall within our understanding before others.

Notes

1. This article deals with whether or not God is the efficient cause of every creature, not how he is their cause. Article two deals with whether or not God is the efficient cause of prime matter. Question 45 deals with the manner in which God causes things.
2. *Metaphysics* II, 2. 996a21–bl.
3. Rom. 11:36.
4. Q. 3, A. 4.
5. Q. 7, A. 1, *ad* 3, and A. 2.
6. *Parmenides* 26. 164C–165E.
7. *Metaphysics* Ia, 1. 993b19–31.
8. Aristotle, *Physics* VIII, 1. 252a32–b6.
9. *Metaphysics* IV, 5. 1015b6–11.
10. Aristotle, *Physics* I, 7. l90a31–bl7.
11. *Confessions* XII, 7. PL 32:828–29.
12. *De generatione et corruptione* II, 10. 336a 31–34.
13. *Timaeus*. 48E–51B.
14. *Metaphysics* XI, 7. 1072b30–1073a5.
15. Q. 44, A. 1.
16. *De divinis nominibus* 5. PG 3:820.
17. *Octoginta trium quaestionum*, Q. 46. PL 40:30.
18. Q. 15, A. 1.
19. St. Thomas cites separate substances (i.e., purely spiritual beings) as examples of species that surpass human beings, but the article makes clear St. Thomas's position that God is the only higher being who is the exemplary cause of creatures.
20. *De divinis nominibus* 11. PG 3:953.
21. *Aristotle, Physics* II, 7. 198a24–27.
22. Prov. 16:4.

ST I
Question 45
On the Manner in Which Things
Emanate from the First Source

[This question is divided into eight articles, the first five of which are included here.]

First Article

Is Creation the Making of Something Out of Nothing?

I proceed in this way to the first article: it seems that creation is not the making of something out of nothing.

Obj. 1. Augustine says in his *Contra adversarium legis et prophetarum*: "To make is to cause what did not exist at all, but to create is to cause something by educing it from what already existed."[1]

Obj. 2. We weigh the excellence of action and motion by their termini. Action that transforms something good into something else good, and one being into another, is thus more excellent than action that transforms nothing into something. But creation seems to be the most excellent action and the most important of all actions. Therefore, creation is not from nothing to something but rather from one being to another.

Obj. 3. The words "out of" imply a causal relationship, and especially a relationship of material causality, as, for example, when we say that a statue is made out of bronze. But "nothing" cannot be the matter of a being or in any way the cause of a being. Therefore, creation is not the making of something "out of nothing."

On the contrary, a gloss on Gen. 1:1, "In the beginning, God created the heavens," etc., says: "To create is to make something out of nothing."[2]

I answer that, as I have said before, we need to consider not only the emanation of a particular being from a particular efficient cause but also the emanation of the whole of being from the universal cause, that is, God,[3] and we indeed designate the latter emanation by the term "creation." Moreover, emanation from the universal cause does not presuppose coming-to-be by a particular emanation; for example, in the case of begetting human beings, the latter did not exist beforehand, but they are produced out of something nonhuman, and something now white is made out of something that was not white. And hence, if we should consider the emanation of the whole of being in general from the first source, such emanation cannot presuppose any being. But "nothing" is the same as nonbeing. Thus, as human beings are begotten out of the nonbeing that is nonhuman, so creation, that is, the emanation of the totality of being, is out of the nonbeing that is nothing.

Reply to Obj. 1. Augustine uses the term "creation" in an equivocal sense, as we say that what is refashioned into something better, is "created"; for example, we say that a person is "created" bishop. But we are not here speaking about creation in this way; rather, we are speaking about creation in the way I described.[4]

Reply to Obj. 2. Changes get their type and worth from their goal, not from their point of origin. Therefore, the more excellent and important the goal of a change, the more perfect and important the change, although the starting point, in contrast to the destination, is less perfect. For example, substantial change is without qualification more excellent and important than accidental change, because substantial forms are more excellent than accidental forms. Nonetheless, lacking a substantial form, which is the starting point in substantial change, is less perfect than its contrary,[5] which is the starting point in accidental change. And creation is likewise more perfect and important than substantial and accidental changes, because its goal is the entire substance of something. But what we understand as creation's starting point, is without qualification nonbeing.

Reply to Obj. 3. When we say that something is made out of nothing, the words "out of" do not designate a material cause but only a relation, as, for example, when we say, "Noon comes out of morning," that is, "Noon comes after morning." But we need to understand that the prepositional words "out of" can include the negation implied in my saying "nothing," or that the negation can include the prepositional words. If in the first way, then the relation is affirmed, and we indicate the relation of something existing to its previous nonexisting. If, however, the negation includes the prepositional words, then the relation is denied, and the meaning is: "Something is made out of nothing," that is, "Something is not made out of anything"; this is as if we should say, "This person is speaking about nothing," because such a person is not speaking about anything. And we find the words "out of" verified in both ways when we say that something is made out of nothing. But the words "out of" in the first way imply a relation, as I have just said; the prepositional words in the second way imply the relationship of a material cause, and the relationship is denied.

Second Article

Can God Create Something?

I proceed in this way to the second article: it seems that God cannot create anything.

Obj. 1. Ancient philosophers accepted as a general conception of the soul that "nothing is made out of nothing," according to the Philosopher in the *Physics*.[6] But God's power does not extend to things contrary to first principles, as, for example, that God cause a whole not to be greater than one of its parts, or that an affirmation and a negation of something be simultaneously true. Therefore, God cannot make something out of nothing or create anything.

Obj. 2. If creating is making something out of nothing, then being created consists in something coming to be. But every coming-to-be consists in a change. Therefore, creation is a change. But every change is out of a subject, as is clear by the definition of change, for change is "the actuality of something that has a potentiality."[7] Therefore, God cannot make anything out of nothing.

Obj. 3. What has been made, needs to be made at some point of time. But we cannot say that something created is being made and simultaneously has been made, because what has been made, already exists. Therefore, something would exist and not exist simultaneously. Therefore, if anything is made, its being made precedes its having been made. But this can be the case only if there pre-exists a subject that supports a being's very coming-to-be. Therefore, nothing can be made out of nothing.

Obj. 4. Crossing an unlimited divide is impossible. But there is an unlimited divide between being and nothing. Therefore, nothing may be made out of nothing.

On the contrary, the Book of Genesis says: "In the beginning, God created the heavens and the earth."[8]

I answer that not only can God create something, but we need to hold that God has created everything, as I have maintained in what I previously set forth.[9] For when anyone makes something out of something else, the person's action presupposes the source out of which the person produces the product, and the action itself does not produce the source; for example, a craftsman works with things of nature, such as wood and bronze, which the action of nature, not the activity of his craftsmanship, causes. But nature itself also causes the things of nature with respect to their form, although nature presupposes matter. Therefore, if God were to act only by means of something else presupposed to exist, he consequently would not cause the thing presupposed. Moreover, I have shown before that there can exist nothing in beings that is not from God, who is the universal cause of all being.[10] And hence we need to say that God brings things into existence out of nothing.

Reply to Obj. 1.   As I have said before, ancient philosophers considered only the emanations of particular effects from particular causes, which causes need to presuppose something in their actions, and the common opinion of those philosophers accordingly was that nothing is made out of nothing.[11] But that adage has no force in the case of the first emanation from the universal source of things.

Reply to Obj. 2.   Creation is change only according to our way of understanding. For it belongs to the nature of change that the same thing be disposed differently now than before. For sometimes there is the same actual being that is disposed differently now than before, as in changes of size, quality, and place, but sometimes there is only the same potential being, as in substantial changes, whose subject is matter. But in the case of creation, which produces the entire substance of things, we can only conceptually understand the same thing to be disposed differently now than before, as if we should understand that something did not exist at all before, and that it exists afterward. Since, however, acting and being acted upon are identical regarding the substance of change but differ only regarding different relationships, as the *Physics* says,[12] only the different relationships in the creator and the creature need to remain when we eliminate change.

But since our way of signifying is the result of our way of understanding, as I have said,[13] we signify creation by way of change and therefore say that to create is to make something out of nothing. And yet the terms "making" and "being made" are more appropriate in this matter than "changing" and "being changed," because making and being made imply relationships of cause to effect, and effect to cause, although making and being made consequently imply change.

Reply to Obj. 3.   When things are made apart from motion, their being made and their having been made exist simultaneously. This is so whether such making is the term of a motion, as in the case of illumination (for an object is being illumined and at the same time has been illumined), or such making is not the term of a motion (as, e.g., concepts are being formed and at the same time have been formed in the mind). What is made in the case of these things, exists, but we signify their existing from another and their not having existed previously, when we speak of their being made. And hence, since creation exists apart from motion, things are being created and simultaneously have been created.

Reply to Obj. 4.   This objection comes from a deceptive imagination, as if there should exist some unlimited entity between nothing and being, and this is evidently false. Moreover, such a deceptive imagination derives from the fact that we signify creation as a sort of change that takes place between two termini.

Third Article

Is Creation Something in the Creature?

I proceed in this way to the third article: it seems that creation is nothing in the creature.

Obj. 1. As we attribute creation, understood in the passive sense, to creatures, so we attribute creation, understood in the active sense, to the creator. But creation in the active sense is nothing in the creator, because it would then follow that something temporal would exist in God. Therefore, creation in the passive sense is nothing in the creature.

Obj. 2. There is nothing in between creator and creature. But we signify creation as something in between the two, for creation is not the creator, since it is not eternal, and it is not the creature, since we would by the same reasoning need to posit a second creation whereby the first creature would be created, and so on in endless regression. Therefore, creation is no thing.

Obj. 3. If creation is something besides a created substance, creation needs to be an accident belonging to the created substance. But every accident is in a subject. Therefore, a created thing would be the subject of creation. And so the same thing would be the subject of creation and its term. And this is impossible, because a subject is prior to its accidents and preserves them, while a term of action is subsequent to the acting and being acted upon whose term it is, and the acting and being acted upon cease when the term exists. Therefore, creation itself is no thing.

On the contrary, it is more important that something be made in its entire substance than in its substantial or accidental forms. But coming to be absolutely or in some respect, whereby something comes to be by a substantial or accidental form, is something in what has come to be. Therefore, much more is creation, whereby something is made in its entire substance, something in the created thing.

I answer that creation puts something in a created thing only by a relation. This is so because created things are not made by motion or change. For what comes to be by motion or change, is made out of something pre-existing, which indeed occurs in the particular productions of some beings, but this cannot happen in the production of the whole of existing by the universal cause of every being, which cause is God. And hence God, when he creates, produces things apart from movement. Moreover, when movement is eliminated from acting and being acted upon, there remains only a relation, as I have said.[14] And hence we conclude that creation in the creature is only a certain relation to the creator as the source of the creature's existing, just as a relation to the source of movement is implied in the state of being acted upon that exists with movement.

Reply to Obj. 1. Creation in the active sense signifies God's action, which is his essence in relation to creatures. But God's relation to creatures is only a conceptual relation, not a real relation, while the relation of creatures to God is real, as I have said before when I dealt with the names of God.[15]

Reply to Obj. 2.   Because we designate creation as change, as I have said,[16] and change is something somehow in between the cause of change and the object changed, so we also designate creation as something in between the creator and creatures. Nonetheless, creation understood in the passive sense exists in the creature and is the creature. And yet there is no need for another creature to be created, because relations, since we say that their very reality consists in being related to something, are related to their objects by themselves, not by other relations, as I have also said before when I dealt with the equality of the Persons.[17]

Reply to Obj. 3.   Creatures are the termini of creation insofar as we designate creation as change. But creatures are the subjects of creation insofar as creation is truly a relation, and creatures are prior to that relation in their existing, as subjects are prior to accidents. Creation, however, has a certain aspect of priority regarding the object toward which creation is appointed, which is the beginning of creatures. But we do not need to say that creatures are being created as long as they exist, because creation implies the relationship of creatures to the creator by a certain newness or beginning.

Fourth Article

Does it Belong to Composite and Subsistent Things to Be Created?

I proceed in this way to the fourth article: it seems that it does not belong to composite and subsistent things to be created.

Obj. 1.   The *Liber de causis* says: "The first thing created is existence."[18] But the existence of a created thing is not subsistent. Therefore, creation in the proper sense does not belong to subsistent and composite things.

Obj. 2.   Everything created is created out of nothing. But composite things do not exist out of nothing but out of their component parts. Therefore, it is inappropriate that composite beings be created.

Obj. 3.   The first emanation in the proper sense produces what we presuppose in succeeding emanations, just as the coming-to-be from nature produces the things of nature that we presuppose in the activity of crafts. But what we suppose in the coming-to-be by nature, is matter. Therefore, it is matter, not a composite, that is in the proper sense created.

On the contrary, the Book of Genesis says: "In the beginning, God created the heavens and the earth."[19] But the heavens and the earth are composite subsistent things. Therefore, creation in the proper sense belongs to them.

I answer that being created is a kind of coming to be, as I have said.[20] But coming-to-be is ordered to the existence of something. And hence coming-to-be and being created belong in the proper sense to what existence belongs. And this is indeed appropriate in the proper sense for subsistent things, whether they be uncomposed, like separate substances,[21] or composite, like material substances. For existence belongs in the proper sense to what possesses existence, that is, what subsists in its own existing. But we do not say that forms and accidents and the like are beings as if they themselves exist, but because things exist by means of them; for example, we call whiteness a being because its subject is white by means of it. And hence, according to the Philosopher, we say in the proper sense that accidents "belong to beings" rather than accidents "are beings."[22] Therefore, as accidents and forms and the like, which do not subsist, are co-existent rather than beings, so we ought to call them co-created rather than created. But subsistent things are created in the proper sense.

Reply to Obj. 1. When the *Liber de causis* says, "The first created thing is existence," the word "existence" does not imply a created subject but the proper nature of the object of creation. For we call something created because it is a being, not because it is this particular being, since creation is the emanation of all existence from the universal being, as I have said.[23] And there is a like way of speaking if we were to say that "the first object of vision is color," although what we see in the proper sense, is a colored object.

Reply to Obj. 2. Creation does not mean constituting something composed of pre-existing sources; rather, we say that composite beings are created in such a way that they are brought into existence along with all their sources.

Reply to Obj. 3. That argument does not prove that only matter is created, but that matter exists only by creation. For creation is the production of all existing and not only the production of matter.

Fifth Article

Does It Belong to God Alone to Create?

I proceed in this way to the fifth article: it seems that it does not belong to God alone to create.

Obj. 1. According to the Philosopher, things able to make things like themselves are perfect.[24] But immaterial creatures are more perfect than material creatures, which make things like themselves; for example, fire generates fire, and human beings beget human beings. Therefore, an immaterial substance can make a substance like itself. But only creation can make an immaterial substance, because an immaterial substance has no matter out of which it may be made. Therefore, a creature can create.

Obj. 2. The greater the resistance by the object made, the greater the power required in its cause. But something contrary resists more than nothing does. Therefore, it belongs to a greater power to make an object out of something contrary, which creatures nonetheless do, than to make something out of nothing. Therefore, much more can creatures make something out of nothing.

Obj. 3. We weigh the power of what makes something, by the measure of what is made. But created beings are limited, as I have proved before when I dealt with the infinity of God.[25] Therefore, only limited power is required to produce something by creation. But it is not contrary to a creature's nature to possess limited power. Therefore, it is possible for a creature to create.

On the contrary, Augustine says in his *De Trinitate* that neither good angels nor bad angels can create anything.[26] Therefore, much less can other creatures do so.

I answer that it is sufficiently apparent at first glance from what I have previously explained, that creating can be the proper action of God alone.[27] For we need to trace more universal effects back to more universal and prior causes. Of all effects, moreover, the most universal is existence itself. And hence that effect needs to be the proper effect of the first and most universal cause, that is, God. And hence also the *Liber de causis* says that neither an intelligence nor an excellent soul bestows existence except inasmuch as it acts by divine action.[28] Moreover, it belongs to the nature of creation to produce existence absolutely, not inasmuch as this particular thing or such a kind of thing exists. And hence creation is evidently the proper action of God himself.

But one thing may share in the proper action of another, not by the former thing's own power but as an instrument of the latter thing, inasmuch as the former acts through the power of the latter; for example, air can by the power of fire heat or ignite something. And some thinkers accordingly thought that, although creation is the proper action of the universal cause, yet some lesser causes, insofar as they act by the power of the first cause, can create. And so Avicenna held that the first separate substance, which God created, afterward creates another separate substance, and the substance of the heavens and its soul, and that the substance of the heavens creates the matter of lower material substances.[29] And the Master in like manner says in the Sentences that God can communicate to a creature the power to create, so that the creature creates as God's minister, not on its own authority.[30]

But such cannot be the case, because a secondary instrumental cause shares in the action of a higher cause only to the extent that it acts dispositively by something proper to itself to produce the effect of the chief cause. Therefore, if a secondary cause were then not to do anything by what is proper to itself, in vain would it be employed in the action, nor would specific instruments be needed for specific actions. For we thus see that an ax, in cutting wood, which power it possesses by a property of its form, produces the form of a footstool, which is the chief cause's own effect. But God's own effect in creating is what all other effects presuppose, namely, existence without qualification. And hence nothing can act dispositively and instrumentally to produce this effect, since creation is not by anything presupposed, something that could be disposed by the action of an instrumental cause. It thus cannot be appropriate for any creature to create, either by its own power or instrumentally, i.e., ministerially.

And it is especially inappropriate to say that a material substance may create, since a material substance acts only by touching or moving something, and so a material substance in its action requires something preexisting, something that could be touched and moved, and this is contrary to the nature of creation.

Reply to Obj. 1. Something perfect sharing in a nature makes something like itself, not indeed by producing that nature absolutely, but by adding the nature to something. For example, particular human beings cannot cause human nature absolutely, because such individuals would thus cause themselves, although individual human beings cause human nature to exist in the individual human beings they have begotten. And so such action by individual human beings presupposes the determined matter by which they are these particular human beings. But as these particular human beings share in human nature, so every created being, if I may so speak, shares in the nature of existing, since God alone is his existing, as I have said before.[31] Therefore, no created being can produce a being absolutely, except inasmuch as a created being causes existence in this particular being, and so it is necessary that the action whereby a created being makes something like itself, presuppose something by which the being is this particular thing.

But in the case of an immaterial substance, we cannot presuppose anything by which such a being is this particular being, because an immaterial substance is this being by its form, by which it has existence, since immaterial substances are subsisting forms. Therefore, an immaterial substance cannot produce another immaterial substance like itself with respect to the other's existing, but only with respect to an additional perfection; this is as if we should say that a superior angel illumines an inferior angel, as Denis says.[32]

And paternity also exists in this way in heaven, as is clear from the words of the Apostle in the Letter to the Ephesians: "And we name every paternity in heaven and on earth from him."[33] And it is also plainly evident by this that no created being can cause anything unless something be presupposed to exist. And the latter supposition is contrary to the nature of creation.

Reply to Obj. 2. Something is by chance made out of its contrary, as the *Physics* says,[34] but something is intrinsically made out of a subject with such a potentiality. Therefore, a contrary resists an efficient cause, inasmuch as the contrary keeps the thing's potentiality from the actuality to which the efficient cause strives to bring the potentiality; for example, fire strives to bring the matter of water to an actuality like itself, but it is impeded from doing so by water's form and contrary dispositions, which restrain the potentiality, as it were, from being brought to actuality. And the more restrained the potentiality, the more power is required in the efficient cause to bring the matter to actuality. And hence much greater power is required in an efficient cause if no potentiality pre-exists. Therefore, it clearly belongs to a far greater power to make something out of nothing than to make something out of its contrary.

Reply to Obj. 3. We weigh the power of what makes something, not only by the substance of the product but also by the manner of its production; for example, greater heat not only heats more but also heats more quickly. Therefore, although creating a limited effect does not demonstrate unlimited power, yet creating such an effect out of nothing does demonstrate unlimited power. And this is evident from what I have said before.[35] For, if the further potentiality is from actuality, the greater the power required in an efficient cause, the power of an efficient cause to produce something out of no presupposed potentiality—and an efficient cause creates in this way—needs to be unlimited. For there is no proportion between no potentiality and some potentiality, which potentiality the power of natural efficient causes presupposes, just as there is no proportion between nonbeing and being. And because no creature has unconditionally unlimited power, just as a creature possesses no unlimited existing, as I have previously proved,[36] it follows that no creature can create.

Notes

1. *Contra adversarium legis et prophetarum* I, 23. PL 42:633.
2. Peter Lombard, *Sentences* II, dist. 1.
3. Q. 44, A. 2.
4. In the body of the article.
5. I.e., lacking an accidental form.
6. *Physics* I, 4. 187a26–29.
7. Aristotle, *Physics* III, 1. 201a10.
8. Gen. 1:1.
9. Q. 44, A. 1.
10. Q. 44, AA. 1, 2.
11. Q. 44, A. 2.
12. Aristotle, *Physics* III, 3. 202b5–8.
13. Q. 13, A. 1.
14. Q. 45, A. 2, *ad* 2.
15. Q. 13, A. 7.
16. Q. 45, A. 2, *ad* 2.
17. Q. 42, A. 1, *ad* 4.
18. *Liber de causis*, prop. 4. This work derives from Proclus.
19. Gen. 1:1.
20. Q. 45, A. 2, *ad* 2.

21. Substances separated from matter, i.e., angels.
22. *Metaphysics* IV, 1. 1028a15–20.
23. Q. 45, A. 1.
24. *Meteorology* IV, 3. 380a11–15.
25. Q. 7, A. 2.
26. *De Trinitate* III, 8. PL 42:875–76.
27. Q. 45, A. 1. Q. 44, AA. 1, 2.
28. *Liber de causis*, prop. 3.
29. *Metaphysics*, tract. 9, chap. 4.
30. Peter Lombard, *Sentences* IV, dist. 5.
31. Q. 7, A. 1, *ad* 3, and A. 2.
32. *De coelesti hierarchia* 8. PG 3:240.
33. Eph. 3:15.
34. Aristotle, *Physics* I, 7. 190b23–29.
35. In the response to the second objection.
36. Q. 7, A. 2.

ST I
Question 46
On the Beginning of the Duration of Created Things

[This question is divided into three articles, the first two of which are included here.]

First Article

Did the Universe of Created Things Always Exist?

I proceed in this way to the first article: it seems that the universe of creatures, which we call the world, had no beginning but always existed.

Obj. 1. If anything began to exist, its existence was possible before it existed; otherwise, its coming-to-be was impossible. Therefore, if the world began to exist, its existence was possible before it began to exist. But what can exist, is matter, and matter has potentiality for existing, which results from form, and potentiality for not existing, which results from lacking a form. Therefore, if the world began to exist, matter existed before the world did. But matter cannot exist without form; rather, matter with form constitutes the world. Therefore, the world existed before it began to exist, and this conclusion is impossible.

Obj. 2. Nothing with power to exist always, exists at one time and does not exist at another time, since a thing exists as long as its power avails. But whatever cannot pass away, has power to exist always, for such a thing does not have only power for a fixed period of time. Therefore, nothing that cannot pass away, exists at one time and does not exist at another time. But everything that begins to be, exists at one time and does not exist at another. Therefore, nothing that cannot pass away, begins to exist. But there are many things in the world that cannot pass away, such as heavenly bodies and all intellectual substances. Therefore, the world did not begin to exist.

Obj. 3. Nothing began to exist that did not come to be.[1] But the Philosopher proves in the *Physics* that matter did not come to be,[2] and he proves

241

in the *De coelo* that the heavens did not come to be.[3] Therefore, the universe of things did not begin to exist.

Obj. 4. There is empty space where no material substances exist but can. But if the world began to exist, no material substances existed beforehand where the world's material substances now are, although they could have been there; otherwise, they would not now be there. Therefore, there was empty space before the world existed, and such a conclusion is impossible.

Obj. 5. Nothing freshly begins to be moved except because a cause of motion or a moveable object is now otherwise disposed than it was before. But something now otherwise disposed than it was before, is moved. Therefore, some motion existed before every newly beginning motion. Therefore, motion always existed. Therefore, a moveable object also always existed, since motion exists only in a moveable object.

Obj. 6. Everything that moves something else, does so either by nature or by free will. But neither nature nor free will begins to move something except by reason of pre-existing motion. For nature always acts in the same way. And hence, unless there should be a preceding change either in the nature of the moving cause or in the moveable object, no previously non-existent movement by a natural cause of motion will begin to exist. And the will, without any change of its own, delays doing what it proposes to do, and this is so only because of a fancied change, at least as regards time itself. For example, one who decides to build a house tomorrow and not today, anticipates that something will exist tomorrow that does not exist today, and at least expects that today will pass away, and that tomorrow will come. And such does not exist without change, since time numbers motion. Therefore, we conclude that a prior motion existed before every newly beginning motion. And so we reach the same conclusion as in the case of the preceding objection.

Obj. 7. Whatever is invariably at a beginning and an end, can neither begin to exist nor cease to exist, because what begins to exist, is not at its end, and what ceases to exist, is not at its beginning. But time always exists at a beginning and an end, since only "now," which is the end of the past and the beginning of the future, belongs to time. Therefore, time cannot begin or cease to exist. And consequently, neither can motion, which time numbers.

Obj. 8. God is prior to the world either only by nature or by duration. Therefore, if God is prior only by nature, since God eternally exists, the world as well eternally exists. But if God is prior by duration, and prior and subsequent events constitute time, then time existed before the world did. And such a conclusion is impossible.

Obj. 9. If we suppose a sufficient cause, we suppose its effect, for a cause with no resulting effect, is an imperfect cause, one that needs something else in order that an effect result. But God is the adequate cause of the world, both the final cause by reason of his goodness, the exemplary cause by reason of his wisdom, and the efficient cause by reason of his power, as is clear from what I have said before.[4] Therefore, since God exists eternally, the world as well existed from eternity.

Obj. 10. One whose action is eternal, produces an eternal effect. But God's action is his substance, and his substance is eternal. Therefore, the world as well existed from eternity.

On the contrary, the Gospel of John says: "Glorify me with yourself, Father, with the glory that I had before the world came to be."[5] And the Book of Proverbs says: "The Lord possessed me at the beginning of his ways, before he initially produced anything."[6]

I answer that only God has existed eternally. And it is indeed possible to hold this. For I have shown before that God's will causes things.[7] Things thus need to exist as much as God needs to will them, for the necessity of an effect depends on the necessity of a cause, as the *Metaphysics* says.[8] Moreover, I have shown before that, absolutely speaking, God does not need to will anything other than himself.[9] Therefore, God does not need to will that the world should always have existed. But the world exists as long as God wills it to exist, since the existence of the world depends on God's will as its cause. Therefore, it is not necessary that the world always exist. And hence neither can such be demonstratively proved.

Nor are the arguments that Aristotle advances to prove the eternity of the world,[10] absolutely demonstrative but demonstrative in one respect, namely, to refute the arguments of the ancient philosophers who held that the world begins in certain ways that are in fact impossible. And this is evident by three considerations. First, indeed, because Aristotle both in the *Physics*[11] and in the *De coelo*[12] sets forth certain views, such as those of Anaxagoras, Empedocles, and Plato, and he brings out arguments that refute those thinkers. Second, because he, whenever speaking about the matter, brings in the testimony of ancient thinkers, and this is the way of one who plausibly persuades, not the way of one who demonstrates. Third, because he expressly says in the *Topics* that there are certain logical problems for which we have no answers, and one such is this one: "Is the world eternal?"[13]

Reply to Obj. 1. It was possible for the world to exist, before it did, not indeed by passive power, which is matter, but by God's active power. And also it was possible that the world exist, before it did, as we call something absolutely possible, not with respect to any power but only by the relationship between mutually compatible terms. And it is in this way that the possible is contrary to the impossible, as the Philosopher makes clear in the *Metaphysics*.[14]

Reply to Obj. 2. If something has the power always to exist, it does not at one time exist and at another time not exist, but it did not exist before it had that power. And hence the argument of this objection, which Aristotle poses in the *De coelo*,[15] does not absolutely demonstrate that things incapable of passing away did not begin to exist. But such reasoning demonstrates that things incapable of passing away did not begin to exist by the natural process whereby things capable of coming to be and passing away begin to exist.

Reply to Obj. 3. Aristotle proves in the *Physics* that matter did not come to be, because it has no subject to which it belongs.[16] Moreover, he proves in the *De coelo* that the heavens did not come to be, because they have nothing contrary out of which they may come to be.[17] And hence it is evident that both texts prove only that matter and the heavens did not begin by coming to be, as some thinkers held, especially about the heavens. But we say that matter and the heavens have been brought into existence by creation, as is clear from what I have said before.[18]

Reply to Obj. 4. It is not enough for the nature of an empty space that nothing exist in it, but there needs to exist a space capable of containing material substances, a space in which no material substance exists, as Aristotle makes clear in the *Physics*.[19] But we say that there existed no place or space before the world existed.

Reply to Obj. 5. The first cause of motion was always disposed in the same way, but the first moveable object was not always disposed in the same way, because, not previously existing, it began to exist. But the first moveable object did not begin to exist by change but by creation, and creation differs from change, as I have said before.[20] And hence the argument of this objection, which Aristotle poses in the *Physics*,[21] is evidently valid against those who held that moveable objects are eternal, but motion not eternal, as the opinions of Anaxagoras and Empedocles explain.[22] But we hold that motion always existed from the moment that moveable objects began to exist.

Reply to Obj. 6. The first efficient cause acts by his free will. And although he had an eternal will to produce an effect, he nonetheless did not produce an eternal effect. Nor do we need to presuppose any change, not even because we imagine a passage of time. For we need to understand this matter in one way in the case of particular efficient causes, which presuppose something to exist and cause something else, and in another way in the case of the universal cause, which produces the whole. For example, particular efficient causes produce forms and presuppose matter, and hence particular efficient causes need to introduce forms proportional to the requisite matter. And hence we reasonably regard in this case that a particular efficient cause brings a form into such matter and not another matter because of the difference of one matter from another. But we do not reasonably regard this to be so in the case of God, who at the same time produces form and matter, although we do reasonably regard in the case of God that he himself produce matter suitable for the form and the end.

Moreover, particular efficient causes presuppose time as well as matter. And hence we reasonably regard in the case of such causes that they act in subsequent and not prior moments of time, by imagining a succession of time, one moment after another. But in the case of the universal cause, which produces things and time, we are not to think that this cause acts now and not before, by imagining one moment of time after another, as if that cause's action presupposes time; rather, we need to regard in the case of the universal cause that he gives as much time to his effects as he willed to give, and as was fitting to manifest his power. For the world more manifestly leads to knowledge of the divine power of the creator if the world did not always exist than if the world were always to have existed. For what has not always existed, evidently has a cause, but having a cause is not so evident in the case of what has always existed.

Reply to Obj. 7. As the *Physics* says,[23] there are successive moments in time insofar as there are successive phases in motion. And hence we need to understand the beginning and end in time as we understand the beginning and end in motion. Moreover, supposing the eternity of motion, we necessarily understand that every phase in motion is the beginning and end of motion, but this does not need to be the case if motion should have a beginning. And the argument is the same with respect to the "now" of time. And so that consideration of the present "now," which is always the beginning and end of periods of time, presupposes the eternity of time and motion. And hence Aristotle advances the argument of this objection in the *Physics* against those who posited the eternity of time but denied the eternity of motion.[24]

Reply to Obj. 8. God is prior to the world by duration. But the term "prior" does not designate a priority of time but the priority of eternity.

Or the term "prior" designates the eternity of the time that we imagine, and not of the time that really exists. For example, when we say, "There is nothing above the heavens," the term "above" designates only a place that we imagine, insofar as we can imagine that other dimensions can be added to those of the heavens.

Reply to Obj. 9. As an efficient cause that acts by nature, produces an effect according to the cause's form, so an efficient cause that acts by free will, produces an effect according to the form that such a cause preconceived and determined, as is clear from what I have said before.[25] Therefore, although God was eternally the sufficient cause of the world, yet we need to hold that he produced the world only as predetermined by his will, namely, that the world more evidently manifest its maker.

Reply to Obj. 10. Supposing action, an effect results as the form that is the source of action, requires. But in the case of efficient causes that act by free will, we understand what such a cause conceives and predetermines, as the form that is the source of the action. Therefore, an eternal effect does not result from God's action, but an effect results from his action in the way in which he willed it to result, namely, that it had existence after not existing.

Second Article

Is It an Article of Faith
that the World Had a Beginning?

I proceed in this way to the second article: it seems that it is not an article of faith but a demonstrable conclusion that the world had a beginning.

Obj. 1. Everything produced has a beginning of its duration. But we can conclusively prove that God is the efficient cause of the world, and the more approved philosophers so held. Therefore, we can conclusively prove that the world had a beginning.

Obj. 2. If we need to say that God produced the world, he therefore did so either out of nothing or out of something. But he did not do so out of something, since the matter of the world would have preceded the world, and the arguments of Aristotle holding that the world did not come to be,[26] are valid against such a position. Therefore, we need to say that God produced the world out of nothing. And so the world has existence after not existing. Therefore, the world needs to have begun to exist.

Obj. 3. Every being that produces by means of an intellect, produces from a certain starting point, as is evident in the case of every artifact. But God produces by means of his intellect. Therefore, he produces from a starting point. Therefore, the world, which is his effect, did not always exist.

Obj. 4. Particular crafts and the population of regions clearly seem to have originated at fixed times. But this would not be the case if the world were always to have existed. Therefore, the world evidently did not always exist.

Obj. 5. It is certain that nothing can be equal to God. But if the world were always to have existed, it would be equal to God in duration. Therefore, it is certain that the world did not always exist.

Obj. 6. If the world always existed, an unlimited number of days preceded today. But nothing passes through what is unlimited. Therefore, the world would never have arrived at today, and this conclusion is evidently false.

Obj. 7. If the world existed eternally, coming-to-be also existed eternally. Therefore, individual human beings have begotten human beings in an infinite series of begettings. But fathers are the efficient causes of their offspring, as the *Physics* says.[27] Therefore, there would be an infinite series of efficient causes, and the *Metaphysics* proves that such an infinite series cannot exist.[28]

Obj. 8. If the world and coming-to-be always existed, an unlimited number of human beings have previously existed. But the human soul is immortal. Therefore, an unlimited number of human souls would now actually exist, which is impossible. Therefore, we can know necessarily that the world had a beginning, and we do not hold this position only by faith.

On the contrary, we cannot demonstratively prove articles of faith, because faith concerns "things not evident," as the Letter to the Hebrews says.[29] But it is an article of faith that God created the world in such a way that the world began to exist, for we say: "I believe in one God," etc.[30]

And Gregory also says in his homilies on the Book of Ezekiel that Moses prophesized about the past when he said that "God created the heavens and the earth in the beginning," whereby he revealed to us the originality of the world.[31] Therefore, we accept the originality of the world only by revelation. And so we cannot prove the newness of the world by demonstration.

I answer that we maintain only by faith that the world did not always exist, and we cannot demonstrate the same, as I have also said before about the mystery of the Trinity.[32] And the reason for this is because we cannot demonstrate the originality of the world by the world itself. For the principle of demonstration is something's essence. Moreover, everything, with respect to its specific nature, abstracts from a particular place and time, and Aristotle consequently says that "universals exist in all places and at all times."[33] And hence we cannot demonstrate that human beings or the heavens or stones did not always exist.

Likewise also, neither can we demonstrate the originality of the world by the world's efficient cause, who produces creatures by his will. For reason can search out God's will only with regard to what God absolutely needs to will, but what he wills in the case of creatures, is not such, as I have said.[34]

But revelation, on which faith rests, can reveal God's will for human beings. And hence we can believe that the world had a beginning, but we cannot demonstrate or have theoretical knowledge of this truth.

And this is useful to be considered, lest anyone, presuming to demonstrate what belongs to faith, should by chance adduce arguments that are not conclusive, and those arguments give material for ridicule to unbelievers, who would think that we believe matters of faith because of such arguments.

Reply to Obj. 1.   Philosophers who posited the eternity of the world held two views, as Augustine says in *The City of God*.[35] For some of these philosophers held that the substance of the world does not exist from God. But this opinion cannot be sustained, and so it is necessarily refuted. Some, however, posited an eternal world in such a way that they nonetheless affirmed that God produced the world. "For they were of the opinion that" the world "does not have a temporal beginning but one by creation, such that the world was in a barely intelligible way always produced."[36]

"And," as the same Augustine says there, "they indicate how they understand this. For, they say, just as there would always be a footprint if a foot were from eternity ever in the dust of the ground, and no one would doubt that a treader produced the footprint, so also the world and its maker have always existed."

And to understand this, we need to reflect that an efficient cause that acts by moving something, necessarily precedes its effect in time, since an effect exists only at the end of such action, while every efficient cause needs to be the starting point of the action. But if an action be instantaneous and not successive, the producer need not be prior in duration to what is produced, as is evident in the case of illumination. And hence, they say, it does not necessarily follow that God is prior to the world in duration if he is the efficient cause of the world, because creation, by which he produced the world, is not successive change, as I have said before.[37]

Reply to Obj. 2. Those who would posit an eternal world, would say that God produced the world out of nothing, not that he produced it after nothing, as we understand by the term "creation," but that he did not produce it out of anything. And so some of them do not reject the term "creation," as Avicenna makes clear in his *Metaphysics*.[38]

Reply to Obj. 3. This objection is the argument of Anaxagoras posed in the *Physics*.[39] But the argument leads to a necessary conclusion only about an intellect that by deliberation studies what is to be done, and this activity is like motion. And the human intellect is such an intellect, while God's intellect is not, as is clear from what I said before.[40]

Reply to Obj. 4. Those who posit the eternity of the world, hold that regions pass from uninhabitable to habitable an unlimited number of times, and vice versa. And they likewise hold that crafts, because of various transformations and events, have been discovered and have also ceased to exist an unlimited number of times. And hence Aristotle says in the *Meteorology* that it is silly to accept a conjecture about the originality of the world on the basis of such particular changes.[41]

Reply to Obj. 5. Even if the world were always to have existed, it would nonetheless not be equal to God in eternity, as Boethius says in his *On the Consolation of Philosophy*.[42] This is so because God's existing is simultaneously whole existing without succession, but this is not so in the case of the world.

Reply to Obj. 6. We always understand transit to be from one terminus to another. Moreover, from any designated past day to another, there is a finite number of days, and this number of days can be traversed. But the objection proceeds as if there would be an infinite number of intermediate points if end points are stipulated.

Reply to Obj. 7. There cannot be an intrinsically infinite series of efficient causes. Such would be the case if causes intrinsically required for an effect were to be multiplied to infinity, as, for example, if a stone were to be moved by a stick, and the stick by a hand, and so on to infinity. But we do consider it possible that there be an infinite series of efficient causes by chance. Such would be the case if all the causes multiplied to infinity should be ordered to a single cause, while their multiplicity be by chance, as, for example, a craftsman by chance works with many hammers because he breaks one after another hammer. Therefore, it is by chance that one after another hammer does the work. And it is likewise by chance that a particular human being, as progenitor, is begotten by another human being, since human beings beget as human beings and not as offsprings of other human beings. For all human progenitors have the same status as efficient causes, namely, the status of particular progenitors. And hence it is possible that individual human beings beget other human beings in an infinite series of begettings. But such would be impossible if begetting by a particular human being were to depend on the particular human being, and on a basic material substance, and on the sun, and so on endlessly.

Reply to Obj. 8. Those who posit the eternity of the world, evade this argument in many ways. For some do not regard it as impossible that an infinite number of souls actually exist, as is evident in the *Metaphysics* of Algazel, who says that such a number is infinite by chance.[43] But I have proved before that this is not so.[44] Others, however, say that the soul passes away with the body. And others say that only one of all the souls abides. Still others, as Augustine says, consequently posited a re-incarnation of souls, namely, that disembodied souls return again to bodies after fixed passages of time.[45] And we need to deal with all of these matters later.[46]

Nonetheless, we need to consider that the argument of this objection concerns only a particular instance. And hence one could say that the world was eternal, or at least that some such creatures as angels were, but that human beings were not. We, however, are now directing our attention generally to whether or not any creature has existed eternally.

Notes

1. The objection speaks of coming to be in the narrow sense, i.e., out of pre-existing matter.
2. *Physics* I, 9. 192a25–34.
3. *De coelo* I, 3. 270a12–14.
4. Q. 44, AA. 1, 3, 4.
5. Jn. 17:5.
6. Prov. 8:22.
7. Q. 19, A. 4.
8. Aristotle, *Metaphysics* IV, 5. 1015a20–35.
9. Q. 19, A. 4.
10. *Physics* VIII, 1. 251a8–252a4.
11. *Physics* VIII, 1. 250b21–251a5.
12. *De coelo* I, 10. 279b14–16.
13. *Topics* I, 11. 104b12–16.
14. Aristotle, *Metaphysics* IV, 12. 1019b22–33.
15. *De coelo* I, 12. 281b18–282a4.
16. See n. 2, *supra*.
17. *De coelo* I, 3. 270a14–22.
18. Q. 45, A. 2.
19. Aristotle, *Physics* IV, 1. 208b25–29.
20. Q. 45, A. 2, *ad* 2.
21. *Physics* VIII, 1. 251a16–28.
22. Ibid. 250b21–251a5.
23. Aristotle, *Physics* IV, 11. 219a22–25.

24. *Physics* VIII, 11. 219a22–25.
25. Q. 19, A. 4. Q. 41, A. 2.
26. See preceding article.
27. Aristotle, *Physics* II, 3. 194b29–32.
28. *Aristotle, Metaphysics* Ia, 2. 994a11–19.
29. Heb. 11:1.
30. Nicene Creed.
31. *Homiliarum in Ezechielem*, I, 1. PL 76:786–87.
32. Q. 32, A. 1.
33. *Posterior Analytics* I, 31. 87.
34. Q. 19, A. 3.
35. *The City of God* XI, 4. PL 41:319.
36. Ibid. X, 31. PL 41:311.
37. Q. 45, A. 2, *ad* 3.
38. *Metaphysics*, tract. 9, chap. 4.
39. Aristotle, *Physics* III, 4. 203a16–b4.
40. Q. 14, A. 7.
41. *Meteorology* I, 14. 352a17–28.
42. *On the Consolation of Philosophy* V, 6. PL 63:859.
43. *Metaphysics* I, tract. 1, chap. 11.
44. Q. 7, A. 4.
45. *Sermo ad populum* 241, 4. PL 38:1135.
46. Q. 75, A. 6. Q. 76, A. 2. Q. 118, A. 6.

ST I
Question 47
On the Diversity of Things in General

[This question is divided into three articles, two of which are included here.]

First Article

Do the Multiplicity and Diversity of Things Come from God?

I proceed in this way to the first article: it seems that the multiplicity and diversity of things do not come from God.

Obj. 1. By nature, one thing always produces one effect. But God is one in the highest degree, as is clear from what I have explained.[1] Therefore, God produces only one effect.

Obj. 2. An image imitates its exemplar. But God is the exemplary cause of what he produces, as I have said before.[2] Therefore, since God is one, he produces only one effect and not diverse effects.

Obj. 3. Means are proportioned to ends. But creatures have only one end, namely, God's goodness, as I have shown before.[3] Therefore, God produces only one effect.

On the contrary, the Book of Genesis says that God "separated light from darkness," and "divided waters" from waters.[4] Therefore, the multiplicity and diversity of things comes from God.

I answer that individual thinkers have ascribed the cause of things' diversity in many ways. For certain thinkers ascribed the cause of things' diversity to matter alone or to matter in conjunction with efficient causes. For example, Democritus and all the ancient philosophers of nature, who held that material causes are the only causes, indeed ascribed the cause of things' diversity to matter alone, and things' diversity, in their view, came about by chance, by the motion of matter.[5] And Anaxagoras, who held that the intellect separates things by abstracting what is confused in matter, ascribed things' diversity and multiplicity to matter and efficient causes jointly.[6]

But such opinions cannot hold for two reasons. First, indeed, because God created even matter itself, as I have shown before.[7] And hence we

251

need to trace even things' diversity, if such comes partly from matter, back to the higher cause. Second, because matter is for the sake of form, and not vice versa. And particular forms differentiate things. Therefore, things do not have diversity because of matter, but rather, conversely, created matter lacks form in order that matter might be adapted to different forms.

And certain thinkers ascribed things' diversity to secondary efficient causes. Avicenna,[8] for example, said that God, in understanding himself, produced the first intelligent being—and there is necessarily a concomitant composition of potentiality and actuality in such a being, since it is not its own existing, as I shall make clear later.[9] The first intelligent being, inasmuch as it understands the first cause, then produced the second intelligent being. And the first intelligent being, inasmuch as it understands itself as something potential, produced the body of the heavens, and the body of the heavens causes motion. And inasmuch as the first intelligent being understands itself as something having actuality, it produced the soul of the heavens.

But this opinion cannot hold for two reasons. First, indeed, because creating belongs to God alone, as I have shown before.[10] And hence God alone produces things that can only be produced by being created, and such are all the things that are not subject to coming-to-be and passing away. Second, because, according to this opinion, the whole universe would result from the conjunction of many efficient causes, not from the aim of the first efficient cause. But we say that such things come about by chance. Therefore, the complement of the universe, which consists in the diversity of things, would exist by chance, and this is impossible.

And hence we need to say that things' diversity and multiplicity come from the aim of the first efficient cause, which is God. For he produced things in existence in order that his goodness be communicated to creatures and be represented by them. And he produced many and diverse creatures because one creature cannot adequately represent his goodness; as a result, one creature supplies what another lacks in representing his goodness. For the goodness that exists simply and uniformly in God, exists in creatures in many ways and separately. And hence the whole universe shares and represents God's goodness more perfectly than any single creature otherwise would.

And because God's wisdom causes things' diversity, Moses says that the word of God, which is the conception of his wisdom, separated things. And this is what the Book of Genesis tells us: "God said, 'Let there be light.' And he divided light from darkness."[11]

Reply to Obj. 1. Efficient causes that cause by nature, do so by means of the forms whereby they exist, and only one form belongs to any one thing. And so such causes produce only one effect. But efficient causes that cause freely—and such is God, as I have shown before[12]—do so by means of forms in the intellect. Therefore, since it is not contrary to God's unity and simplicity for him to understand many things, as I have shown before,[13] we conclude that he, though one, can make many things.

Reply to Obj. 2. The argument of this objection would hold about an image that perfectly represents its exemplar, and such an exemplar is multiplied only in a material sense. And hence there is only one uncreated image,[14] which is perfect. But no creature perfectly represents the first exemplar, which is the divine essence. And thus many things can represent the first exemplar.

And yet, insofar as we call ideas exemplars, the plurality of ideas in God's mind corresponds to the plurality of things.

Reply to Obj. 3. In theoretical matters, there is only one means of demonstration, which definitively proves a conclusion, although there are many probable means of proof. And likewise in practical matters, if the means is equivalent to the end, so to speak, there need be only one means. But creatures are not so related to the end that is God. And hence there needed to be many creatures.

Third Article

Is There Only One World?

I proceed in this way to the third article: it seems that there is not only one world but several worlds.

Obj. 1. As Augustine says in his work *Octoginta trium quaestionum*, it is inappropriate to say that God created things without a reason.[15] But he could create many worlds for the same reason that he created one, since his power is not limited to the creation of a single world but is unlimited, as I have shown before.[16] Therefore, God produced more than one world.

Obj. 2. Nature does what is better, and much more does God do so. But it would be better if several worlds exist than if only one does, since more goods are better than fewer. Therefore, God produced more than one world.

Obj. 3. Things that possess forms in matter, can be numerically many but specifically the same, since numerical multiplicity derives from matter. But the world has a form in matter. For, just as I signify a form when I say "human being," but I signify that form in matter when I say "this human being," so we signify a form when we say "the world," but we signify that form in matter when we say "this world." Therefore, nothing prevents many worlds from existing.

On the contrary, the Gospel of John says: "He produced the world."[17] And the Gospel there says "world" in the singular, as if only one world exists.

I answer that the very order that exists in the things God so created, manifests the oneness of the world. For we call this world one by the one-ness of its order, as some things are ordered to other things. But every-thing from God has a relation to every other thing and to God himself, as I have shown before.[18] And hence everything needs to belong to one world.

And so those who held that chance, not an ordering wisdom, causes the world, could posit several worlds. One such was Democritus, who said that the juncture of atoms produced this world and an infinite number of other worlds.[19]

Reply to Obj. 1. The argument shows why the world is one, because every-thing needs to be ordered by one order and toward one end. And Aristotle in the *Metaphysics* consequently inferred the oneness of God, who governs the universe, from the oneness of the order that exists among the things of the universe.[20] And Plato from the oneness of the exemplar proves the one-ness of the world, a copy of the exemplar, as it were.[21]

Reply to Obj. 2. No efficient cause strives for a plurality of matter as its goal, since a large number of material objects has no fixed limit but extends endlessly, and the unlimited is incompatible with the nature of limit. Moreover, if we say that several worlds are better than one, we do so by the largeness of the number of material objects. But such a "better" is not part of the intention of God when he causes, because one could by the same reasoning say that, if he were to have produced two worlds, it would be better that three exist, and so on to infinity.

Reply to Obj. 3. The world consists of its entire matter. For no other earth than this one can exist, since nature would bring every earth to a particular center, wherever that center would be.[22] And the reasoning is the same in the case of the other material substances that are parts of the world.

Notes

1. Q. 11, A. 4.
2. Q. 44, A. 3.
3. Q. 44, A. 4.
4. Gen. 1:4, 7.
5. See Aristotle, *Physics* I, 4. 187; III, 4. 203; VIII, 9. 265.
6. Ibid.
7. Q. 44, A. 2.
8. *Metaphysics*, tract. 9, chap. 4.
9. Q. 50, A. 2, *ad* 3.
10. Q. 45, A. 5.
11. Gen. 1:3–4.
12. Q. 19, A. 4.
13. Q. 15, A. 2.
14. I.e., the Son.
15. *Octoginta trium quaestionum*, Q. 46. PL 40:30.
16. Q. 25, A. 2.

17. Jn. 1:10.
18. Q. 11, A. 3. Q. 21, A. 1, *ad* 3.
19. See Aristotle, *Physics* III, 4. 203.
20. *Metaphysics* XI, 10. 1076a3–4.
21. *Timaeus*. 31A, B.
22. St. Thomas, like his contemporaries and the ancients, thought that the earth was the center of the universe.

ST I
Question 48
On the Diversity of Creatures in Particular

[This question is divided into six articles, the first four of which are included here.]

First Article

Is Evil Some Sort of Nature?

I proceed in this way to the first article: it seems that evil is a certain nature.

Obj. 1. Every genus is some sort of nature. But evil is a certain genus, for the *Categories* says that "good and bad do not fall within a genus but are the genera of other things."[1] Therefore, evil is some sort of nature.

Obj. 2. Every constitutive specific difference is some sort of nature. But evil is the constitutive specific difference in moral matters, for a bad habit differs specifically from a good one. For example, generosity differs specifically from stinginess. Therefore, evil signifies some sort of nature.

Obj. 3. Contrary things have different kinds of natures. But evil and good are opposed as contraries, not as privation is opposed to characteristic disposition; this the Philosopher proves in the *Categories* by the fact that there is something in between good and evil, and by the fact that something can revert to good.[2] Therefore, evil designates some sort of nature.

Obj. 4. What does not exist, does not cause anything. But evil causes something, since it destroys good. Therefore, evil is some sort of being and nature.

Obj. 5. Only beings and certain natures belong to the perfection of the universe. But evil belongs to the perfection of the universe, for Augustine says in his *Enchiridion* that "the wonderful beauty of the universe consists of everything, and what is evil in the universe, when rightly ordered and kept in its place, more excellently recommends what is good."[3] Therefore, evil is some sort of nature.

On the contrary, Denis says in his *De divinis nominibus*: "Evil is neither anything that exists, nor anything good."[4]

I answer that we know one contrary by the other, as, for example, we know darkness by light. And so also we need to understand evil by the nature of good. Moreover, we have said before that good is what is desirable,[5] and so we need to say that the existence and perfection of every nature possesses the nature of goodness, since every nature desires its own existence and perfection. And hence evil cannot signify a way of existing or a certain form or a nature. We conclude, therefore, that we signify a certain absence of good by the term "evil." And we accordingly say that evil "is neither anything existing nor anything good," because being as such is good, and so the removal of both is the same.

Reply to Obj. 1.   Aristotle is speaking in the cited text about the opinion of the Pythagoreans, who thought that evil was some sort of nature, and thus posited good and evil as genera.[6] For Aristotle usually, and especially in his works on logic, posed examples that some contemporary philosophers regarded as likely.

Or, as the Philosopher says in the *Metaphysics*, "the prime contrary opposition is between privation and characteristic disposition,"[7] because, to be sure, such contrary opposition is maintained in the case of every set of contraries. For one of two contraries is always imperfect with respect to the other, as, for example, black is imperfect with respect to white, and bitter imperfect with respect to sweet. And we accordingly say that good and evil are genera, not absolutely but as contraries, since, as every form has the nature of good, so every privation as such has the nature of evil.

Reply to Obj. 2.   Good and evil constitute specific differences only in moral matters, which take their species from their goal, i.e., the object of the will, on which moral matters depend. And because good has the nature of an end, good and evil accordingly are specific differences in moral matters, good as such but evil as taking away a due end. Nonetheless, taking away a due end constitutes a species in moral matters only insofar as the taking away is connected with an undue end, just as we find privation of a substantial form in things of nature only when such a privation is connected with another form. Thus the evil that constitutes the specific difference in moral matters, is some sort of good linked to the privation of another good; for example, an intemperate person indeed does not aim to be deprived of the good of reason but to gain a sensibly pleasurable good apart from the order of reason. And hence evil as such does not constitute a specific difference but does so by reason of a connected good.

Reply to Obj. 3.   The preceding response makes clear the answer to the third objection. For the Philosopher is speaking in the cited text about good and evil as we find these in moral matters. For thus do we find something in between good and evil, insofar as we call good what is ordered, and call evil what is not only disordered but also harmful to another. And hence the Philosopher says in the *Ethics* that a prodigal person is indeed vain but not evil.[8]

And things may also revert to good from what is morally evil but not from every evil. For example, a blind person cannot revert to sight, although blindness is nonetheless one kind of evil.

Reply to Obj. 4. We say that something causes in three ways. In one way, as a formal cause, in the way we say that whiteness makes something white. And we thus say that evil, even by reason of privation itself, destroys good, because evil is the very destruction or privation of good. We say in a second way that something causes as an efficient cause, as, for example, we say that a painter makes a wall white. In the third way, we say that something causes by way of a final cause, as we say that a goal, by moving an efficient cause to act, causes the effect. In the latter two ways, however, evil as such, that is, as a privation, does not cause anything except insofar as there is some good connected with evil. For every action exists by some form, and everything desired as an end is some perfection. And so, as Denis says in his *De divinis nominibus*, evil causes and is desired only by virtue of a connected good, while evil as such is "indeterminate" and "beyond our power to will and our intention."[9]

Reply to Obj. 5. As I have said before,[10] parts of the universe have an order to one another, as one part acts on another and is the end and model of another. Such things, however, as I have said,[11] are inappropriate for evil except by reason of a connected good. And hence evil neither belongs to the perfection of the universe nor is included in the order of the universe, except by accident, i.e., by reason of a connected good.

Second Article

Do We Find Evil in Things?

I proceed in this way to the second article: it seems that we do not find evil in things.

Obj. 1. Everything we find in the world is either a being or the privation of a being, which is nonbeing. But Denis says in his *De divinis nominibus* that evil differs from what exists, and differs still more from what does not exist.[12] Therefore, we in no way find evil in things.

Obj. 2. "Being" and "thing" are convertible. Therefore, if evil is a being in things, evil is consequently a certain thing. And this is contrary to what I have said before.[13]

Obj. 3. "Something is whiter if it has less admixture of black," as Aristotle says in the *Topics*.[14] Therefore, something is better if it has less admixture of evil. But God, much more than nature, always produces what is better. Therefore, we find nothing evil in the things that God produced.

On the contrary, all prohibitions and punishments, which are only concerned with evils, would accordingly be eliminated.

I answer that, as I have said before, the perfection of the universe requires dissimilarity in things, so that every grade of goodness be realized.[15] Moreover, one grade of goodness is such that there is something good that can never be wanting. And another grade of goodness is such that there is something good in such a way that it can fall short of good. And we find these grades of goodness in existing itself. For there are certain things, such as immaterial things, that cannot lose their existence, while there are other things, such as material things, that can. Therefore, as the perfection of the universe requires that there be not only things that cannot pass away, but also things that can pass away, so the perfection of the universe requires that there be certain things that can fall short of goodness, and such things consequently do sometimes fall short. But the nature of evil consists in this, namely, that something fall short of what is good. And hence we evidently find evil in things, just as we find that things pass away, for passing away itself is also an evil.

Reply to Obj. 1. Evil differs both from being unconditionally and from nonbeing unconditionally, because evil does not exist as a disposition or a pure negation but as a privation.

Reply to Obj. 2. We speak of being in two ways, as the *Metaphysics* says.[16] In one way, as being signifies the reality of something, as we divide being into ten categories, and "being" is in this way convertible with "thing." And no privation is a being in this way, and so no evil is either. In the second way, we say that being signifies the truth of a proposition. And the truth of a proposition consists in its composition, which the word "is" indicates. And this is the being that answers the question: Is it? And we say in this way that there is blindness in the eye, or that there is any other privation. And we also in this way call evil a being.

But because of ignorance of this difference, some thinkers who considered the fact that we call some things evil, or that we say that there is evil in things, believed that evil was some sort of thing.

Reply to Obj. 3. God and nature and every efficient cause produce something that is better on the whole, but not something better in every particular except in relation to the whole, as I have said before.[17] But the very whole that is the created universe, is better and more perfect if certain things exist in it that can fall short of good, and that sometimes do fall short of good unless God prevents their failing. For it belongs to providence to maintain, not destroy, nature, as Denis says in his *De divinis nominibus*,[18] but it belongs to the very nature of things that, if they can fall short, they sometimes do. Things also can and do fall short because, as Augustine says in his *Enchiridion*, God is so powerful that he can even act well in the case of evil.[19] And hence many good things would be eliminated if God were to allow no evil to exist. For example, fire would not come to be unless air were to be consumed, nor would the life of lions be preserved unless asses were to be killed, nor would either retributive justice or patient suffering be praised unless injustice were to exist.

Third Article

Is Evil in Something Good as Its Subject?

I proceed in this way to the third article: it seems that evil is not in something good as its subject.

Obj. 1.   Everything good is something that exists. But Denis says in his *De divinis nominibus* that "evil is nothing that exists, nor is it in things that exist."[20] Therefore, evil is not in something good as its subject.

Obj. 2.   Evil is not a being, but good is. But nonbeing does not require any being as a subject in which to exist. Therefore, neither does evil require any good as a subject in which to exist.

Obj. 3.   One contrary is not the subject of the other. But good and evil are contraries. Therefore, evil is not in something good as its subject.

Obj. 4.   We say that a subject in which there is whiteness, is white. Therefore, a subject in which there is evil, is likewise evil. Therefore, if evil is in something good as its subject, good is consequently evil, contrary to what the prophet Isaiah says: "Woe to you who call evil good, and good evil."

On the contrary, Augustine says in his *Enchiridion* that there is evil only in something good.[21]

I answer that evil implies the taking away of good, as I have said.[22] But we do not say that every taking away of good is evil. For we can understand taking away good both by way of privation and by way of negation. Thus taking away good, when understood in the sense of negation, does not have the nature of evil; otherwise, things that in no way exist, would consequently be evil, and likewise everything that did not possess the good of something else, would consequently be evil. For example, human beings would be evil because they did not possess the swiftness of a deer or the strength of a lion.

But we say that taking away good, when understood in the sense of privation, is an evil; for example, we call being deprived of sight blindness. Moreover, the subject of a privation or a form is one and the same thing, namely, a potential being. This is so whether the being be unconditionally potential, as in the case of prime matter, which is the subject of a substantial form and of the privation of a contrary form, or the being be in one respect potential but unconditionally actual, as in the case of a transparent material substance, which is the subject of darkness and light. But the form by which a being is actual, is evidently a certain perfection and a certain good, and so every actual being is some kind of good. And likewise, every potential being as such is some kind of good insofar as it is ordered to good. For as something is a potential being, so also is it a potential good. We conclude, therefore, that the subject of evil is something good.

Reply to Obj. 1. Denis understands that evil is not in existing things as a part or a natural property of any existing thing.

Reply to Obj. 2. Nonbeing understood in the sense of negation does not require a subject. But privation is negation in a subject, as the *Metaphysics* says,[23] and such nonbeing is an evil.

Reply to Obj. 3. The subject of an evil is not the good contrary to the evil but some other good; for example, the subject of blindness is not sight but an animal.

Nonetheless, as Augustine says,[24] it seems that the rule of logic that contraries cannot exist at the same time, fails here. But we need to understand this by the general understanding of good and evil and not as we particularly understand a particular good and a particular evil. Moreover, because white and black, sweet and bitter, and like contraries are in certain fixed genera, we understand them only in a particular way. But good encompasses every genus, and so one good can at the same time exist along with the privation of another good.

Reply to Obj. 4. The prophet invokes "woe" on those who say that good as such is evil. But such does not follow from what I have set forth, as is clear from what I have said.[25]

Fourth Article

Does Evil Destroy Good in Its Entirety?

I proceed in this way to the fourth article: it seems that evil destroys good in its entirety.

Obj. 1. One of two contraries completely eliminates the other. But good and evil are contraries. Therefore, evil can destroy good in its entirety.

Obj. 2. Augustine says in his *Enchiridion* that evil inflicts harm inasmuch as evil "takes away good."[26] But good is the same and uniform. Therefore, evil completely takes away good.

Obj. 3. Evil, while it exists, inflicts harm and takes away good. But if one continually takes away part from a whole, the whole comes to an end at some point of time, unless the whole be infinite, and we cannot say this about any created good. Therefore, evil completely destroys good.

On the contrary, Augustine says in his *Enchiridion* that evil cannot completely destroy good.[27]

I answer that evil cannot completely destroy good. And for evidence of this, we need to consider that there are three kinds of good. There is one kind of good that evil completely takes away, and such is the good that is contrary to an evil; for example, darkness completely takes away light, and blindness completely takes away sight. But there is another kind of good that evil neither completely takes away nor diminishes, namely, the good that is the subject of evil; for example, darkness does not diminish any part of the air's substance. And there is a kind of good that evil indeed diminishes but does not completely take away, and such a good is the aptitude of a subject for actuality.

But we do not understand the diminution of such a good by way of subtraction, as in the case of quantitative diminutions, but by way of contraction, as in the case of qualitative and formal diminutions. Moreover, we understand contraction of this aptitude in contrast to its expansion. For this kind of aptitude is expanded by the dispositions whereby matter is prepared for actuality, and the more these dispositions are increased in a subject, the more apt the subject is to receive perfection and form. And conversely, this kind of aptitude is contracted by contrary dispositions, and the more these dispositions are increased in the matter, and the more intense they are, the more the potentiality for actuality is contracted.

Therefore, if contrary dispositions cannot be increased and expanded endlessly but only up to a fixed limit, neither is the aforementioned aptitude endlessly lessened or contracted, as is evident in the case of active and passive qualities of the elements. For example, coldness and wetness, which lessen or contract the aptitude of matter for the form of fire, cannot be endlessly increased.

But if contrary dispositions can be increased indefinitely, the aforementioned aptitude is also indefinitely lessened or contracted. Nonetheless, the aptitude is not completely taken away, because it always abides in its source, which is the substance of the subject. For example, if opaque material substances were interposed between the sun and air to infinity, the aptitude of air for light would be infinitely lessened, but the aptitude is not completely taken away as long as the air, which is by its nature transparent, remains. In like manner, sins, which always more and more lessen the aptitude of the soul for grace, can be increased to infinity, and these sins are indeed obstacles, as it were, interposed between ourselves and God, as the prophet Isaiah says: Our sins "create division" between ourselves and "God."[28] And yet the aforementioned aptitude is not completely taken away from the soul, for the aptitude results from the soul's nature.

Reply to Obj. 1. The good that is contrary to an evil, is completely taken away, but other goods are not completely taken away, as I have said.[29]

Reply to Obj. 2. The aforementioned aptitude is in between a subject and the subject's actuation. And hence evil diminishes the part of an aptitude whereby the aptitude reaches actuality, but the part of the aptitude whereby the aptitude is included with its subject, remains. Therefore, although good as such is the same, it is nonetheless, on account of its relation to different things, not completely taken away but partially.

Reply to Obj. 3.   Certain thinkers, imagining the diminution of the aforementioned good to be like quantitative diminution, said that, as a continuum is infinitely divisible by the same ratio (as, e.g., that we should take a half of a half, or a third of a third), so it happens in the case of the matter under discussion.

But this argument is not valid here. For we always take away less and less in the case of divisions maintaining the same proportion, since half of a half is less than half of the whole. But a subsequent sin does not necessarily less diminish part of the aforementioned aptitude than a preceding sin does; rather, a subsequent sin may by chance diminish the aptitude in equal or greater measure.

Therefore, we need to say that that aptitude, although finite, is nonetheless endlessly decreased, not intrinsically but by chance, as contrary dispositions are also endlessly increased, as I have said.[30]

Notes

1. Aristotle, *Categories* 11. 14a23–25.
2. Ibid. 10. 13a18–36; 11. 13b36.
3. *Enchiridion* 10, 11. PL 40:236.
4. *De divinis nominibus* 4. PG 3:717.
5. Q. 5, A. 1.
6. See Aristotle, *Metaphysics* I, 5. 986.
7. *Metaphysics* IX, 4. 1055a33–35.
8. *Ethics* IV, 1. 1121a21–27.
9. *De divinis nominibus* 4. PG 3:717.
10. Q. 2, A. 3. Q. 19, A. 5, *ad* 2. Q. 21, A. 1, *ad* 3. Q. 44, A. 3.
11. In the previous response.
12. *De divinis nominibus* 4. PG 3:716.
13. Q. 48, A. 1.
14. *Topics* III, 5. 119a27–28.
15. Q. 47, A. 2.
16. Aristotle, *Metaphysics* IV, 7. 1017a22–35.
17. Q. 47, A. 2, *ad* 1.
18. *De divinis nominibus* 4. PG 3:733.
19. *Enchiridion* 11. PL 40:236.
20. *De divinis nominibus* 4. PG 3:733.
21. *Enchiridion* 14. PL 40:238.
22. Q. 48, A. 1.
23. Aristotle, *Metaphysics* III, 2. 1004a9–16.
24. See n. 21, *supra*.
25. In the body of the article.
26. *Enchiridion* 12. PL 40:237.
27. Ibid.
28. Is. 59:2.
29. In the body of the article.
30. In the body of the article.

ST I
Question 49
On the Cause of Evil

[This question is divided into three articles, all of which are included here.]

First Article

Can Good Cause Evil?

I proceed in this way to the first article: it seems that good cannot cause evil.
Obj. 1. The Gospel of Matthew says: "A good tree cannot bear bad fruit."[1]
Obj. 2. One of two contraries cannot cause the other. But evil is contrary to good. Therefore, good cannot cause evil.
Obj. 3. A deficient effect only comes from a deficient cause. But evil, supposing it to be caused, is a deficient effect. Therefore, evil has a deficient cause. But everything deficient is evil. Therefore, only evil causes evil.
Obj. 4. Denis says in his *De divinis nominibus* that evil has no cause.[2] Therefore, good does not cause evil.

On the contrary, Augustine says in his *Contra Iulianum*: "Only good could at all be the source of evil."[3]

I answer that we need to say that every evil is in some sort of way caused. For evil is the deficiency of a good that is produced by nature and ought to be possessed. Moreover, only a cause drawing something away from its natural and requisite disposition can bring it about that the thing lacks its proper disposition. For example, only something driving moves something heavy upward, and an efficient cause likewise fails in its activity only if there is some hindrance. But it can belong only to something good to cause, since nothing can cause except inasmuch as it really exists, and every being as such is good. And if we should consider particular kinds of causes, efficient causes and forms and ends imply some kind of perfection that is proper to the nature of good. And matter also, inasmuch as it is a potentiality for good, has the nature of good.

And what I have already previously set forth, indeed makes clear that

264

good causes evil by way of a material cause. For I have shown that good is the subject of evil.[4] Moreover, evil has no formal cause but rather consists in the deprivation of a form. And likewise, neither does evil have a final cause but rather consists in the deprivation of an order to a requisite end, since the useful, which is ordered to an end, as well as the end, have the nature of good. Evil, however, does have a cause by way of an efficient cause, albeit by chance and not intrinsically.

And for evidence of this, we need to recognize that evil is caused in one way in actions and in another way in effects. A deficiency in any source of action, whether in the action's chief or instrumental efficient cause, indeed causes there to be evil in an action. For example, either weakness in the power of locomotion, as in the case of the young, or merely the incapacity of the means of locomotion, as in the case of the lame, can cause deficiency in an animal's movement.

On the other hand, sometimes the power of an efficient cause, and sometimes a deficiency of the cause or the matter, causes evil to result in something, although not in the cause's proper effect. The power or perfection of an efficient cause indeed causes evil in something when the form that the cause strives for, necessarily results in the deprivation of another form; for example, the form of fire results in the deprivation of the form of air or water. Thus, as the more perfect the power of fire, the more perfectly it imprints its form, so also the more perfectly does it destroy its contrary, and hence the perfection of fire also causes air and water to pass away. But this destruction is by accident, since fire does not strive to cause the deprivation of water's form but to introduce its own form, although fire by so doing also accidentally causes the deprivation of water's form.

But if there should be a deficiency in the proper effect of fire, for example, that fire fails to heat, this happens either because of a deficiency in the action—which redounds to a deficiency in some source, as I just said—or by an indisposition of the matter that fails to receive the action of the fire acting on it. And yet the very fact that there is deficient existing, befalls something good, to which activity intrinsically belongs. And hence it is true that evil is in no way caused except by accident. And thus does good cause evil.

Reply to Obj. 1. As Augustine says in his *Contra Iulianum*, "The Lord calls a bad will a bad tree, and a good will a good tree."[5] Moreover, a good will does not produce a morally bad act, since we judge an act to be morally good by a will that is itself good. And yet rational creatures, which are good, cause the very movement of a bad will. And thus does good cause evil.

Reply to Obj. 2. Good does not cause the evil that is contrary to itself, but some other evil; for example, fire's goodness causes water's evil, and human beings, who are good by their nature, cause an act that is morally bad. And this very evil happens by accident, as I have said.[6]

Moreover, we find that even one of two contraries causes the other by accident; for example, exterior cold enveloping an object causes heat, inasmuch as the object's heat recedes to the interior.

Reply to Obj. 3. Evil has a defective cause in the case of freely willed things otherwise than in the case of things of nature. For a natural efficient cause, produces the same kind of effect as itself unless something external prevents it from doing so, and this very thing is a sort of defect in it. And hence evil never results in an effect unless something else evil pre-exists in the efficient cause or the matter, as I have said.[7] But in the case of freely willed things, the deficiency of an action comes from an actually defective will, inasmuch as such a will does not actually subject itself to its norm. And yet this deficiency is not a fault, but fault results because a will acts with such a deficiency.

Reply to Obj. 4. Evil is not caused intrinsically but only by accident, as I have said.[8]

Second Article

Does the Highest Good, That Is, God, Cause Evil?

I proceed in this way to the second article: it seems that the highest good, that is, God, causes evil.

Obj. 1. The prophet Isaiah says: "I am the Lord, and there is no other God, the Lord who produces light and creates darkness, who causes peace and creates evil."[9] And the prophet Amos says: "Will there be in a city any evil that the Lord did not cause?"[10]

Obj. 2. We trace the effect of a secondary cause back to the primary cause. But good causes evil, as I have said.[11] Therefore, since God causes every good, as I have shown before,[12] every evil as well is consequently from God.

Obj. 3. There is the same cause of a ship's well-being and its peril, as the *Physics* says.[13] But God causes the well-being of everything. Therefore, he causes all perdition and evil.

On the contrary, Augustine says in his work *Octoginta trium quaestionum* that God "is not the author of evil, because he does not cause things to strive for nonexistence."[14]

I answer that the deficiency of an efficient cause always causes the evil that consists in defective action, as is clear from what I have said.[15] But in God, there is no deficiency but the highest perfection, as I have shown before.[16] And hence the evil that consists in defective action, or the evil that a defective efficient cause causes, is not traceable to God as its cause.

But the evil that consists in some things passing away, is traceable to God as its cause. And this is evident both in the case of the things of nature and in the case of freely willed things. For I have said that an efficient cause, inasmuch as it by its power produces a form from which the destruction and deficiency of another form results, by its power causes such destruction and deficiency.[17] Moreover, the form that God chiefly strives for in created things, is evidently the good of the universe's order. And the order of the universe requires, as I have said before,[18] that there exist certain things that can pass away, and at some point of time do so. And so, by causing the universe's order in things, God consequently and as if by accident causes things to pass away, as the First Book of Samuel says: "The Lord inflicts death and causes life."[19] But we understand the saying of the Book of Wisdom that "God did not cause death,"[20] to mean "as if striven for as such."

And the order of justice, which requires that punishment be inflicted on sinners, also belongs to the order of the universe. And God is accordingly the author of the evil that consists of punishment, but he is not the author of the evil that consists of wrongdoing, for the reason stated above.[21]

Reply to Obj. 1. Those scriptural authorities are speaking about the evil of punishment and not about the evil of wrongdoing.

Reply to Obj. 2. We trace the effect of a deficient secondary cause back to the nondeficient primary cause with regard to what has reality and perfection but not with regard to what has any deficiency. For example, the power of locomotion causes whatever movement there is in limping, but the leg's curvature, not power of locomotion, causes what belongs to the limp in the limping. And in like manner, we trace whatever belongs to reality and activity in a bad action, back to God as its cause, but a secondary, deficient cause, not God, causes what is deficient in such an action.

Reply to Obj. 3. We assign the cause of a ship's sinking to its captain, because the captain fails to do what is necessary for the safety of the ship. But God does not fail to do what is necessary for well-being. And hence there is no comparison.

Third Article

Is There One Supreme Evil that Causes Every Evil?

I proceed in this way to the third article: it seems that there is one supreme evil that causes every evil.

Obj. 1. Contrary causes produce contrary effects. But we find contrariety in things, as the Book of Sirach says: "Good is contrary to evil, and" death "contrary to" life; "so also are sinners contrary to the upright."[22] Therefore, there are contrary sources of these effects, one the source of good, the other the source of evil.

Obj. 2. If one of two contraries exists in the constitution of the world, the other does too, as the *De coelo says*.[23] But the highest good exists in the constitution of the world and causes every good, as I have shown before.[24] Therefore, there is a contrary highest evil that causes every evil.

Obj. 3.   As we find in the world good and better things, so do we find bad and worse things there. But we speak of good and better with respect to best. Therefore, we speak of bad and worse with respect to something that is the supreme evil.

Obj. 4.   We trace everything that exists by sharing, back to something that exists by essence. But evils in our world are not evil by essence but by sharing. Therefore, we need to discover a highest evil that is evil by essence, and causes every evil.

Obj. 5.   We trace everything that exists by accident, back to something that exists intrinsically. But good causes evil by accident. Therefore, we need to posit some highest evil, which intrinsically causes evils. Nor can we say that evil is only caused by accident and not intrinsically, because then evil would exist in relatively few cases and not in most cases.

Obj. 6.   We trace the evil in an effect back to evil in its cause, because a deficient effect comes from a deficient cause, as I have said before.[25] But we cannot regress endlessly in deficient causes. Therefore, we need to posit one first evil that causes every evil.

On the contrary, the highest good causes every being, as I have shown before.[26] Therefore, there can exist no contrary source that causes evils.

I answer that what I have said before, makes clear that there is no one first source of evil as there is one first source of good.

First, indeed, because the first source of good is good by essence, as I have shown before.[27] But nothing can be bad by essence, for I have shown that every being as such is good, and that there is evil only in a subject that is good.[28]

Second, because the first source of good is the highest and perfect good, which in itself possesses all goodness, as I have shown before.[29] But a highest evil cannot exist. For I have shown that evil, although it always diminishes good, nonetheless can never completely destroy good, and so nothing wholly and completely evil can exist if there always remains something good. And the Philosopher consequently says in the *Ethics* that "if something were evil in its entirety, it would destroy itself," because evil itself, whose subject is good, is taken away if everything good is destroyed—which is required for something to be entirely evil.[30]

Third, because the nature of evil is inconsistent with the nature of a first source. This is so both because something good causes every evil, as I have shown before,[31] and because evil can only cause something by accident and so cannot be a primary cause, since an accidental cause is secondary to an intrinsic cause, as the *Physics* makes clear.[32]

But those who posited two first causes, one good and the other bad, fell into this error from the same source from which the other odd positions of ancient philosophers also originated, namely, that they considered only the particular causes of particular effects, not the universal cause of the totality of being. Thus, for example, if they found something to be by the power of its nature harmful to something, they thought the nature of the harmful thing to be bad, as if, for instance, one should say that the nature of fire is bad because fire burned down the house of a poor man.

We should not, however, understand our judgment about the goodness of anything by its relation to a particular thing but as such and by its relation to the whole universe, in which everything has its place in a most ordered way, as is clear from what I have said.[33]

Likewise, because they found two contrary particular causes of two contrary particular effects, they also did not know how to trace these contrary particular causes back to their common universal cause. And so they judged there to be contrariety in causes even in the case of primary causes.

Since all contraries agree in one thing that is common to them, however, we need in their case to discover one common cause superior to their own contrary causes. For example, we find the power of heavenly bodies superior to the contrary qualities of the elements. And we likewise find one first source of existence superior to everything, however it exists, as I have shown before.[34]

Reply to Obj. 1. Contraries agree in one genus and in the aspect of existing. And so, although they have contrary particular causes, we nonetheless need to arrive at one first common cause.

Reply to Obj. 2. Nature causes privation and disposition to come about in the case of the same thing. But the subject of privation is a potential being, as I have said.[35] And hence evil, since it is the privation of good, as is clear from what I have said before,[36] is contrary to the good linked to potentiality, but not to the highest good, which is pure actuality.

Reply to Obj. 3. Each thing is increased according to its own nature. But as form consists in a certain perfection, so privation consists in a certain taking away of perfection. And hence every form and perfection and good is increased by approaching a perfect end, while privation and evil is increased by receding from such an end. And hence we do not call things bad or worse by reason of their approaching a highest evil in the way that we call things good or better by reason of their approaching the highest good.

Reply to Obj. 4. We do not call anything evil by reason of its sharing but by reason of its privation of sharing. And hence we do not need to trace evil back to anything that is evil by essence.

Reply to Obj. 5. Evil can only by accident be caused, as I have shown before.[37] And hence it is impossible to trace evil back to anything that as such causes evil.

Moreover, it is absolutely false to say that evil exists in most cases. For things that can come to be and pass away, in which alone natural evil happens to exist, are a rather small part of the whole universe. And also the deficiencies of nature in each species occur in rather few cases. But only in the case of human beings does there seem to be evil in most cases. This is so because, although the good of human beings regarding the senses is not the good of human beings as such, that is, the good regarding reason, most human beings follow their senses rather than their reason.

Reply to Obj. 6. We do not regress endlessly in the case of causes of evil; rather, we trace all evils back to a cause that is good, from which evil by accident results.

Notes

1. Mt. 7:18.
2. *De divinis nominibus* 4. PG 3:732.
3. *Contra Iulianum* I, 9. PL 44:670.
4. Q. 48, A. 3.
5. *Contra Iulianum* I, 9. PL 44:672.
6. In the body of the article.
7. In the body of the article.
8. In the body of the article.
9. Is. 45:6–7.
10. Amos 3:6.
11. Q. 49, A. 1.
12. Q. 2, A. 3. Q. 6, AA. 1, 4.
13. Aristotle, *Physics* II, 3. 195a11–14.
14. *Octoginta trium quaestionum*, Q. 21. PL 40:16.
15. Q. 49, A. 1.
16. Q. 4, A. 1.
17. Q. 49, A. 1.
18. Q. 22, A. 2, *ad* 2; Q. 48, A. 2.
19. 1 Sam. 2:6.
20. Wis. 1:13.
21. At the beginning of the body of the article.
22. Sir. 33:14–15.
23. Aristotle, *De coelo* II, 3. 286a23–25.
24. Q. 2, A. 3. Q. 6, AA. 2, 4.
25. Q. 49, AA. 1, 2.
26. Q. 2, A. 3. Q. 6, A. 4.
27. Q. 6, AA. 3, 4.
28. Q. 5, A. 3. Q. 48, A. 3.
29. Q. 6, A. 2.
30. *Ethics* IV, 5. 1126a12–13.
31. Q. 49, A. 1.
32. Aristotle, *Physics* II, 6. 198a5–13.
33. Q. 47, A. 2, *ad* 1.
34. Q. 2, A. 3.
35. Q. 48, A. 3.
36. Ibid.
37. Q. 49, A. 1.

ST I
Question 103
On the Governance of Things in General

[This question is divided into eight articles, all of which are included here.]

First Article

Does Someone Govern the World?

I proceed in this way to the first article: it seems that no one governs the world.

Obj. 1. It belongs to things that are moved or act for the sake of an end, to be governed. But the things of nature, which constitute a large part of the world, are not moved or do not act for the sake of an end, since they do not know ends. Therefore, the world is not governed.

Obj. 2. Being governed belongs in a proper sense to things that are moved toward something. But the world does not seem to be moved toward something; rather, the world in itself is stable. Therefore, the world is not governed.

Obj. 3. What is in itself necessarily determined to one result, does not need any external thing to govern it. But a certain necessity determines the more important parts of the world to one result in their actions and movements. Therefore, the world does not need governance.

On the contrary, the Book of Wisdom says: "But you, Father, govern" everything "by your providence."[1] And Boethius says in his *On the Consolation of Philosophy*: "O you who govern the world by an eternal plan."[2]

I answer that certain ancient philosophers eliminated governance from the world, saying that everything is done by chance.[3] But two considerations show this position to be impossible. First, indeed, because of what things themselves evidence. For we see that what is better, either always or for the most part, comes about in the case of things of nature, and that such would not happen unless a providence were to direct things of nature toward the end of some good. And this is governance. And hence the very fixed order of things clearly demonstrates the world's governance. Similarly, if someone were to enter a well-ordered home, one would, from the home's very arrangement, study the plan of the person who arranged the home, as Cicero in his work *De natura deorum* cites the words of Aristotle.[4]

Second, moreover, the same point is evident by considering God's goodness, which brings things into existence, as is clear from what I have said before.[5] For, since "it belongs to the best to produce the best,"[6] it is inappropriate that the supreme goodness of God not bring the things produced to a perfect state. But the final perfection of each thing consists in the attainment of an end. And hence it belongs to God's goodness to bring things to their ends, just as his goodness brings things into existence. And to do so is governance.

Reply to Obj. 1.   Things are moved or act for the sake of ends in two ways. In one way, by moving themselves to their ends, as human beings and other rational creatures do, and it belongs to such to know the nature of ends and of means to ends.

But we say that things are moved or act for ends as if something else acts on them and directs them to ends. For example, an arrow aimed by an archer is propelled to a target, and the archer knows the arrow's goal, although the arrow does not. And hence, as the movement of an arrow toward a fixed goal clearly indicates that a knowing being aims the arrow, so the fixed course of things of nature, which lack knowledge, clearly reveals that a plan governs the world.

Reply to Obj. 2.   Something stable, at least prime matter, exists in all created things, and something belonging to motion if we also include operations under motion. And regarding both, things need governance, because the very element that is stable in them, would fall into nothingness (because it is made from nothing) if a governing hand were not to preserve it, as I shall make clear later.[7]

Reply to Obj. 3.   The necessity from nature that inheres in things determined to one result, is a certain impulse from God, who directs them to their ends. Similarly, the necessity by which an arrow is propelled as it strives for a fixed target, is an impulse from the archer and not from the arrow. But there is a difference between God and the archer, because what creatures receive from God, is their nature, but what human beings impress on things of nature supplementary to such things' nature, belongs to physical force. And hence, as the necessity of the physical force in the arrow's propulsion indicates the direction of the arrow, so the necessity from nature indicates the governance of God's providence.

Second Article

Is the End of the World's Governance Extrinsic to the World?

I proceed in this way to the second article: it seems that the end of the world's governance is nothing extrinsic to the world.

Obj. 1. The end to which governed things are brought, is the goal of things' governance. But the end to which things are brought, is a good in things themselves, as, for example, a sick person is brought to health, which is something good in that person. Therefore, the end of things' governance is not an extrinsic good but one that exists in things themselves.

Obj. 2. The Philosopher says in the *Ethics* that "some ends are operations, some are works,"[8] that is, products. But nothing extrinsic to the entire universe can be a product, and operations exist in the very beings that act. Therefore, nothing extrinsic to the entire universe can be the end of things' governance.

Obj. 3. The good of a multitude seems to consist in order and peace, which is "the tranquility of order," as Augustine says in *The City of God.*[9] But the world consists in a certain multitude of things. Therefore, the end of the world's governance is a peaceful order, which exists in things themselves. Therefore, the end of things' governance is not an extrinsic good.

On the contrary, the Book of Proverbs says: "God produced everything for his sake."[10] But he is outside the entire order of the universe. Therefore, the end of things is an extrinsic good.

I answer that, since an end corresponds to a source, it cannot be the case that we do not know the end of things when we know their source. Therefore, since the source of things is something extrinsic to the entire universe, namely, God, as is clear from what I have said before,[11] the end of things also needs to be an extrinsic good.

And this is clear from reason, for good evidently possesses the nature of an end. And hence the particular end of a particular thing is a certain particular good, while the universal end of all things is a certain universal good. But the universal good is something intrinsically and essentially good, which is the very essence of goodness, while a particular good is something good by sharing. Moreover, there is evidently nothing good in the entire created universe that is not good by sharing. And hence the good that is the end of the entire universe, needs to be a good extrinsic to the entire universe.

Reply to Obj. 1. We acquire something good in several ways. In one way, we acquire a good as a form that exists in ourselves, such as health or knowledge. In a second way, we acquire a good as something we produce, as, for example, a builder achieves his goal by building a house. In a third way, we acquire a good as a good held or possessed, as, for example, buyers achieve their goal by possessing land. And hence nothing prevents the end to which the universe is brought, from being an extrinsic good.

Reply to Obj. 2. The Philosopher is speaking about the ends of skills, some of which have their very activities as their ends, as, for example, the goal of a lyre player is to play the lyre. But other skills have as their end a product, as, for example, the goal of a builder is a house, not building the house. Some external things, however, may be an end both as an object produced and as an object possessed or held, or even as an object represented, as, for example, if we should say that Hercules is the end of a statue produced to represent him. Thus we can say that a good extrinsic to the entire universe is the end of things' governance as an object possessed and represented, because everything strives to share in that good and is made like that good insofar as possible.

Reply to Obj. 3. The end of the universe is indeed a good that exists in itself, namely, the order of the universe itself. This good, however, is not the universe's final end but is ordered to an extrinsic good as the final end, as, for example, an army's disposition is ordered to its commander, as the *Metaphysics* says.[12]

Third Article

Does One Ruler Govern the World?

I proceed in this way to the third article: it seems that one ruler does not govern the world.

Obj. 1. We judge about causes by their effects. But in things' governance, things evidently are not moved and do not act in uniform ways; for example, some things do so in a contingent way, while others do so by necessity, and they do so in other different ways. Therefore, one ruler does not govern the world.

Obj. 2. Subjects that one ruler governs, are at odds with one another only because of the inexperience or incapacity of the ruler, and inexperience and incapacity are far removed from God. But created things are at odds and contend with one another, as is evident in the case of contraries. Therefore, one ruler does not govern the world.

Obj. 3. We always find in nature what is better. But "two persons together are better than only one," as the Book of Ecclesiastes says.[13] Therefore, several rulers, not one, govern the world.

On the contrary, we profess one God and one Lord, according to the saying of the Apostle in the First Letter to the Corinthians: "There is for us only one God, the Father . . . , and one Lord."[14] And both of these titles belong to governance, for governance of subjects belongs to the Lord, and we understand the name "God" from providence, as I have said before.[15] Therefore, a single ruler governs the world.

I answer that we need to affirm that a single ruler governs the world. For, since the end of the world's governance is something intrinsically good, which is the best, governance of the world needs to be the best. Moreover, the best governance is one that a single ruler carries out. And this is so because governance is nothing other than directing the governed to an end, which is some good. But unity belongs to the nature of goodness, as Boethius demonstrates in his *On the Consolation of Philosophy*, because, as all things desire good, so do they desire unity, without which they cannot exist.[16] For everything exists as much as it is one, and hence we see that things resist their division as much as they can, and that their breakup comes about by their deficiency. And so the end at which the ruler of a multitude aims, is unity or peace.

Moreover, the cause of unity is intrinsically one. For several rulers evidently can unite or harmonize many things only if the several things are themselves somehow united. But what is intrinsically one, can more suitably and more perfectly cause unity than many rulers in concert can. And hence one ruler governs a multitude better than several rulers do.

Therefore, we conclude that the best governance of the world is one by a single ruler. And this is what the Philosopher says in the *Metaphysics*: "Beings do not wish to be poorly disposed, and a plurality of rulers is a bad thing. Therefore, there needs to be only one ruler."[17]

Reply to Obj. 1. Motion is "the actuality of a moveable object that a cause of motion effects."[18] Therefore, different kinds of motions result from different kinds of moveable objects, whose differences the perfection of the universe requires, as I have said before,[19] and not from different kinds of rulers.

Reply to Obj. 2. Contraries, although they disagree regarding their proximate ends, nonetheless agree with respect to their final end, as they are included in the single order of the universe.

Reply to Obj. 3. Two persons are better than one in the case of particular goods, but no goodness can be added to what is essentially good.

Fourth Article

Does Governance of the World Produce Only One Effect?

I proceed in this way to the fourth article: it seems that governance of the world produces only one effect.

Obj. 1. Governance seems to produce what governance effects in the governed. But this is a single effect, namely, the good of order, as is clear in the case of an army. Therefore, the world's governance produces a single effect.

Obj. 2. Nature brings it about that only one kind of effect results from one kind of thing. But one ruler governs the world, as I have shown.[20] Therefore, governance of the world likewise produces only one effect.

Obj. 3. If the effect of the world's governance is not a single effect by reason of a single ruler, there need to be as many effects as there are subjects governed. But we cannot count the number of subjects governed. Therefore, we cannot include the effects of the world's governance in a discrete number.

On the contrary, Denis says that "the Deity contains all things and fulfills all of them by his providence and perfect goodness."[21] But the world's governance belongs to providence. Therefore, there are particular determined effects of God's governance of the world.

I answer that we can weigh the effect of any action by its goal, for actions bring about the attainment of ends. But the end of the world's governance is an intrinsic good that everything strives to share and assimilate. Therefore, we can understand the effect of the world's governance in three ways.

In one way, we can understand the effect of the world's governance regarding its very purpose, and the world's governance in this way has only one effect, namely, to be likened to the supreme good.

In the second way, we can consider the effect of the world's governance with respect to the means whereby creatures are produced to be like God. And so, in general, the world's governance has two effects. For creatures are likened to God in two respects, namely, one regarding God's goodness, inasmuch as creatures are good, and the other regarding the fact that God causes the goodness of other things inasmuch as creatures cause the goodness of other creatures. And hence the world's governance produces two effects, namely, the preservation of things in goodness, and their movements to produce good.

In the third way, we can consider the effect of the world's governance in particular, and in this way, we cannot count the effects.

Reply to Obj. 1. The order of the universe includes both the preservation of the different things that God has constituted, and their movements. For we find order in the world in both of these ways, namely, as one thing is better than another, and as one thing causes another.

Replies to Objs. 2 and 3. The answers to objections two and three are clear from what I have said.[22]

Fifth Article

Is Everything Subject to God's Governance?

I proceed in this way to the fifth article: it seems that some things are not subject to God's governance.

Obj. 1. The Book of Ecclesiastes says: "I saw under the sun that the race is not to the swift, nor combat to the strong, nor bread to the wise, nor riches to the learned, nor favor to the skillful, but that time and chance exist in everything."[23] But things subject to someone's governance do not occur by chance. Therefore, things under the sun are not subject to God's governance.

Obj. 2. The Apostle says in his First Letter to the Corinthians that "God has no charge over oxen."[24] But a person has charge of the subjects that he governs. Therefore, some things are not subject to God's governance.

Obj. 3. Something capable of self-governance does not seem to need to be governed by another. But rational creatures can govern themselves, since they are masters of their actions, and act by themselves and are not merely acted upon by another. And being acted upon by another seems to be characteristic of those subject to governance. Therefore, some things are not subject to God's governance.

On the contrary, Augustine says in *The City of God*: "God endowed with suitable parts not only the heavens and the earth, not only human beings and angels, but also the meagre and despicable bowels of animals and the wings of birds and the flowers of plants and the leaves of trees."[25] Therefore, everything is subject to his governance.

I answer that it belongs to God to govern things and to cause them for the same reason, because it belongs to him to produce things and to give them their perfections, and such is the characteristic of governance. But God indeed not only causes particular kinds of things but every single being, as I have shown before.[26] And hence, as nothing can exist that God does not create, so nothing can exist that is not subject to his governance.

The nature of the end of governance also makes the same point clear. For a ruler's governance reaches as far as the end of his governance can reach. But the end of God's governance is his very goodness, as I have shown before.[27] And hence, since nothing can exist that is not ordered to God's goodness as its end, as is clear from what I have said before,[28] nothing belonging to beings can be withdrawn from his governance.

Therefore, foolish was the opinion of those who said that God does not govern things here below that can pass away, or even individuals, or even human affairs. And out of the mouths of such persons, Ezekiel says: "The Lord has abandoned the earth."[29]

Reply to Obj. 1. We say that things exist "under the sun" that come to be and pass away by reason of the sun's motion. And we find chance in all those things, not such that everything that comes to be in them, is by chance, but because we find an element of chance in all of them. And the very fact that we find an element of chance in such things, shows that they are subject to governance. For unless a higher being were to govern such things that can pass away, especially things that lack knowledge, they would not strive toward anything, and so nothing would result in them different from what they strive for, and such constitutes the nature of chance. And hence, to show that things of chance come about by the ordering of a higher cause, the writer of Ecclesiastes does not say unconditionally that he sees chance in everything, but he says that he sees "time and chance" in everything, namely, that we find accidental deficiencies in those things regarding some temporal order.

Reply to Obj. 2. Governance is a certain change effected by a ruler in his subjects. But every motion is "the actuality of a moveable object that the cause of motion effects," as the *Physics* says.[30] Moreover, every actuality is proportioned to the potentiality of which it is the actuality. And so even every movement by a single cause needs to move different moveable objects in different ways. Thus the single craftsmanship of God as ruler governs things in different ways according to their differences. For certain things by their nature, as masters of their actions, act intrinsically. And God governs such things not only because he himself acting interiorly on them moves them, but also because he draws them by commands and prohibitions, rewards and punishments, away from evil and toward good. But God does not so govern irrational creatures, which do not act and are only acted upon. Therefore, when the Apostle says that God has no charge of oxen, he does not entirely withdraw oxen from the charge of God's governance but only with respect to the way that in the proper sense belongs to rational creatures. *Reply to Obj. 3.* Rational creatures govern themselves by their intellects and wills, both of which God's intellect and will need to rule and perfect. And so God needs to govern rational creatures over and above the governance whereby such creatures govern themselves as masters of their actions.

Sixth Article

Does God Directly Govern Everything?

I proceed in this way to the sixth article: it seems that God directly governs everything.

Obj. 1. Gregory of Nyssa[31] censures the opinion of Plato, who divided providence into three parts; Plato said that the first providence indeed belongs to the most excellent God, who provides for heavenly beings and everything in general, and that a second providence, namely, one that regards things involved in coming to be and passing away, belongs to secondary gods, who circle the heavens, and that a third providence belongs to supernatural beings, who are the guardians on earth of human actions. Therefore, it seems that God directly governs everything.

Obj. 2. It is better, if possible, that one rather than many accomplish something, as the *Physics* says.[32] But God can by himself directly govern everything. Therefore, it seems that he directly governs everything.

Obj. 3. Nothing in God is defective or incomplete. But that a ruler govern through intermediaries, seems to belong to a deficiency in the ruler; for example, an earthly king, because he cannot do everything and is not present everywhere in his kingdom, consequently needs to have personnel to administer his governance. Therefore, God directly governs everything.

On the contrary, Augustine says in his *De Trinitate*: "As finer and more powerful bodies rule denser and inferior bodies by a certain order, so rational living spirits rule every body, and dutiful and upright rational living spirits rule the unfaithful and sinners, and God himself rules dutiful and upright rational living spirits."[33]

I answer that we need to consider two things in the matter of governance, namely, the essence of governance, which is providence itself, and the execution of governance. Therefore, concerning the essence of governance,

God governs everything directly, but concerning the execution of govern-ance, he governs certain things by means of others.

And this is so because we should attribute each thing to God according to what is most good in it, since God is the very essence of goodness. But the best in every way or plan or practical knowledge (and such is the essence of governance) consists in knowing actual particular things. For example, the best doctor is not one who considers only universal things, but one who can also weigh the least particulars. And other examples illustrate the same point. And hence we need to say that God possesses the essence of the gov-ernance of everything, even the least particular.

But since governance ought to bring the governed to perfection, the greater the perfection that a ruler shares with his subjects, the better will be his governance. Now, it is a greater perfection that things, in addition to being intrinsically good, cause goodness in others, than if things were to be good only intrinsically. And so God governs things in such a way that, in governing the world, he constitutes certain ones the causes of others, just as if a master were to cause his pupils not only to be knowledgeable but also to be teachers of others.

Reply to Obj. 1. Gregory censures the opinion of Plato because the latter held that God does not directly govern everything even with respect to the essence of governance. And this is evident because Plato divided provi-dence, that is, the essence of governance, into three parts.

Reply to Obj. 2. Causal perfection would be withdrawn from things if God alone were to govern. And hence one thing would not cause the whole that many things cause.

Reply to Obj. 3. For an earthly king to have personnel to execute his gov-ernance belongs not only to his imperfection but also to his kingly dignity, because administrative ranks render kingly power more illustrious.

Seventh Article

Can Anything Happen outside the Order of God's Governance?

I proceed in this way to the seventh article: it seems that things can happen outside God's governance.

Obj. 1. Boethius says in his *On the Consolation of Philosophy* that "God disposes everything by what is good."[34] Therefore, if nothing happens in the world outside the order of his governance, nothing evil would consequently exist in the world.

Obj. 2. Nothing that comes about as a ruler pre-ordains, exists by chance. Therefore, if nothing happens in the world outside the order of God's gov-ernance, nothing in the world would consequently exist by luck or chance.

Obj. 3. The order of God's governance is fixed and unalterable, because it exists by his eternal plan. Therefore, if nothing could happen in the world outside the order of God's governance, it follows that everything comes about by necessity, and that there is nothing contingent in the world. And this is not appropriate. Therefore, things can happen in the world outside the order of God's governance.

On the contrary, the Book of Esther says: "Lord God, almighty king, all things have been placed in your power, and there is no one who can resist your will."[35]

I answer that an effect can come about outside the disposition of particular causes but not outside the disposition of the universal cause. This is so because nothing comes about outside the disposition of a particular cause unless another cause impedes the latter, and we indeed need to trace the other cause back to the first universal cause. For example, an impediment like the coarseness of food may cause indigestion outside the disposition of the nutritive power, and we need to trace the food's coarseness back to another cause, and so on back to the first universal cause. Therefore, since God is the first universal cause not only of one kind of being but of every being without exception, nothing can happen outside the order of his governance. An effect needs to rest on the order of God's governance with respect to a particular cause, however, precisely because the effect seems from one perspective to depart from the same order with respect to another cause.

Reply to Obj. 1. We find nothing in the world that is entirely bad, because evil is always founded on good, as I have shown before.[36] And so we call something evil because it departs from the disposition of a particular good. But if something were to depart entirely from the order of God's providence, it would be nothing at all.

Reply to Obj. 2. We say that some things exist in the world by chance in relation to particular causes, and such things happen outside the disposition of those causes. But with respect to God's providence, "nothing happens in the world by chance," as Augustine says in his *Octoginta trium quaestionum.*[37]

Reply to Obj. 3. We call some effects contingent in relation to proximate causes, which can fail to produce their effects, not because anything can arise outside the entire order of God's governance. For the fact that something happens outside the disposition of a proximate cause, itself results from a cause subject to God's governance.

Eighth Article

Can Anything Resist the Order of God's Governance?

I proceed in this way to the eighth article: it seems that some things can resist the order of God's governance.

Obj. 1. Isaiah says: "Their tongues and their deeds are against the Lord."[38]

Obj. 2. No king justly punishes those who do not resist his ordinances. Therefore, God would punish no one justly if there were no resistance to his disposition.

Obj. 3. Everything is subject to the order of God's governance. But one thing wars against another. Therefore, there are some things that resist his governance.

On the contrary, Boethius says in his *On the Consolation of Philosophy*: "There is nothing willing or able to stand in the way of this supreme good. Therefore, the supreme good firmly rules and agreeably disposes everything,"[39] as the Book of Wisdom says of God's wisdom.[40]

I answer that we can consider the order of God's providence in two ways. In one way, in general, namely, as that order comes from the cause that governs the whole world; in the second way, in particular, namely, as that order comes from a particular cause, which executes his governance.

In the first way, therefore, nothing resists the order of God's governance. And two considerations make this evident. First, indeed, because the order of God's governance strives entirely for good, and everything in its activity and effort strives only for good, "for no one acts looking for something bad," as Denis says.[41] The same point is evident in a second way, because every tendency of a thing, whether by nature or free will, is nothing other than a certain impulse from the first cause of motion, as I have said before.[42] For example, the tendency of an arrow toward a fixed target is nothing other than a certain impulse from an archer. And hence everything that acts, whether by nature or free will, arrives at the end for which God ordains the thing, as if by its own will. And so Boethius says that God "disposes everything agreeably."

Reply to Obj. 1. We say that some persons think or speak or act against God, not because they entirely resist the order of his governance, for even sinners intend some good, but because they resist a certain fixed good suitable for them by their nature or condition. And so God justly punishes them.

Reply to Obj. 2. And the above response makes clear the answer to the second objection.

Reply to Obj. 3. The fact that one thing wars against another, shows· that something can resist the order that arises from a particular cause, but not the order that depends on the universal cause of everything.

Notes

1. Wis. 14:3.
2. *On the Consolation of Philosophy* III, 9. PL 63:758.
3. E.g., Democritus, Epicurus.

4. *De natura deorum* II.
5. Q. 44, A. 4. Q. 65, A. 2.
6. Cf. Plato, *Timaeus*. 30A.
7. Q. 104, A. 1.
8. *Ethics* I, 1. 1094a3–5.
9. *The City of God* XIX, 13. PL 41:640.
10. Prov. 16:4.
11. Q. 44, A. 1.
12. Aristotle, *Metaphysics* XI, 10. 1075a13–15.
13. Eccl. 4:9.
14. 1 Cor. 8:6.
15. Q. 13, A. 8.
16. *On the Consolation of Philosophy* III, 11. PL 63:771–72.
17. *Metaphysics* XI, 10. 1075b37–1076a4.
18. Aristotle, *Physics* III, 3. 202a13–14.
19. Q. 47, A. 1. Q. 48, A. 2.
20. Q. 103, A. 3.
21. *De divinis nominibus* 12. PG 3:969.
22. In the body of the article.
23. Eccl. 9:11.
24. 1 Cor. 9:9.
25. *The City of God* V, 11. PL 41:154.
26. Q. 44, AA. 1, 2.
27. Q. 103, A. 2.
28. Q. 44, A. 4. Q. 65, A. 2.
29. Ez. 9:9.
30. Aristotle, *Physics* III, 3. 202a13–14.
31. Nemesius, *De natura hominis* 44. PG 40:793–96. St. Thomas erroneously attributed this work to Gregory of Nyssa.
32. Aristotle, *Physics* VIII, 6. 259a8–13.
33. *De Trinitate* III, 4. PL 42:873.
34. *On the Consolation of Philosophy* III, 12. PL 63:779.
35. Esther 13:9.
36. Q. 48, A. 3.
37. *Octoginta trium quaestionum*, Q. 24. PL 40:17.
38. Is. 3:8.
39. *On the Consolation of Philosophy* III, 12. PL 40:17.
40. Wis. 8:1.
41. *De divinis nominibus* 4. PG 3:732.
42. Q. 103, A. 1, *ad* 3, and A. 5, *ad* 2.

On the Effects of God's Governance of the World in Particular

[This question is divided into four articles, all of which are included here.]

First Article

Does God Need to Preserve Creatures?

I proceed in this way to the first article: it seems that God does not need to preserve creatures.

Obj. 1. What cannot not exist, does not need to be preserved in existence, just as what cannot pass away, does not need to be preserved from passing away. But there are certain creatures that by their nature cannot not exist. Therefore, God does not need to preserve every creature in existence.

I prove the minor premise thus. What intrinsically belongs to something, needs to exist in it, and the contrary cannot belong to it. For example, multiples of two are even numbers and cannot be odd numbers. But existence intrinsically results from form, because each thing is an actual being insofar as it has form. Moreover, certain creatures are subsistent forms, as I have said about angels,[1] and so existence intrinsically belongs to such creatures. And the reasoning is the same regarding those creatures whose matter has potentiality for only one form, as I have said about heavenly bodies.[2] Therefore, such creatures by their nature necessarily exist and cannot not exist. For potentiality for nonexistence can be based neither on their form, which is intrinsically a consequence of existing, nor on the matter underlying their form, which matter they cannot lose, since such matter has no potentiality for another form.

Obj. 2. God is more powerful than any created efficient cause. But a created efficient cause can communicate preservation in existence to its effects even after the cause's activity ceases; for example, a house abides after the activity of its builder ceases, and water stays hot for some time after fire's activity ceases. Therefore, much more can God bring it about that his creatures be preserved in existence after his causal action ceases.

Obj. 3. Nothing physically forced can arise apart from an efficient cause. But to tend toward nonexisting is contrary to the nature of, and physically forced on, any creature, since every creature by nature desires to exist. Therefore, creatures can tend toward nonexisting only by a cause that acts to bring about their passing away. But there are certain creatures, such as spiritual substances and heavenly bodies, that no cause can make pass away. Therefore, such creatures cannot tend toward nonexisting even if God's activity ceases.

Obj. 4. If God preserves things in existence, this will be by some action. But every action by an efficient cause, if the action be efficacious, produces something in the effect. Therefore, God's preserving action needs to produce something in creatures.

But this does not seem to be so. For such action does not produce the very existence of creatures, since something already existing is not produced. Nor, moreover, does God's action add anything else to creatures, because either God would thus not continually preserve creatures in existence, or he would continually add something to creatures—and either alternative is inappropriate. Therefore, God does not preserve creatures in existence.

On the contrary, the Letter to the Hebrews says that God sustains "everything by his powerful word."[3]

I answer that both faith and reason require us to affirm that God preserves creatures in existence. And to prove this, we need to consider that one thing preserves another in two ways. In one way, indirectly and by accident, as we say that one who removes a destructive cause, preserves something; for example, we say that one who keeps watch over a child lest the child fall into a fire, preserves the child. And so also we say that God preserves some things—but not everything, since certain things have no destructive causes that need to be removed in order to preserve them.

We say in a second way that one thing preserves another intrinsically and directly, namely, insofar as the thing preserved depends on the preserving thing in such a way that the former cannot exist without the latter. And all creatures need God to preserve them in this way. For every creature's existing depends on God, so that no creature could exist even for a moment without being annihilated, if the activity of God's power were not to preserve them in existence, as Gregory says.[4]

And we can examine this matter as follows. Every effect depends on its cause as such. But we need to consider that a particular efficient cause causes only its effect's coming-to-be and not directly the effect's existence. And this indeed happens both in the case of man-made objects and in the case of things of nature. For example, a builder causes a house's coming-to-be but not directly its existing. For the house's existing itself evidently results from the house's form, and the house's form consists in the house's composition and arrangement, and the latter result from the natural capacities of certain things. As a cook cooks food by using a natural causal power, namely, fire, so a builder builds a house by using rubble, stones, and timber, materials that can support and preserve a house's composition and arrangement. And hence the house's existing depends on the nature of such materials, just as the house's coming-to-be depends on the activity of the builder.

And we need by like reasoning to consider causality in the case of things of nature. For if a particular efficient cause does not cause a form as such, the cause will not intrinsically cause the existing that results from such a form, but only the effect's coming-to-be.

Moreover, it is evident that one of two things belonging to the same species cannot intrinsically cause the form of the other as such, because the first would thus cause its own form, since both have the same nature. But one thing can cause such a form in another as that form exists in matter, that is, as this particular matter acquires this particular form. And this is to cause something's coming-to-be, as, for example, when human beings beget human beings, and fire causes fire. And so, whenever nature produces an effect to receive from the effect's efficient cause essentially the same imprint that exists in the cause, then the effect's coming-to-be but not its existing depends on the cause.

But sometimes nature does not produce an effect to receive from the effect's efficient cause an imprint essentially the same as the imprint in the cause, as is evident in the case of efficient causes that do not produce effects specifically like themselves. For example, heavenly bodies cause material substances here below, which are specifically unlike heavenly bodies, to come to be. And such efficient causes can cause forms as essentially such and not only as acquired in particular matter. And so such causes cause things not only to come to be but also to exist.

Therefore, as something's coming-to-be cannot continue when the action of the efficient cause causing an effect's coming-to-be ceases, so neither can something's existing continue when the action of the efficient cause causing both an effect's coming-to-be and its existing ceases. And this is the reason why hot water retains heat after the heating action by fire ceases, while air does not remain illuminated, not even for a moment, after the sun's illuminating action ceases. For, to be sure, water's matter can receive from fire essentially the same heat that exists in fire. And hence, if water's matter should be brought completely to the form of fire, water's matter will retain heat forever. But if water's matter should imperfectly share some of the form of fire in a certain inchoative way, the heat will not remain forever but for a period of time, because the water's matter shares weakly in the source of heat. On the other hand, nature in no way produces air to receive light essentially the same as the light existing in the sun, namely, to receive the sun's form, which is the source of light. And so light, since it does not have its source in air, immediately ceases when the sun's action ceases.

Moreover, every creature is disposed toward God as air is disposed toward the sun illuminating it. For, as the sun by its nature shines, while air becomes luminous by sharing in light from the sun, albeit not by sharing in the nature of the sun, so God alone is a being by essence, because his essence is his existing. But every creature is a being by sharing, not such that its essence is its existing. And so, as Augustine says in his *Super Genesim ad litteram*, "If the power of God were at some point of time to cease from things created to be ruled, their nature would also at the same time cease, and every nature would perish."[5] And he says in the same work that, "as air becomes lucid when there is light, so human beings are illuminated when God is present in them, and they are immediately in darkness when he is absent from them."[6]

Reply to Obj. 1.   Existing intrinsically results from a creature's form, but God's influence is presupposed, just as light results from the translucence of air if the sun's influence is presupposed. And hence the potentiality for nonexisting in spiritual creatures and heavenly bodies exists in God, who can withdraw his influence, rather than in the form or matter of such creatures.

Reply to Obj. 2.   God cannot communicate to any creature that it be preserved in existence were his activity to cease, just as he cannot communicate to any creature that it cause its existence. For God needs to preserve creatures in existence as much as the existing of an effect depends on the cause of existing. And hence there is no comparison to an efficient cause that causes only coming-to-be, not existing.

Reply to Obj. 3.   That argument is valid with respect to preservation by removing a destructive cause, but not all creatures need such preservation, as I have said.[7]

Reply to Obj. 4.   God does not preserve things by a new action but by continuing the action whereby he bestows existing, and this action is indeed motionless and timeless. Similarly, too, the continuous influence of the sun preserves the light in air.

Second Article

Does God Directly Preserve Every Creature?

I proceed in this way to the second article: it seems that God directly preserves every creature.

Obj. 1.   God preserves creatures by the same action whereby he creates them, as I have said.[8] But God directly creates everything. Therefore, he also directly preserves them.

Obj. 2.   Everything is more like itself than like anything else. But God cannot communicate to a creature that it preserve itself. Therefore, much less can God communicate to a creature that it preserve another. Therefore, God preserves everything apart from any intermediate cause doing so.

Obj. 3. What causes both an effect's coming-to-be and its existing, keeps the effect in existence. But all created causes, it seems, cause only their effects' coming-to-be, for created causes cause only by changing things, as I have maintained before.[9] Therefore, there are no such causes that preserve their effects in existence.

On the contrary, things are preserved by the same thing whereby they have existence. But God bestows existence on things by means of some intermediate causes. Therefore, he preserves things in existence by means of some intermediate causes.

I answer that, as I have said,[10] something keeps something else in existence in two ways: in one way, indirectly and by accident, because something removes or blocks action by a destructive cause; in the second way, directly and intrinsically, because the existing of something else depends on it, as an effect's existing depends on a cause. We find, moreover, that a created thing preserves another created thing in both ways. For even in the case of corporeal things, there are evidently many things that prevent destructive acts, and we consequently say that such things preserve other things. For example, salt preserves meats from putrefying, and it is likewise in many other cases.

We also find that the existence of some effects depends on some creatures. For, when there are many ordered causes, effects indeed need to depend first and chiefly on a primary cause but secondarily on all the intermediate causes. And so the primary cause indeed chiefly preserves effects, but all the intermediate causes do so secondarily, and the more so as an intermediate cause happens to be higher and more akin to the primary cause. And hence we attribute the preservation and perdurance of things to their higher causes, even in the case of corporeal things. The Philosopher accordingly says in the *Metaphysics* that the first movement, namely, the daily cycle, causes the continuity of coming to be, while the second movement, that is, the motion by the zodiac, causes differences regarding coming to be and passing away.[11] And astronomers likewise attribute to Saturn, the uppermost planet, fixed and perduring things.

We thus need to say that God preserves certain things in existence by means of some intermediate causes.

Reply to Obj. 1. God directly created everything. But in the very creation of the world, he established an order among things, such that some depend on others, by which they are secondarily preserved in existence, although we presuppose that God himself chiefly preserves them.

Reply to Obj. 2. An appropriate cause can preserve an effect dependent on it. For this reason, as no effect can be endowed with the ability to cause itself, but it can be endowed with the ability to cause something else, so also no effect can be endowed with the ability to preserve itself, but it can be endowed with the ability to preserve something else.

Reply to Obj. 3. Creatures can cause other creatures to acquire a new form or disposition only by way of some change, because creatures always act with subjects of change presupposed. But after a creature has brought about a form or disposition in an effect, the creature preserves such a form or disposition without any change in the effect. For example, we understand that there is some sort of change in air when it is freshly illuminated, but only the presence of the illuminating source preserves the light, without any change on the part of the air.

Third Article

Can God Annihilate Anything?

I proceed in this way to the third article: it seems that God cannot annihilate anything.

Obj. 1. Augustine says in his *Octoginta trium quaestionum* that "God does not cause any tendency toward nonexisting."[12] But such would happen if he were to annihilate any creature. Therefore, God cannot annihilate anything.

Obj. 2. God by his goodness causes things to exist, since "we exist inasmuch as God is good," as Augustine says in his *De doctrina Christiana.*[13] But God cannot not be good. Therefore, he cannot cause things not to exist. And such would be the case if he were to annihilate them.

Obj. 3. If God were to annihilate some things, he would need to do so by some action. But such cannot be the case, because the final end of every action is some being. And hence the final end even of action by a destructive cause is something produced, because the coming-to-be of one thing is the passing away of another. Therefore, God cannot annihilate anything.

On the contrary, Jeremiah says: "Chastize me, O Lord, but in just measure and not in your anger, lest, perchance, you annihilate me."[14]

I answer that certain thinkers held that God brought things into existence by acting out of a necessity of nature. And if this were to be true, God could not annihilate anything, since, by his nature, he cannot vary. But this position, as I have maintained before,[15] is false and utterly foreign to the Catholic faith, which professes that God brought things into existence by his free will, as the Psalm says: "The Lord did whatsoever he wished to do."[16] The fact that God communicates existing to creatures, therefore, depends on his will. Nor does he otherwise preserve things in existence than as he continuously pours existence into them, as I have said.[17] Therefore, as he was able not to communicate existing to them before they existed, and thus not to produce them, so he is able not to pour existence into them after he has already produced them, and thus they would cease to exist. And the latter is to annihilate them.

Reply to Obj. 1. Nonexisting does not have an intrinsic cause. For things can cause only insofar as they are beings, and, strictly speaking, beings cause existing. Thus God cannot cause tending toward nonexisting, although creatures as such have a tendency not to exist, insofar as they are made from nothing. But God can accidentally cause things to be annihilated, namely, by withdrawing his activity from them.

Reply to Obj. 2. God's goodness does not cause things by a necessity of nature, as it were, because his goodness does not depend on created things, but God's goodness causes things by his free will. And hence, as God was able not to bring things into existence without prejudice to his goodness, so he is able not to preserve things in existence without detriment to that goodness.

Reply to Obj. 3. If God were to annihilate anything, this would not result from any activity by him but from the fact that he ceases to act.

Fourth Article

Is Anything Annihilated?

I proceed in this way to the fourth article: it seems that some things are annihilated.

Obj. 1. Ends correspond to beginnings. But only God existed at the beginning. Therefore, things will be brought to the end that nothing but God exists. And so creatures will be annihilated.

Obj. 2. Every creature has limited power. But no limited power extends endlessly, and hence the *Physics* proves that limited power cannot cause motion in unlimited time.[18] Therefore, no creature can perdure without limit. And so creatures will at some point of time be annihilated.

Obj. 3. Forms and accidents do not have matter as one of their constituent parts. But forms and accidents at some point of time cease to exist. Therefore, they are annihilated.

On the contrary, Ecclesiastes says: "I have learned that every work of God endures forever."[19]

I answer that certain things that God has done with respect to creatures, come about in the natural course of things, but that he does certain other things miraculously outside the natural order implanted in creatures, as I shall explain later.[20] And we can from the very natures of things consider what God will do by the natural order implanted in things. But things happening miraculously are arranged to manifest his favor, as the Apostle says in his First Letter to the Corinthians: "The manifestation of the Spirit is given to each one for a benefit."[21] And he then applies this to the working of miracles, among other things.

Moreover, creatures' natures show that none of them are annihilated, because either they are immaterial and thus have no potentiality for nonexisting, or they are material and thus always remain, at least regarding their matter, which cannot pass away, as the existing subject of coming to be and passing away. Nor does annihilating a being belong to manifesting God's favor, since God rather manifests his power and goodness by preserving things in existence. And hence we need to say unconditionally that nothing at all will be annihilated.

Reply to Obj. 1. The fact that things are brought from nonexistence into existence, reveals the power of the one who produces them. But if things were to be annihilated, that would hinder such a manifestation, since God's power is most manifested in his preserving things in existence, as the Apostle says in the Letter to the Hebrews: God sustains "everything by his powerful word."[22]

Reply to Obj. 2. A creature's potentiality for existing is merely receptive, but active power belongs to God himself, who pours out existence. And hence the fact that beings perdure without limit, is a consequence of the infinity of God's power. Nonetheless, a power to remain for a limited time is determined for certain beings, inasmuch as they can be prevented from receiving his outpouring of existence by a contrary efficient cause, which a limited power can resist for only a limited, not an unlimited, period of time. And so things that do not have a contrary, albeit they have limited power, perdure forever.

Reply to Obj. 3. Forms and accidents, since they do not subsist, are not complete beings, but each of them is part of a being, for we call each a being because something exists by reason of it. And yet they are not entirely annihilated, in the way in which they exist, because they remain in the potentiality of matter or the subject, not because any part of them remains.

Notes

1. Q. 50, AA. 2, 5.
2. Q. 66, A. 2.
3. Heb. 1:3.
4. *Moralia* XVI, 37. PL 75:1143.
5. *Super Genesim ad litteram* IV, 12. PL 34:304.
6. Ibid. VIII, 12. PL 34:383.
7. In the body of the article.
8. Q. 104, A. 1, *ad* 4.
9. Q. 45, A. 3.
10. Q. 104, A. 1.
11. *Metaphysics* XI, 6–7. 1072a9–23.

12. *Octoginta trium quaestionum*, Q 21. PL 40:16.
13. *De doctrina Christiana* I, 32. PL 34:32.
14. Jer. 10:24.
15. Q. 19, A. 4.
16. Ps. 135:6.
17. Q. 104, A. 1, *ad* 4.
18. Aristotle, *Physics* VIII, 10. 266a12–24.
19. Eccl. 3:14.
20. Q. 105, A. 6.
21. 1 Cor. 12:7.
22. Heb. 1:3.

ST I
Question 105
On Change in Creatures by God

[This question is divided into eight articles, four of which are included here.]

Fourth Article

Can God Move Created Wills?

I proceed in this way to the fourth article: it seems that God cannot move created wills.

Obj. 1. Everything that something extrinsic moves, is compelled. But the will cannot be compelled. Therefore, something extrinsic does not move it. And so God cannot move the will.

Obj. 2. God cannot make contradictory propositions be true at the same time. But such would follow if he were to move the will, for to be moved of one's own accord is to be moved intrinsically and not by another. Therefore, God cannot move the will.

Obj. 3. We attribute motion to the cause of motion rather than to the moveable object, and hence we do not attribute intentional homicides to stones but to those who throw stones. Therefore, if God were to move the will, we would consequently not impute freely willed actions to human beings for their praise or blame. But this conclusion is false. Therefore, God does not move the will.

On the contrary, the Letter to the Philippians says: "God works" in us "to will and accomplish."[1]

I answer that, as the intellect is moved by its object and by him who bestowed the power to understand, as I have said,[2] so the will is moved by its object (which is the good) and by him who bestowed the power to will. Moreover, although the will's object, any good, can move the will, only God can adequately and efficaciously move the will. For nothing can adequately move something moveable unless the active power of the motion's cause exceeds, or at least equals, the moveable thing's passive power. And the will's passive power extends to good in general, for the will's object is universal

292

good, as the intellect's object is universal being. But every created good is a certain particular good, while God alone is universal good. And hence he alone fulfills the will and suffices to move it as its object.

And likewise God alone also causes the power to will. For willing is nothing other than the tendency of the will toward its object, which is universal good. But it belongs to the first cause of motion, to whom the final end is proportioned, to incline the will to universal good, just as, in the case of human affairs, it belongs to the person in charge of a people to direct them toward the good of the community.

And hence it belongs to God to move the human will in both ways but especially in the second way, by interiorly inclining the will.

Reply to Obj. 1. We say that something moved by another is compelled if something is moved contrary to its own tendency, but not if it is moved by another that bestows on it its own tendency. For example, a heavy object, when moved downward by the cause producing it, is not compelled. Thus God, by moving the will, does not compel it, since he gives it its own tendency.

Reply to Obj. 2. To be moved of one's own accord is to be moved intrinsically, that is, by an intrinsic source, but that intrinsic source can exist by reason of another source that is extrinsic. And so being moved intrinsically is not inconsistent with being moved by another.

Reply to Obj. 3. If something else were to move the will in such a way that the will would not at all move itself, we would not impute willed actions to human beings for their praise or blame. But because being moved by another does not exclude being moved intrinsically, as I have said,[3] so God's action consequently does not take away the reason for merit or demerit.

Fifth Article

Does God Act in Every Efficient Cause?

I proceed in this way to the fifth article: it seems that God does not act in every efficient cause.

Obj. 1. We should attribute no inadequacy to God. Therefore, if God acts in every efficient cause, he acts adequately in each one of them. Therefore, it would be superfluous were any created efficient cause to do anything.

Obj. 2. A single action does not simultaneously come from two efficient causes, just as a numerically single movement cannot belong to two moveable objects. Therefore, if a creature's action comes from God acting in the creature, such action cannot at the same time come from the creature. And so no creature does anything.

Obj. 3. We say that the maker of something causes the product's activity, inasmuch as the maker gives the product the form by which the product acts. Therefore, if God causes the activity of the things created by him, this will be so because he gives them the power to act. And this happens at the beginning, when he makes them. Therefore, it seems that he does not act further in creatures' activity.

On the contrary, Isaiah says: "You, O Lord, have wrought in us all our deeds."[4]

I answer that certain thinkers understood God to act in every efficient cause in such a way that no created power would cause anything in things; rather, God alone would directly cause everything.[5] For example, fire would not heat things, but God would do so in the fire, and similarly in every other case.

But this theory is impossible. First, indeed, because it would take the order of cause and effect away from created things. And this involves lack of power on the part of the creator, for it is by an efficient cause's power that a cause imparts to its effect the power to act.

Second, the theory cannot stand because we would erroneously attribute to things the active powers we find in them, if they were to do nothing by means of those powers. Indeed, every created thing would seem to be somehow purposeless if it were to be deprived of its own activity, since everything exists for the sake of its activity. For what is incomplete, always exists for the sake of what is more complete. Therefore, as matter exists for the sake of form, so form, which is a first actuality, exists for the sake of its activity, which is a second actuality, and so activity is the goal of created things. We thus need to understand that, although God acts in things, the things themselves have their own activity.

And to prove this, since there are four kinds of causes, we need to consider that matter is not a source of action but disposed as the subject that receives the effects of action. Ends and efficient causes and forms, however, are disposed as sources of action, albeit in a certain order. For the first source of action is indeed the end that moves an efficient cause to act; the second source of action is the efficient cause; the third source of action is the form of what the efficient cause brings to the thing to be produced, although the efficient cause itself also acts by means of its form. This is evident in the case of man-made objects. For a goal, that is, the product itself (e.g., a box or a bed) causes a craftsman to act, and he brings to his action the ax that cuts the wood with its sharp edge.

God thus acts in three ways in everything that acts. First, indeed, by reason of the action's end. For, since every action is for the sake of some real or apparent good, and something is really or apparently good only insofar as it shares some likeness to the highest good, which is God, God himself consequently causes every action as its end.

We should likewise note that, in the case of several ordered efficient causes, the second cause acts in the power of the first, for the first causes the second to act. And everything accordingly acts in the power of God himself, and so he causes the actions of every efficient cause.

Third, we need to consider that God not only moves things to act by applying their forms and powers to actions, as it were, just as a craftsman applies his ax to cutting wood, although he sometimes has not given the ax its form, but God also gives created efficient causes their forms and preserves creatures in existence. And hence God causes actions inasmuch as he bestows the forms that are the sources of actions; for example, we say that the producer of heavy and light objects causes their movement. But God also causes actions by preserving things' forms and powers; for example, we say that the sun causes colors to be manifest inasmuch as the sun gives and preserves the light whereby colors are manifested. And because a thing's form exists within the thing—and the more so as we consider the form as prior and more universal—and because God himself in the strict sense causes the very universal existing present in everything, which existing is, above all, innermost to things, God consequently most intimately acts in everything. And sacred Scripture consequently ascribes the actions of nature to God acting in nature, as it were, as Job says: "You have clothed me with skin and flesh, you have composed me with bones and sinews."[6]

Reply to Obj. 1. God adequately acts in things as the primary efficient cause, nor are the actions of secondary causes thereby superfluous.

Reply to Obj. 2. A single action does not come from two efficient causes of one and the same rank, but nothing prevents one and the same action coming from a primary and a secondary efficient cause.

Reply to Obj. 3. God not only bestows forms on things, but he also preserves the forms in existence and applies the forms to the things to be produced, and is the end of everything, as I have said.[7]

Sixth Article

Can God Do Anything outside the Order Imparted to Things?

I proceed in this way to the sixth article: it seems that God cannot do anything outside the order imparted to things.

Obj. 1. Augustine says in his *Contra Faustum*: "God, the author and creator of all natures, does nothing contrary to nature."[8] But something outside the order imparted to things by nature seems to be contrary to nature. Therefore, God cannot do anything outside the order imparted to things.

Obj. 2. As the order of justice comes from God, so also does the order of nature. But God cannot do anything outside the order of justice, for he would then do something unjust. Therefore, he cannot do anything outside the order of nature.

Obj. 3.   God established the order of nature. Therefore, if God should do something outside the order of nature, it seems that he would vary. And this is inappropriate.

On the contrary, Augustine says in his *Contra Faustum* that "God at times does things contrary to the usual course of nature."⁹

I answer that every cause results in an order in its effects, since every cause has the nature of source. And so also a multiplicity of causes multiplies the orders in effects, and one order is included in another order, just as one cause is included in another cause. And hence a higher cause is not included in the order of a lower cause, but the converse is true. And an example of this is evident in human affairs, for the order of a household depends on the father of the household, and the order of a household is included in the order of a local community, and the order of a local community comes from its administrator, while the latter order is likewise included in the order of a king, who orders an entire kingdom.

Therefore, if we should consider the order of things as that order depends on the primary cause, then God cannot do anything contrary to the order of things, for he would do something contrary to his foreknowledge or his will or his goodness if he were to do so.

But if we should consider the order of things as that order depends on any secondary cause, then God can do something outside the order of things. For he is not subject to the order of secondary causes; rather, such an order is subject to him, proceeding from him, as it were, by the choice of his will, not by a necessity of nature, since he could have established a still different order of things. And hence he can, when he has so willed, also do things outside the order he has established—for example, by producing the effects of secondary causes apart from those causes, or by producing some effects beyond the reach of secondary causes. And so also Augustine says in his *Contra Faustum* that "God does things contrary to the usual course of nature, but he in no way acts contrary to the supreme law or contrary to himself."¹⁰

Reply to Obj. 1.   It can happen in two ways that something comes about in things of nature outside the nature imparted. In one way, by the action of an efficient cause that did not give things of nature their natural tendency, as when a human being moves a heavy material substance upward but did not endow the material substance with its tendency to move downward. And this is contrary to nature. In the second way, something comes about in things of nature outside their nature by the action of an efficient cause on which the action by nature depends. And this is not contrary to nature. Such action, for example, is evident in the ebb and flow of the sea, which action is not contrary to nature but is outside the natural downward movement of water. For impulses from heavenly bodies cause the tides, and the natural tendency of material substances here below depends on such impulses.

Therefore, since God causes the order of nature imparted to things, it is not contrary to nature if he should do something outside that order. And hence Augustine says in his *Contra Faustum* that "what he who causes every measure, number, and order of nature, produces, is natural for every being."[11]

Reply to Obj. 2. The order of justice exists in relation to the first cause, which is the norm of all justice. And so God can do nothing outside this order.

Reply to Obj. 3. God imparted a fixed order to beings in such a way that he nonetheless reserved to himself what he would sometimes for good reason do otherwise. And hence he does not vary when he acts outside that fixed order.

Seventh Article

Is Every Deed of God
outside the Natural Order of Things a Miracle?

I proceed in this way to the seventh article: it seems that some deeds of God outside the natural order of things are not miracles.

Obj. 1. God causes both the world and souls to be created, and the un-righteous to be made righteous, outside the order of nature, for the action of no natural cause produces such effects. And yet we do not call these things miracles. Therefore, some deeds of God outside the natural order are not miracles.

Obj. 2. We call miracles "difficult and unusual things transcending the capacity of nature and the expectation of those who wonder at them."[12]

But certain things occur outside the order of nature even though they are not difficult, for such things occur in unimportant matters, for example, recovery of jewels or healing of the sick.

Nor are certain things outside the order of nature unusual, since they happen frequently, as when the sick were placed in the streets to be cured by Peter's shadow.[13]

Nor are certain things outside the order of nature above the capacity of nature, as when some persons are cured of fever.

Nor are certain things outside the order of nature beyond expectation, as, for example, all of us expect the resurrection of the dead, even though the resurrection of the dead occurs outside the order of nature.

Therefore, some things arising outside the order of nature are not miracles.

Obj. 3. We derive the word "miracle" from wonderment. And wonderment concerns things evident to the senses. But things sometimes happen outside the order of nature in things not evident to the senses, as, for example, the Apostles were endowed with knowledge without study or learning on their part.[14] Therefore, some things arising outside the order of nature are not miracles.

On the contrary, Augustine says in his *Contra Faustum* that "when God does anything contrary to the commonly known and customary course of nature, we call such things great or wonderous events."[15]

I answer that we derive the word "miracle" from wonderment. And wonderment arises when effects are apparent, but their cause is hidden; for example, one wonders when one sees an eclipse of the sun but does not know the cause, as the Philosopher says in the beginning of the *Metaphysics*.[16] Moreover, one person can know an evident effect's cause even though other persons do not. And hence something is wonderous to one person and not wonderous to others; for example, a peasant wonders at an eclipse of the sun, but an astronomer does not. But we say that miracles are wonder-full, as it were, namely, that they have a cause absolutely hidden from absolutely everyone. And this cause is God. And hence we call things produced by God outside causes known to us miracles.

Reply to Obj. 1.   Although God alone produces the creation of the world and the justification of the unrighteous, we nonetheless do not, properly speaking, call them miracles. For other causes do not by nature produce them, and so they do not occur outside the order of nature, since such do not belong to the order of nature.

Reply to Obj. 2.   We call difficult things miracles because such things surpass the capacity of nature, not because of the excellence of the things in which they arise.

We likewise call things unusual because they occur outside the customary course of nature, not because they occur infrequently.

Moreover, we say that something is above the capacity of nature not only because of the substance of what has been done, but also because of the manner and order of doing it.

We also say that miracles are beyond the expectation of nature, not beyond the expectation of grace, which is by faith, by which we believe in the future resurrection.

Reply to Obj. 3.   The Apostles' knowledge, although it was not apparent as such, was nonetheless manifested in its effects, whereby it seemed wonderous.

Notes

1. Phil. 2:13.
2. Q. 105, A. 3.
3. Reply to Obj. 2.
4. Is. 26:12.
5. The reference is to John the Saracen. See Averroes, *In libros Metaphysicorum*

IX (VIII in the Bekker notation), comm. 7; XII (XI in the Bekker notation), comm. 18.

6. Job 10:11.
7. In the body of the article.
8. *Contra Faustum* XXVI, 3. PL 42:480.
9. Ibid. PL 42:481.
10. Ibid.
11. Ibid. PL 42:480.
12. Cf. Augustine, *De utilitate credendi* 16. PL 42:90.
13. Acts 5:15.
14. Acts 2:4.
15. *Contra Faustum* XXVI, 3. PL 42:481.
16. *Metaphysics* I, 2. 982b11–21.

Glossary

ACCIDENT. *An attribute that inheres in another and cannot subsist in itself.* What does not inhere in another but subsists in itself, is a substance. John, for example, is a substance, while his height is an accident; the latter cannot exist apart from the former. *See* Actuality, Property, Substance.

ACTION. *Activity.* In the broad sense, the term applies to immanent as well as transient activity. In the strict sense, however, the term refers to transient activity in contrast to immanent activity. In transient action, the active being produces an effect in something else. In short, transient action in the strict sense is efficient causality. *See* Cause, Operation.

ACTUALITY. *The perfection of a being.* Existence is the primary actuality of every being; a specific (substantial) form actualizes all finite beings and distinguishes one kind of being from another; particular (accidental) characteristics further actualize all finite beings. Joan, for example, is perfected and actualized by her act of existence, her human form, and her particular attributes (her knowledge, her virtue, her physical attributes). *See* Accident, Form, Matter, Potentiality, Substance.

APPETITE. *The active tendency of finite beings to actualize their capacities.* Inanimate material beings have natural appetites; plants have additional vegetative appetites (for nourishment, growth, and reproduction); animals have additional sense appetites (concupiscible, irascible); human beings have an additional intellectual appetite (rational).

CAUSE. *A being that influences the being or coming-to-be of something else.* In common parlance, the term refers primarily to an efficient cause, that is, the cause that by its activity produces an effect; a builder and those who work under him, for example, are the efficient causes of the house they build. Efficient causes can be univocal or equivocal. An efficient cause is univocal when it and its effect belong to the same species; human beings, for example, beget human beings. An efficient cause is equivocal when it and its effect do not belong to the same species. God, for example, equivocally causes creatures because he not only does not share a species with any creature, but he does not belong to any genus or species.

But there are other causes than efficient causes. A final cause is the end for the sake of which an efficient cause acts; a builder, for example, builds a house to make money (subjective purpose) and to provide a shelter for someone (objective purpose). An exemplary cause is the idea or model of a desired effect in the mind of an intellectual efficient cause that preconceives the effect; a builder, for example, conceives the form of the house that he intends to build.

Efficient, final, and exemplary causes are extrinsic to an effect. In addition, form, which makes an effect to be what it is, and matter, which receives a form, are correlative intrinsic causes; a house, for example, is composed of bricks and wood (matter), which are given a structure or shape (form). *See* Form, Matter, Principle.

300

COMING TO BE. *See* Generation and Corruption.

EFFICIENT CAUSE. *See* Cause.

ESSENCE. *What makes something to be what it substantially is.* The human essence, for example, makes human beings to be what they are as substances, namely, rational animals. When the essence of a being is considered as the ultimate source of the being's activities and development, it is called the being's nature; human nature, for example, is the ultimate source of the human activities (activities of reason and activities according to reason) whereby human beings develop themselves. *See* Accident, Form, Property, Substance.

EQUIVOCAL CAUSE. *See* Cause.

EXEMPLARY CAUSE. *See* Cause.

FINAL CAUSE. *See* Cause.

FORM. *The cause that makes a being to be substantially or accidentally what it is.* The human form, for example, makes John to be what he is as a substance, and other forms make him to be what he is accidentally (tall, thin, red-headed). *See* Accident, Substance.

FORMAL CAUSE. *See* Cause.

GENERATION AND CORRUPTION. *The coming-to-be and passing away of a material substance.* In substantial change, matter (prime) gains a particular form (substantial), and so a new material substance comes to be (generation). The same matter also loses a particular form, and so the previous material substance as such ceases to exist (corruption). *See* Form, Matter.

GENUS. *See* Species.

HABIT. *The characteristic disposition or inclination to act in a certain way.* Habits may belong to the intellect or will, be innate or acquired, natural or supernatural, good or bad. For example, logical argumentation is a habit of the intellect; moderation is a habit of the will; timidity may be an innate habit; cleanliness is an acquired habit; courage is a natural habit; faith is a supernatural habit; generosity is a good habit; stinginess is a bad habit. *See* Virtue.

IDEAS (GOD'S). *The forms or natures of actual or possible creatures in God's mind.* Because God knows himself as imitable, he knows the forms or natures of every being that he creates or could create. These ideas are identical with God's knowing himself, and God's knowing is in turn identical with his substance.

INTELLECT. *The power of understanding.* The human intellect does so by apprehending the essences of material things, forming judgments, and reasoning discursively. God's intellect is one of pure understanding.

MATERIAL CAUSE. *See* Cause.

MATTER. *The cause or "stuff" out of which and with which something material is produced.* The material causes of a house, for example, are its bricks, mortar, wood.

Prime matter individualizes and so limits a specific substantial form, and it provides the subject and capacity for material things to change from one substance into another. Although prime matter is no-thing, it is a principle or cause in everything material. It can receive any communicable substantial form and so has a limitless capacity for any such form. *See* Cause, Form, Potentiality.

MOTION. *Movement.* Motion literally and primarily refers to locomotion, that is, change of position. But the term can refer more broadly to any change or transition from one state or condition to another. According to St. Thomas, it is a self-evident first principle of understanding that whatever undergoes motion, does so as a result of causal action by something else.

NATURE. *See* Essence.

OPERATION. *Immanent activity.* In a broad sense, the term can refer to any activity, whether transient or immanent. In the strict sense, however, the term refers to immanent activity in contrast to transient activity. Immanent activity, unlike transient activity, perfects the being that acts. Plants have the immanent activities of nutrition, growth, and reproduction. Animals have the additional immanent activities of sense knowledge and sense appetites. Human beings have the additional immanent activities of understanding and willing. God alone has perfectly immanent activity, that is, understanding and willing apart from any effect distinct from his substance. *See* Action.

PASSING AWAY. *See* Generation and Corruption.

POTENTIALITY. *The capacity to be or become something.* The potentiality of a being limits its actuality; frogs, for example, can swim, but they cannot fly. Finite beings can change accidentally; John, for example, can go bald. Finite material beings can also change from one substance into another; grass, for example, when consumed by a cow, becomes part of the cow. Potentiality in the active sense is the same as power. *See* Accident, Actuality, Matter, Power.

POWER. *The active capacity to perform a certain type of activity.* For example, the power of sight. *See* Potentiality.

PREDICABLE. *One of the five most general kinds of attributes that can be predicated of the subject of a proposition.* Genus, species, specific difference, property, accident. *See* Accident, Property, Species.

PREDICAMENT. *One of ten fundamental categories of being that can be affirmed of a subject in predication.* For example, John is a human being (substance), big (quantity), white (quality), living in New York City (place) on January 1, 1991 (time), the husband of Jane (relation).

PRINCIPLE. *That from which something else comes.* The essence of a frog, specifically its form, for example, is an ontological principle or cause, that is, the principle or cause governing the frog's being and activity. The premises of an argument, on the other hand, are logical principles. From the premises that all men are mortal, and that Socrates is a man, the intellect can conclude that Socrates is mortal. *See* Cause.

PROPERTY. *A quality or characteristic that necessarily belongs to a substance; a proper accident.* Joan's ability to use language, for example, unlike the color of her hair, is a characteristic proper to her as a human being. *See* Accident, Predicable, Substance.

PRUDENCE. *The intellectual virtue whereby a person is characteristically disposed to reason rightly in the choice of means to achieve excellence.* Human prudence governs the moral virtues. *See* Virtue.

SCIENCE (ARISTOTELIAN). *Knowledge of beings through their causes.* Science consists in understanding not only the efficient but also the material, formal, and final causes of beings. Physical, psychological, and social sciences study the secondary causes of material composites, while philosophy studies the first causes of all being. Philosophy (metaphysics) is the highest Aristotelian science. For St. Thomas, however, theology, which studies God in the light of revelation, is the highest science.

SLAVERY. *Involuntary servitude.* The slavery (*servitudo*) that Aquinas mentions, is the medieval variety, of which serfdom was the principal institution. The medieval slave was subject to the disposition of his master, but he enjoyed, at least in theory, rights that his master was bound to respect. This type of slavery should be distinguished from that of ancient Greece and Rome and from that of the antebellum American South, in which slaves had no (or negligible) rights, and masters had no duties toward them. So also "slave" ("*servus*").

SOUL. *The substantial form of a living material being.* The soul is the ultimate intrinsic source whereby living material beings differ from nonliving material beings. There are three different kinds of souls: the vegetative soul capable of nutrition and growth, the sensory soul capable of sense perception, and the rational soul capable of intellection. These souls are virtually but not actually distinct in human beings. Only the rational soul is intrinsically independent of matter for its existence and activity. *See* Form, Substance.

SPECIES. *The substantial identity of material beings insofar as that identity is common to many.* The species concept (e.g., human being) is composed of a genus concept (e.g., animal), which indicates the essence of certain material beings in an incompletely determined way, and of a specific difference between things of the same genus (e.g., rational). The species concept, or definition, thus expresses the whole substance or essence of a particular kind of material being.

SPECIFIC DIFFERENCE. *See* Species.

SUBJECT. *The substance underlying accidental characteristics and activities.* In an extended sense, prime matter can be called the subject of substantial form. In logic, the subject of a proposition. *See* Accident, Form, Matter, Substance.

SUBSTANCE. *What exists in itself and not in another.* Finite individual substances "stand under" (Lat.: *substare*) accidents and persist through accidental changes. Human beings, for example, are composed of substance (body-soul) and accidents (size, shape, color, etc.). *See* Accident, Property, Subject.

VIRTUE. *Human excellence.* Like its Greek equivalent (*aretē*), the Latin-derived term indicates a perduring quality of an individual human being and so a characteristic disposition to act in a properly human or Christian way. Aquinas distinguishes three kinds of virtue: intellectual, moral, and theological. Intellectual virtues have for their objects intellectual activities. Concerning theoretical truth, intellectual virtues include understanding or insight (skill in judging), science (skill in reasoning), and wisdom or contemplation (skill in understanding the ultimate causes of things). Concerning practical truth, intellectual virtues include practical wisdom or prudence (skill in making right judgments about the propriety of human actions) and art (skill in making right judgments about things to be made). Moral virtues have for their objects characteristic readiness to act in particular matters as prudence dictates; these virtues are acquired. The four cardinal virtues are prudence, fortitude, temperance, and justice. There are also for St. Thomas the theological virtues of faith, hope, and charity, and the infused moral virtues. *See* Habit.

Select Bibliography

On Aristotle's philosophical system, see:
Grene, Marjorie. *A Portrait of Aristotle*. Chicago: University of Chicago Press, 1967.
Veatch, Henry. *Aristotle: A Contemporary Appreciation*. Bloomington: Indiana University Press, 1974.

On the introduction of Aristotle into Western Europe, see:
van Steenberghen, Fernand. *Aristotle in the West: The Origins of Latin Aristotelianism*. Translated by L. Johnson. New York: Humanities Press, 1970.

For a guide to the context of St. Thomas's thought, see:
Pieper, Josef. *Guide to Thomas Aquinas*. Translated by Richard and Clara Winston. New York: Pantheon, 1962.

For an excellently written and expert life of St. Thomas, see:
Chesterton, G.K. *St. Thomas Aquinas*. Garden City, N.Y.: Image Books, 1956.

For a summary of St. Thomas's philosophy, see:
Copleston, Frederick. *Aquinas*. New York: Penguin, 1955.
————. *A History of Philosophy* 2: 302–424, especially 336–74. Westminster, Md.: Newman, 1950. Also available in Image Books, Doubleday (vol. 2, part 2).
Gilson, Etienne. *The Christian Philosophy of St. Thomas Aquinas*, especially part 1. New York: Random House, 1956.

For an explanation of textual terms, see the Blackfriars' Latin text and English translation (McGraw-Hill).

On the origin of the five ways St. Thomas proves God's existence in the *Summa*, see:
Sillem, Edward. *Ways of Thinking about God*. New York: Sheed and Ward, 1961.

On the progression of the five ways, see:
Dewan, Lawrence. "The Number and Order of St. Thomas' Five Ways." *Downside Review* 92 (1974): 1–18.

For an excellent Neo-Thomistic perspective, especially on participation and analogy, see:
Clarke, W. Norris. *The Philosophical Approach to God*. Winston-Salem, N.C.: Wake Forest University Philosophy Dept., 1979.

For a transcendental Thomist perspective, see:
Lonergan, Bernard. "The Natural Desire to See God." In *Collection*. New York: Herder and Herder, 1967.

On creation, see:
Schmitz, Kenneth L. *The Gift: Creation*. Milwaukee: Marquette University Press, 1982.

Index

Action, kinds of, 153
Algazel, 249
Almaric, 48
Ambrose, Saint, 63, 95, 100, 173, 203
Analogy: of being, 55; of predication, 64, 98–100, 104–5
Anaxagoras, 243, 244, 248, 251
Annihilation, 288–90
Anselm, Saint, 133, 139, 183
Appetite, 63, 117, 132–33, 157–58, 171–72, 175–76, 189
Aristotle, 49, 98, 137, 219, 243–44; on action, 153; on being, 67, 123, 140, 259, 275; on causality, 132, 266, 268, 278, 298; on change, 115, 149, 232, 233, 241–42; on contraries, 243, 257, 267; on ends, 162, 273, 274; on eternity of the world, 243, 245, 246; on evil, 215, 256, 257; on first principles, 38–39; on God, 114, 119, 153, 160, 176, 182, 215, 224, 254; on the good, 57, 60, 61–62, 63, 66, 128; on the infinite, 71, 246; on knowledge, 103, 104, 111, 112, 117, 193; on life, 148, 149, 150; on love, 177; on mathematical objects, 223; on motion, 158, 244, 245, 277, 287, 288; on necessary beings, 224; on necessary causes, 194, 225; on necessary conclusions, 243; on order, 272; on the possible, 214, 243; on power, 212, 213; on practical wisdom, 189, 190; on privation, 261; on relations, 101, 103; on sense appetites, 176, 182, 189; on sense perception, 144, 145; on separate forms, 69, 127; on time, 80, 81–82, 245; on truth and falsity, 132, 134, 136, 143, 144, 145; on understanding, 89, 91; on will, 157, 176
Athanasian Creed, 81
Augustine, Saint, 112, 154, 218; on creation, 164, 225, 230, 237, 247, 253, 288, 295; on the divine ideas, 126, 128, 276;

on eternity, 81; on evil, 43, 171, 256, 259, 260, 261, 264, 265, 266; on God's eternity, 107; on God's goodness, 61, 66, 94, 219; on God's governance of the world, 277–78; on God's immutability, 77; on God's knowing, 114, 115, 117; on God's love and providence, 179, 194; on God's power, 286; on God's presence in the world, 73; on God's will, 164; on the good, 57, 69, 162, 273, 288; on miracles, 296, 297, 298; on predestination, 169, 171, 199, 203, 206, 208; on predication about God, 93, 101; on re-incarnation, 249; on theology, 37; on truth and falsity, 132, 138, 139, 140, 142, 143, 144, 145
Averroes, 53, 160
Avicenna, 84, 133, 237, 248, 252

Beauty, 61, 62
Beings: contingent and necessary, 41–42, 214, 215, 223, 224; gradations of, 43, 259
Boethius: on creatures' goodness, 69; on God's eternity, 79, 80, 81, 248; on God's governance of the world, 271, 281; on God's providence, 189, 195, 279; on the good, 57, 58, 274; on justice, 181, 183; on knowledge, 39, 89; on pure forms, 107

Causes, efficient: accidental, 268; chief, 128, 152, 265; contingent, 121–24, 169–71, 195; created, 283, 287, 295; deficient, 170, 265, 266–67, 268; destructive, 284, 286, 287; equivocal (nonunivocal), 55–56, 66–67, 100, 134, 285; first, 42, 43, 47, 51, 65, 69, 115, 163, 191, 212, 228, 244, 252, 280; free, 192–93, 245, 252, 266; imperfect, 228; inferior, 216, 296; infinite series of, 246, 247, instrumental, 152, 237–38, 265; intermediate, 169, 170, 287;

307

Will, 157–58; free, 173, 192, 201, 202,
204–5, 207, 292–93; God's absolute,
160–61, 203, 247; God's antecedent,
165–66, 203; God's consequent, 161,
165–66, 203; God's in general, 157–
73, 217

Wisdom: God's, 77, 78, 217, 218, 227,
252; practical, 188–89; of the world,
214, 216